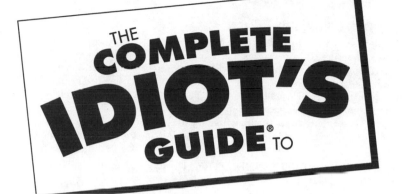

THE COMPLETE IDIOT'S GUIDE® TO

Women's Spirituality

by Mary Faulkner

ALPHA

A Pearson Education Company

Publisher: *Marie Butler-Knight*
Product Manager: *Phil Kitchel*
Managing Editor: *Jennifer Chisholm*
Senior Acquisitions Editor: *Randy Ladenheim-Gil*
Development Editor: *Deborah S. Romaine*
Senior Production Editor and Copy Editor: *Christy Wagner*
Illustrator: *Chris Eliopoulos*
Cover/Book Designer: *Trina Wurst*
Indexer: *Julie Bess*
Layout/Proofreading: *Svetlana Dominguez, Mary Hunt, Cheryl Lynch, Nancy Wagner*

Contents at a Glance

Contents

Foreword by Donna Fontanarose Rabuck, Ph.D.

You hold in your hands *The Complete Idiot's Guide to Women's Spirituality*, a book with an amusing title and a powerful purpose. In my experience over the past decade as a writer, teacher, ritual leader, and independent scholar in this field, I have never read a text which conveys as well as this one the depth and breadth of women's spirituality: what it is, what its roots are, its many expressions and embodiments, and how it is connected to personal, political, and planetary evolution.

Mary Faulkner reminds me of Spider Woman, the Native American goddess of weaving and culture, creatrix of worlds, as she skillfully lays out all the diverse strands of women's spirituality and answers questions anyone interested in the subject would want to know, such as how do you define women's spirituality? We learn that it is organic, inclusive, broad in scope, "a work in process," and that each woman participates in it as she questions what her values and beliefs are and how to live them out in the world. It also helps women claim their authority and gain their voices as they come to understand that they, too, share in divinity. Through her work, Ms. Faulkner remembers, restores, and reweaves the threads of women's power and possibility.

This book includes discussions and examples of women expressing their spirituality within organized religion, outside of it, and women who integrate both. Ms. Faulkner shares the stories of African American women; Native women; Jewish women; Catholic and Protestant women; women who worship the goddess; women who practice Wicca; women who create their own altars, rituals, and ceremonies; women who engage in holistic healing, and women who have changed and are changing the course of history as their spirituality and activism push them forward to work for change in society and a return to the feminine values of partnership and equality.

One of the gifts of this book is Ms. Faulkner's understanding of the political strands of women's spirituality, how the personal and political are, in fact, intertwined. Through her sharing of the stories of Sojourner Truth, Harriet Tubman, Elizabeth Cady Stanton, Mary McLeod Bethune, Margaret Sanger, and others, she powerfully demonstrates how we have a heritage of female leaders for whom racial equality, social equality, and spiritual autonomy were one and the same.

Deeply woven into this work is also the awareness that each individual woman is the authority on her own life and that the answers lie within. As the author says, "Spirituality is about finding wholeness, and that is a process of self-discovery. You must find your truth, stop along the way and sort through your old beliefs, and find out what is true and not true for you." This book is a companion into the realms of self-awareness and personal reflection that are so much a part of women's spirituality.

Additionally, this is an experiential work which encourages us not only to think about, but also to practice ways of integrating body, mind, and spirit through hands-on information, practical suggestions, and living examples. It can be used as a source for personal growth, as a text for a women's studies class, or shared in a circle of women. I find it a valuable guidebook that can lead others to learn, explore, and perhaps come to say, as one woman in the book does, "I am doing the work I feel I was born to do, and I love doing it. I have followed my visions, my intuition, and my inner guidance, and it has served me well."

This book reminds me of an enormous cape designed from many different materials and threads. The cape is made up of sewn-together sections, each original and complete in and of itself, as the chapters are. The cape becomes even more magnificent to behold as we recognize how all the pieces are woven together to express the diversity, the beauty, and the power of women's spirituality.

By the end of the book may you take this beautiful cape, put it on, and recognize that the pattern has been spun for centuries upon centuries by sisters near and far. May you recognize that it belongs to you, that it belongs to each and every one of us and all of us together. May you use the knowledge to set yourself free in the areas where you most need to. May you continue to work for peace and justice in your own way, knowing that you are blessed by a heritage of women who have come before you. May you pass this book on to your mother, your daughter, your sister, your friends. May you use it to name and claim your own spirituality.

Donna Fontanarose Rabuck, Ph.D.

Donna Fontanarose Rabuck, Ph.D. is a writer, teacher, scholar, seminar and ritual leader, and director of the Center for the Sacred Feminine in Tucson, Arizona, where she offers women's circles, workshops, and retreats. She is also an educator at the University of Arizona. She can be reached at the Center for the Sacred Feminine, 3400 E. Speedway, #118-130, Tucson, AZ 85716, drabuck@u.arizona.edu, or expage.com/sacredfeminine.

Foreword by Patricia Monaghan, Ph.D.

Suddenly the goddess is news. Across the globe, whenever women look for a divinity who reflects their lives, they find her. In dreams and in poems, in rituals, and in silence, women find the image of the goddess opening up to them an inclusive, accepting, celebratory spirituality, one that does not lock the doors against them as participants or leaders.

But new as the goddess seems at the turn of the millennia, she is as old as the human heart. Ancient sculptures attest to her significance to people who lived thousands and even tens of thousands of years ago. We may not know the names by which those unknown ancestors called her, but the art and artifacts they left behind in bone and stone, clay, and fiber show her as an ample embracing deity, one who we can envision caring like a mother for her many human children. From this maternal goddess descend the many forms she takes in the imagination of her worshipers: huntress and poet, wanton and crone, magician and healer.

The great diversity of goddess imagery is one of its most appealing features, and women of all ages, races, and walks of life can discover a powerful divine image who speaks directly to them. Men are not excluded from this search, for they recognize in the goddess their daughters, lovers, mothers, and friends. In the shadow of the goddess, half of the human race comes forth into the light.

In *The Complete Idiot's Guide to Women's Spirituality*, Mary Faulkner introduces you to this exciting, emerging arena of spirit. She not only gives an accessible and thorough description of the historical goddess; she also explores some of the many avenues available to those who wish to further pursue awareness of the feminine aspect of divinity. Beyond Neopaganism and Wicca, she charts the Native American and black womanist traditions, the important influences of Jewish thought, and the impact of Celtic religion. And throughout the book, we hear the wisdom of the sages as well, in poignant and evocative passages that give a hint of the breadth and depth of women's knowledge.

Whether you are a novice or an adept, this book will bring you new insights into one of the most profound and moving religious impulses of today, a movement that reconnects with the wisdom of ages past and gives hope for a better future.

Patricia Monaghan, Ph.D.
DePaul University

Patricia Monaghan is the author of the definitive encyclopedia of goddesses, in print continuously for more than 20 years—*The New Book of Goddesses and Heroines*—as well as six additional books on the subject. She is a member of the interdisciplinary faculty of DePaul University in Chicago.

Introduction

Women's spirituality is not separate from women's lives. Women's spiritual or religious history is not separate from their political history. In telling the stories in the book, I focused on experiences that have a particular relationship to spiritual or religious expression. But as you will see, women's activities almost always directly engage the political and social realities of their world.

About 6,000 years ago, the Western world separated God's kingdom into two different realms. Men were said to have greater access to the heavens, and women were given the earth. God became "he," and the earth became "she." The stories in the book echo this primal theme, showing how women's spirituality is connected to the earth and to the body. Women know the sanctity of the living earth and the spirituality of giving birth. Whether they personally choose to have children is not necessary; they know that life is sacred and that the living presence of the divine is here, now, in each of us and in the world.

This book begins by establishing a working definition of women's spirituality. It gives the history of the movement—both its political and spiritual components. It goes on to identify the specific agenda of this emerging spirituality, allowing for the broadest possible interpretation of how that agenda is addressed. We will look at the hierarchical paradigm we've been living with for thousands of years and explore a new paradigm that is more relational and inclusive of women's values. Throughout the book, the point is made that women's spirituality is not about reversing the dynamics of a hierarchical order and putting women in charge; it is about creating a new game based on partnership.

Theologians and scholars from a variety of disciplines have gathered a body of work to support this spirituality. They have corrected errors in translation and reinterpreted biblical material that has justified keeping women in subordinate positions in society. As you read about the women who dominated the social and religious world of the young America, you will quite possibly be as amazed as I was at their insight and fervor. They worked tirelessly to ensure constitutional rights were extended to include freedom for all people, the right for everyone to cast a vote, and to secure basic education and healthcare for women. Elizabeth Cady Stanton's mandate to women in her time, urging them to disregard scriptural texts when it served to oppress women, is as relevant today as it was then. Today it is extended to include governmental and business policies as well. The words of Sojourner Truth, "Ain't I woman?" still echo in our ears today as we watch women around the globe being denied the most elemental security and humane treatment.

We will look at our ancient history and meet the goddess, the symbol of women's innate value and divine presence in the world. The goddess stands as a symbol for all people, and she is particularly important for women who have been seen as different and treated as an "other." In learning about the world before patriarchy, I caution you not to idealize something we cannot ever really know. Exploring matriarchy isn't about going back; it's about going forward with new images of power and dignity. Women's spirituality encourages women to take responsibility for their spirituality. Whether through building a personal altar, performing ceremonies to honor life passages, or howling at the moon, it provides a framework for developing a spirituality that empowers.

Throughout the book you will hear directly from women on a variety of paths who find spiritual expression through different means. Women's spirituality can be practiced along with traditional religion, and we will hear from women who are doing that in creative ways. A few bottom lines that I would like to draw regarding women's spirituality are that it celebrates diversity of expression, honors the divine presence in the here and now, and understands the interconnected web of life. I close with the Lakota prayer that is said many times each day to honor the relationship of all; that is: *Mitkuye Oyassin* ("To all our relations").

What You'll Discover in This Book

The book is divided into five parts:

Part 1, "Women Are Gathering," presents a working definition of the movement, the theological underpinnings, and an understanding of its political and spiritual components.

Part 2, "Meeting Goddess," explores the ancient civilizations in which the divine was honored as female and discovers how she becomes an empowering symbol for women today, as well as harkening ecological responsibility.

Part 3, "Continuing the Legacy: Inside the Organization," introduces you to women who express their spirituality in traditional arenas. You'll have an opportunity to explore the legacy of women abolitionists, suffragettes, and those who worked for basic rights for women.

Part 4, "People of the Earth," begins with Native American spirituality, explores our Celtic roots, as well as the modern-day Neopagan movement. It looks at spiritual truths contained in the body and how you can connect with your innate wisdom to help you make life decisions.

Part 5, "Mending the Split in the Patriarch's Pants," looks at holistic spirituality and how women are putting body and soul back together and expressing spirituality through creativity, education, and healing arts.

In the appendixes you'll find more interesting information. There is a glossary of terms used in the book, a list of books for further reading, and resources that will help you find many of the women whose stories appear in the book.

Helpful Hints for the Reader

You'll no doubt notice the helpful and interesting information contained in the sidebars throughout the text. They each contain a particular kind of information.

Goddess Guide

Goddess Guide boxes provide additional historic information about the goddess and common practices associated with the practice of women's spirituality.

Mother Knows Best

Mother Knows Best boxes correct mistaken beliefs about women's spirituality, or religion, and also give warnings on how to better keep you on your spiritual path.

Womanspeak

Womanspeak boxes define terms that might not be familiar to you or words that have a specific meaning to women's spirituality.

Wise Words

Wise Words boxes contain quotations and comments about spirituality or religion by famous people.

Sophia's Wisdom

Sophia's Wisdom boxes include additional and interesting information that is helpful to traditionalists, showing how many of the beliefs and practices of women's spirituality are the same as beliefs in Western religion.

Acknowledgments

Special thanks go to Elizabeth D. Wise, whose painting, *Confirmation*, appears on the cover of the book. Her art represents all that is beautiful, strong, mysterious, and classically female. (To find out how to see more of Wise's work, check Appendix C.) Special thanks to my technical editor, Jo Searles, who has lived the goddess path for many years and instructs other women in her ways. Special thanks to Sarah and Martha Leigh, who kept me fed and exercised during the project. Special thanks to my agent and good friend, Linda Roghaar, who took me camping in August when I needed it the most, my acquisitions editor Randy, development editor Debbie, and production editor and copy editor Christy—and all the others at Alpha who helped make this a great book. A special thanks to the women whose scholarship made the writing of this book possible, many of whom are listed in the back of the book. I want to acknowledge my teachers, Carol Christ, Mary Daly, Rosemary Radford, Sallie McFague, Starhawk, Luisah Teish, and Buck Ghosthorse. Special thanks to good friend Margaret McClemons, who is part of this journey with me, and to friends and mentors Jennie Adams and Betty Lackey, who are wise women in my life.

Special Thanks to the Technical Reviewer

The Complete Idiot's Guide to Women's Spirituality was reviewed by an expert who double-checked the accuracy of what you'll learn here, to help us ensure that this book gives you everything you need to know about women's spirituality today. Special thanks are extended to Jo C. Searles.

Jo is a retired professor of English and women's studies from Penn State University. She has researched the goddess images, dance, culture, and music of women in Brazil, Malaysia, Greece, Hawaii, and Mexico. She has published poetry and essays and has lectured and given workshops in the areas of women's spirituality and older women's writings. These days she focuses on working with the image of the Crone and the (largely unrecognized) importance of her place in our culture.

Trademarks

All terms mentioned in this book that are known to be or are suspected of being trademarks or service marks have been appropriately capitalized. Alpha Books and Pearson Education, Inc., cannot attest to the accuracy of this information. Use of a term in this book should not be regarded as affecting the validity of any trademark or service mark.

Part 1

Women Are Gathering

All over the country, women are gathering. They're gathering in upstate New York, Washington, Montana, New Mexico, Florida, Alaska, and every place in between. They're meeting in homes and apartments—sometimes on the beach or out in a field. They talk about their lives and create ceremonies to celebrate being female. Who are these women, and why are they gathering?

They are gathering together to reconnect to their spiritual and religious roots. They are talking about the things that have meaning for them, identifying beliefs and values they want to see reflected in the world. They are becoming a strong voice and are claiming their spiritual history as women. It is a fascinating movement, with a sociological, political, and deeply spiritual dimension. It is pulling women from every tradition and socio-economic group together, and they are pushing at the established boundaries and defining new religious turf.

In this part, we'll explore this emerging tradition, read about the beliefs and practices, learn about the remarkable women of the past who left their imprints on the world as we know it, and meet today's spiritual pioneers and hear their stories.

Women's Spirituality: What Is It?

In This Chapter

- This thing called women's spirituality
- Twinges, inklings, and spirituality
- How some women have found answers
- Politics and religion: not such strange bedfellows

You might begin by thinking of women's spirituality as a verb rather than a noun because it is a process rather than a doctrine. It's a process of becoming aware of your own sacred nature and of the presence of the sacred in the world, as well as a way of seeing the things you hold sacred respected in society. It begins at the most intimate personal level, becomes political, and then gets practical.

Is this spirituality for women only, or can men practice women's spirituality? Much of this spirituality is about respecting the same innate presence of the divine in one another and in nature that many men and other religious groups also value. However, in women's spirituality, the focus is on the feminine, and our focus in this book will be on women. As you read more about the values of women's spirituality, you will recognize that they exist in many other places, too.

Asking Questions

Often this phenomenon called women's spirituality is a spirituality of questioning. It questions many of the traditional understandings about power, authority, and who and what God is. Of course, these are many of the same questions that both men and women have always asked. The difference is in who gets to answer the questions, who gets to define what is sacred. Women's spirituality doesn't accept all the traditional responses. It points to the fact that for thousands of years, women's voices have been silent. The great religions of the world are based on men's interpretations, and women believe they bring a different perspective and have valuable information to add to this collection of religious material.

Women's spirituality provides a process and a place where women can allow their questions to surface, a place where they can explore spiritual possibilities. It does not teach or preach a specific theology. Women's spirituality is about empowering women to have a voice in the world. In so doing, it does not go to the traditional religious sources for answers, but instead goes to where revelation has always occurred—within. Answers come from our everyday encounters with the divine presence all around us. An answer might be found in the eyes of another creature, while walking through the woods, or in a conversation with a stranger or a loved one. Revelation comes through a sense of deepened connection with your self that is gained in those divine moments. This spirituality honors creation's interconnected web and opens your mind and heart to new spiritual perceptions.

Sophia's Wisdom

Women have always gathered together in one way or another. Since the beginning of time, women have met on riverbanks to pound their clothes with rocks while they discussed the latest comings and goings of the people. It's how they kept a finger on the village pulse. While few women long for the "good old days" of doing the laundry on the riverbank, many do feel the loss of gathering time.

Women's spirituality values insight. It does this by asking questions such as: What are the things you hold sacred? Where do you feel most connected to God? Who or what is God for you? Where do you go for spiritual nourishment? How do you define "spirituality"? What kind of work do you find meaningful? What feeds your spirit and still puts bread on the table? Again, these questions have been floating around since the beginning of time. The difference is that in women's spirituality, each woman contributes her truth based on how she experiences life, and most important, all answers are valid. This is how spiritual and religious "truth" expands.

The women you'll be hearing from in this book are asking themselves questions about sexuality, economics, political power, religion, ecology, family structure, community, health, well-being, sickness, death, and life after death—all under the heading of women's spirituality. In women's spirituality, *you* are the expert. *You* have the answers that are right for you.

Wise Words

"The highest spiritual state is curiosity. When we have a question we are ready to receive a new revelation. The Kingdom is advancing by increments."

—Sister Maura, Sisters of St. Joseph, Holy Angels Academy in Minneapolis, Minnesota (1957)

Spiritual "Inklings"

If you have ever sat quietly and had a woman-to-woman talk with yourself about any of the questions just mentioned, you have something in common with women's spirituality. If you have ever come away from your church or synagogue wondering "Is that all there is?" you have something in common with women's spirituality.

Women's spirituality begins with a feeling—or maybe even earlier than a feeling—with an "inkling." It is an intuitive twinge coming from inside. Most of us are trained to not pay attention to inklings. They're usually as quickly dismissed as they are felt. We get busy and push them to the back of our mind or down into our stomach. Other than in very exceptional cases, we are pretty well conditioned to ignore emotional signals and follow the rules—whatever they are. If the inklings are unpleasant, we "tighten the bandages and keep walking," as a friend of mine used to say. If the twinge is a desire stirring inside us, our "shouldn't" buzzer goes off. Either way, intuition plays second fiddle to intellect almost all the time, and nowhere is this more true than in matters of religion and spirituality.

Women's spirituality begins with a feeling. It stems from the understanding that feelings contain good information and that if we "sit" with them and talk about them with others, we learn something important. Those twinges are spiritual messages. Women's spirituality starts with a twinge, which leads to a question, which is followed by an answer—and something quite creative usually happens. A big difference between women's spirituality and any other form of inquiry is *where* you go for the answer. In women's spirituality, the answer comes from the same place as the twinge—within.

Why do women turn to women's spirituality? They do it for a variety of reasons. Often they are drawn to it out of their growing dissatisfaction, lack of fulfillment, boredom, and sometimes even anger. Women tend to interpret their feelings as a sign that something is wrong with them. Yet their feelings refuse to go away no matter how "good" they are, no matter how well they perform, no matter how much they accommodate. They still feel "wrong."

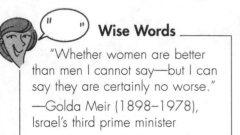

Wise Words

"Whether women are better than men I cannot say—but I can say they are certainly no worse." —Golda Meir (1898–1978), Israel's third prime minister

One day one woman hears another woman talking about feeling that way, too. In that moment a veil lifts. Women's spirituality acts as a sounding board for feelings such as these and as a source of validation. As women begin to discover that the feelings they're having are actually leading them somewhere—and that many other women have the same feelings, too—they begin the process of finding their own spirituality. As they learn that there are cultural influences that have defined them and shaped their reality, they begin to get their spiritual power back. Here are two women's journeys.

Finding Missing Pieces

"I love religion and have always looked forward to services. I sing in the choir, and that is important to me," said Karen. "However, for quite a while, I was finding that my religion was just not scratching where I itched. I would come away from services feeling empty. I blamed myself. I had to be doing something wrong! Everyone else was finding satisfaction there, what was 'wrong' with me? So I kept quiet and tried harder. The harder I tried the emptier I got. Finally I couldn't stand it any longer. I had to walk out. Mind you, I don't think there is anything wrong with my church—I love my church, that's why this was so puzzling—yet the urge to get up and leave was so compelling I couldn't ignore it."

Karen followed her urge. It led her to the spiritual writings of the women *mystics*. "I began to hear reflected back to me some of the things I 'knew' but couldn't find words for. I knew of a few other women who were beginning to ask similar questions. I heard about a group who were meeting and exploring spirituality. They came from many different traditions but were discovering their own version of religion. I was fearful at first. I had never dared to voice any of my feelings about this. I was frightened of what I would hear and where that would take me, but that urge I talked about kept me moving in that direction. As luck would have it, they were planning a retreat the night I showed up. That sounded safe to me."

Womanspeak

Mystics are men and women who belong to a tradition of prayer and meditation. They are in communication with the sacred presence within them; their writings and teachings are important contributions to religion and spirituality. Mystics traditionally live in monasteries or convents and are found within all religions.

"I went with them to a retreat center where we attended a workshop on Sophia. The whole weekend was about reading scripture and going within to find what meaning it had for us. I was totally amazed. We laughed, cried, danced, drummed, asked questions, and found our answers. My experience that weekend taught me that women have a different approach to spirituality than men do. We are more intuitive. We have to be able to connect to the God we feel within. That was the emptiness I was feeling at church. Church was all about the external God and other people's meanings. I value their interpretations, but not at the expense of my own! Today, many years later, I feel filled up again. I now attend both my women's spiritual circle and my traditional church."

Sophia's Wisdom

Sophia is the Greek word for "wisdom." Her name appeared in the Hebrew scripture as God's female partner in creation of the world and throughout time. Over the years many references to her were removed, and her material was identified by the concept "Wisdom." Here she speaks in Proverbs 8:27–31:

> When God set the heavens in place, I was present, when God drew a ring on the surface of the deep, when God fixed the clouds above, when God fixed the wells of the deep, when God assigned the sea its limits—and the waters will not invade the land—when God established the foundations of the earth, I was by God's side, a master craftswoman, delighting God day after day, ever at play by God's side, at play everywhere in God's domain, delighting to be with the children of humanity.

Making Conscious Choices

Sandy Solomon was raised Jewish. She has not been actively involved in her religion for the last few years but believes she'll be back some day. "I'm on sabbatical!" she notes for the record. Sandy doesn't have any quarrel with her religion; she just needed time to sort some things out. On a friend's recommendation, she joined a women's circle where the women were exploring spirituality.

"I can't separate creativity from spirituality," says Sandy. "To be alive is to be creative. The question becomes, are you creating consciously or unconsciously? You can create peace of mind or anxiety through your choices. I want peace of mind. The spiritual challenge for me is to create a life that brings that peace of mind. Then that's what I am putting into the world—that's my creation! So many people are creating stress, and that is their spiritual legacy. I want to leave a legacy of peace. That means making the choices that will allow me peace of mind.

"Once you decide what your legacy is to be, the real work begins. For example, I want peace. What brings me peace? As I begin to identify what brings me peace, I develop a criteria by which to measure decisions. We all make decisions that affect the kind of relationship we have with each other and with the world around us. I want mine to be conscious choices. How is this different than traditional approaches to religion? It's different because I'm working for what I feel is important. You might have your own ideas, and we can work on them together."

Yes, but What Is Women's Spirituality?

Women in the United States in this moment in time probably enjoy more freedom of expression, have more choices, and have more access to education, jobs, and money, than has ever been true in any culture throughout recorded history. This leaves many women and men wondering why certain women see a problem where others do not. What are these women looking for? And for crying out loud, what is this thing called women's spirituality?"

Wise Words

"I am only one; but still I am one.
I cannot do everything,
But still I can do
Something; I will not
Refuse to do the
Something I can do."

—Helen Keller (1898–1978). Left deaf and blind after a childhood illness, Helen Keller was instructed by her famous teacher, Anne Sullivan, and overcame the results of her handicap. Helen educated others in issues of justice, knowing much blindness comes from illnesses linked to poverty. Her story was published as *The Miracle Worker* in 1959.

Many believe we stand on the brink of a major cultural shift in consciousness. This shift in consciousness is being aided by women claiming their power and becoming a vital force in shaping the world. That's a lofty declaration, one that might energize some women but send many running for cover. "I don't want to be a vital force in the world. I just want to be a vital force in my own life," they might say. And there you have it, in a nutshell. *Women's spirituality is about women becoming a vital force in their own lives.*

This spirituality helps women identify what is important to them, the things they most value, and discover ways they can have more of what is valuable in their lives. Whether it's in the home, at the office, in a science laboratory, in business or industry, in the arts, in entertainment, or in religious life doesn't matter. It's about choices and possibilities.

Mother Knows Best

Don't bump your head! While the social and political systems are now officially open to women, many women don't feel the necessary entitlement that would allow them to move ahead with their lives, and many still hit the proverbial glass ceiling. Women's spirituality isn't a "therapy," but the results of practicing it can be healing. It is more than a course in women's history (although learning more about the accomplishments of women is an important part of the process); its great value lies in supporting feminine values.

Community of Seekers

Women's spirituality is a community. The community can be as small as one other friend, but it involves bouncing ideas around with someone. Although the women who gather in this spirituality may come from a variety of religions or backgrounds, they have something very much in common—they are seekers. They are seeking their spiritual identity and new ways of expressing spirituality in the world. It's been called a new religion, a political movement, an emerging tradition. It is somewhat characterized by its spontaneity because there is no "super" structure.

The community of women's spirituality has defining characteristics or principles by which it is guided. The women of this community share a common worldview that sees power as responsibility rather than privilege, honors a sacred relationship with creation, and explores new ways of experiencing relationships.

Within women's spirituality, you will find women who belong to mainstream religion; women who have left that world to explore a new spiritual territory; women who have never practiced a formal religion; women of all ages, races, and economic and political backgrounds— sometimes all in one circle. A description that might fit is somewhere between creative and progressive—or maybe a combination of these two descriptive words, creative/progressive, because these women are inventing something new, and they're moving on.

Wise Words

"We've chosen the path to equality, don't / Let them turn us around."

—Geraldine A. Ferraro (1935–), first female vice presidential candidate on a national party ticket (1984)

Goddess Guide _____

There aren't any specific demographics available on how many women practice women's spirituality or who they are. However, it seems that there are more white women than women of color, slightly more Catholic women than other Christian women, and more Jewish women than Protestant. Catholic and Jewish women have a well-developed sense of ritual and may feel more comfortable in this spirituality. The exclusion of women from the priesthood in Catholicism has resulted in many women leaving their tradition to seek other ways of expressing themselves spiritually.

Is It Religion or Spirituality?

"Spirituality" is one of the buzzwords of the time, yet there probably isn't an agreed-upon definition of it or a clear understanding of how spirituality differs from religion. One view is that while all religion has spirituality, not all spirituality has religion. Spirituality is how you express your values in the world, and your values may not necessarily be attached to a formal religious tradition.

Religion has a defined system of beliefs and carefully governed practices. It draws distinct lines of separation between itself and "others." Spirituality can incorporate a variety of beliefs. It's a connecting kind of thing rather than a way of distinguishing one from another. Women's spirituality has no problem crossing spiritual or religious lines. It gathers eggs from a variety of nests, borrowing freely from many traditions.

An observer can identify influences from Buddhist, Hindu, Native American, Celtic, Wiccan, Neopagan, Christian, African/Caribbean, Jewish, and Christian beliefs; Jungian psychology; and assorted folklore. Within this context, women's spirituality is an emerging spirituality, characterized by some common principles and recognizing its status as a work in progress.

Politics and Spirituality: Strange or Sacred Bedfellows?

It may surprise some readers to know that all spirituality has a _political_ underbelly. As you will find out later in the book, American women have been working in the United States to secure political and religious rights for women since the day the Pilgrims landed. These women have always understood the political and the spiritual as different sides of the same flapjack. The process of women's spirituality is an awakening to understanding the religious and political dynamics of the culture.

Women's politics periodically catches the public's attention and then seems to quiet down. However, it doesn't really go away. After a time of relative quiet following the end of

World War II, the movement began to resurface in the late 1960s and early 1970s, often in the form of women's gatherings called consciousness-raising groups. A debate arose between women who positioned themselves as political and those who favored a spiritual approach. This debate was characterized as a squabble that permanently marked the women's movement and continues to mar its image to some extent today. However, there is an increased awareness that the two approaches, spiritual and political, are really two wings on the same bird. In order to fly, they must work together.

Womanspeak

Politics is the totality of interrelationships in a particular area of life involving power, authority, or influence, and is capable of manipulation.

Mother Knows Best

Don't think you can divorce politics from religion. They are two sides of the same issue. The political beliefs of a culture flow out of their religious beliefs.

Checking and Raising Consciousness: Sacred Poker Club

I belonged to an unconventional consciousness-raising group in the 1970s—we called it the Sacred Poker Club. Rather than consciousness-raising, we thought of it as raising a few eyebrows and maybe a little hell along the way. We were becoming aware of the sexism and racism all around us. Our "social critique" consisted of thumbing our nose at the establishment. We rebelled by getting together once a week to play poker, and it was scandalous. We became known far and wide—meaning for at least two counties in every direction.

We had a definite feminist bent no doubt—for example, Queens beat Kings! We were separatist—no men allowed. We would have welcomed any black woman, but the lines between the races at that time in our town made that extremely unlikely. A couple of us did give money to Ida Mae's campaign when she was running for city council in her all-black neighborhood. We talked about anything that was on our minds, which meant we talked about male dominance in our town, our county, our state, our country, and the world, and what it would be like if we ran things.

Mary McCarthy's *The Group* was a best-selling book in the 1960s. McCarthy's characters discussed the politics and morality of their day with Ivy League polish and sophistication we sorely lacked. We drank and smoked, cussed, and played 15-cent limit, quarter on the third raise, nothing wild but the dealer poker. Now as I look back, it was a consciousness-raising experience, although we would never have called it that. We were putting the pieces together, understanding our reality—creating our political analysis, as the movement says. Most important, we gave each other support for our hopes and dreams.

"As we come to trust and love our internal guide, we lose our fear of intimacy because we no longer confuse our intimate others with the higher power we are coming to know. In short, we are learning to give up idolatry—the worshipful dependency on any person place or thing. Instead we place our dependency on the source itself. The source meets our need through people, places or things."

—Julia Cameron, *The Artist's Way* (1992)

Putting Down a Taproot

Woman positioned on the spiritual side of the movement believe in the same vision as their political sisters but find that without direct connection to the spirituality that shapes and supports their political action, burnout is extremely high. They find that working strictly from a political base, without a taproot firmly anchored in the soul of the matter, the spirit cannot be sustained. They believe this is what happened to a lot of women who spent many years on the front lines of the feminist movement—they ran out of gas. Spiritual feminists see social change as the political flowering of the spirit—and for them it has soul.

Upon closer inspection, though, the two groups are more alike than they are different. Each in their own way addresses the same issues: a new understanding of relationship, concern for the environment, and the desire for a global community of nonviolence. They differ in how they go about it.

Sophia's Wisdom

Spiritual feminists work politically by working spiritually. They are introspective and meditative and create rituals to strengthen the spirit. Political feminists are pragmatic. They believe the changes that both groups of women are wanting to effect can only be done in confrontation with the existing political structures. For them, the sound of tom-toms, the smell of sage, and sweet grass do not a democracy make! There are women who pitch a tent in both camps.

Building a Better Mousetrap

Spiritual feminists say religious beliefs are at the core of the politics that both groups abhor. Their spirituality gives them personal support, and it functions another way, too.

They believe that without going deeper into the religious assumptions that lie at the heart of politics, nothing really changes. Those who create the political world will recreate it again in the same way because their religious beliefs support it. For example, when religion supports supremacy of any one group over another, politics will support it, too. These women understand that political change is an outcropping of religious transformation.

They are not alone in their belief. History confirms what they're saying. In recent times, one has only to look at the African American struggle for civil rights for a good example. This struggle was powered by deeply felt spiritual and religious beliefs. Its message of liberation was biblical. It confronted the politics of the time and changed the law.

> **Wise Words**
>
> "If you want to know how a culture is structured, look at their creation myth. It will tell you about their relationship to God, their relationship to each other, and how they organize their society."
>
> —Xan Griswold (1960–), student of Christian education, Scarrett Graduate School (1984)

In choosing to work toward social and political change from the spiritual or faith level, spiritual feminists believe they will ultimately be more successful. They are creating a new model of spirituality in the process. People don't let go of the way they are doing something, even when it isn't working, until a different way is in place in the society. They operate from the "build better mousetrap theory." Once a new system has been created, if people don't beat a path to your door, they will, at least, find the system and use it.

> **Sophia's Wisdom**
>
> A new idea goes through three stages. In the first, an alarm is sounded. Someone realizes what is going on isn't working. These are societies' prophets. The second phase begins with the building of new models. These builders are the visionaries; they can see new ways to do things. The third happens when society moves into the new model. This requires educators and facilitators. All three roles are important and necessary in making creative changes.

The Least You Need to Know

- Women's spirituality is a community of women who provide a place to ask questions about the religious and political realities we all live in.
- Women's spirituality has sociological, political, and spiritual characteristics. It has roots that go far back into history.

◆ Women's spirituality includes a process of coming to greater awareness of what you hold sacred and finding ways of expressing your spiritual beliefs in the world.

◆ There isn't a particular set of religious beliefs or written rules in women's spirituality; it works from common principles. You can belong to your traditional religion and practice women's spirituality, too.

New Paradigm: Women on Top?

In This Chapter

◆ The paradigm shift

◆ The great wound of Western culture

◆ Why 6,000 years is long enough

◆ Becoming more colorful

◆ Front and center with the Mother Goddess

You've just found out a bit about women's spirituality, some of the concerns and hopes behind it, and why it is gaining popularity. Now let's look at the religious and political influences that have spawned the re-emergence of this spirituality. To understand the circumstances this movement has developed out of, we'll look back to history to our cultural roots and see where we are now and where we want to go.

Patriarchy to Partnership

Patriarchy comes from the Latin words *pater*, meaning "father," and *arches*, meaning "to rule." It is literally a social system in which the father or eldest son is recognized as the head of the family or tribe. Western society has been organized on a patriarchal model since the beginning of its written history.

After thousands of years, we are shifting to a new organizational structure. You may have heard of the term *paradigm shift*. It describes a basic change in how we organize society. Women's spirituality is a way women are defining a new paradigm that they believe will be more attuned to the needs of all the people and all creation.

Womanspeak

Patriarchy is a combination of two Latin words, *pater,* meaning "father," and *arches,* meaning "to rule." It means rule by father or oldest son, or rule by men. A **paradigm** is a pattern or model upon which an organization or society is built.

The new paradigm in based on partnership. It begins as partnering with the sacred and includes creating partnerships with one another and with creation. In this new model, the whole creation is considered holy. All power is seen to come from God, and no one part of it has any more power than any other part.

Patriarchy: The Old Paradigm

Approximately 12,000 to 6,000 years ago, many societies in the near East and old Europe began the slow shift from tribal cultures to urban centers. This shift, which was characterized by patriarchal rule, would become the dominating paradigm of Western civilization.

Many believe that the tribal societies were (and are) based on maintaining a careful balance or partnership with the natural world. However, there are theories that say this wasn't always true, that as tribal societies' population grew, they exploited the earth's resources in their area and moved on. It's probably fair to say that tribal people of the past faced some of the same challenges we do today, and they had a different relationship with the earth than urban cultures have.

Urbanization brought with it a belief that nature was something to be subdued or conquered. Male dominance and the stratification of social systems became the primary organizing principle of the urban cultural centers. The principles of patriarchal thought were reflected in the development of the Western religious tradition, as well.

Wise Words

"Patriarchy is the religion of the planet."

—Mary Daly (1900–), author and associate professor in the Department of Theology at Boston College, where she teaches feminist ethics

Religious patriarchy has its origins in Hebrew scripture with Abraham, Isaac, Jacob, and his 12 sons, who were the founders of the first ancient Hebrew families or tribes. Judaism, Christianity, and Islam are all based on the scriptures and share this common patriarchal heritage. All societal structures—religion, government, military, education, economy, medicine, and family—were built on this model. Western culture continues to operate on this paradigm today.

Characteristics of patriarchy are a hierarchical ranking structure, laws originating at the top and applied to those below, and exclusively male leadership. The religious patriarchal structure defines God as a male and from that definition draws the rationale for male privilege. In addition, God is perceived to exist outside of creation. Matters of spirit are considered to be more important than earthly concerns.

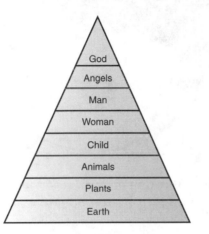

This vertical structure shows how a religious hierarchy might be represented. Each level of the pyramid has power over those below.

Duality: Hearing from the Other Side

One way of understanding spiritual wholeness is through the principle of *duality*. Duality means that all things contain their opposite within them. You have to go to Eastern philosophy for a symbol, the *yin/yang*, to understand duality because we don't have a symbol for it in our Western culture.

Principles of yin/yang describe life's duality. Yin and yang are not genders but describe basic characteristics that are found throughout all of nature and within both males and females. Yang is considered "male," and yin is "female," as many of the characteristics can be observed within the corresponding gender. Males have more yang, females have more yin, and each contains aspects of the other. That is the basic principle of duality—things containing their opposite.

What does this have to do with women's spirituality?

Western culture has a different perception. We see opposites as separate structures rather than as two parts of a whole. They see one aspect as better than the other. These two components are seen in competition with one another. This is called *dualism*. Dualism is always characterized by a one-up, one-down mentality. In our culture women are the "one down" part of the equation. Duality, on the other hand, would see male and female as two equal genders, two equal aspects of human beings.

The classic Chinese yin/yang symbol shows how combining opposites creates wholeness. Each half contains a particle of the other.

Women's spirituality is based in dua**lity** rather than dual**ism**. It sees men and women as equal partners. It sees humans and nature as partners. It sees humans in partnership with the creator.

Womanspeak

Duality describes the understanding that each individual part of nature has two opposite aspects that are complementary. **Dualism** describes the understanding that nature is composed of two opposite and opposing forces usually seen as good and evil. **Yin** symbolizes the principle of darkness, negativity, and femininity in Chinese philosophy that is the complement of yang. **Yang** symbolizes the principle of light, heat, impetus, and masculinity in Chinese philosophy that is the complement of yin.

The characteristics are of neutral or equal value in themselves until a culture assigns a value to them. In a society in which male and female are equally valued, the characteristics remain valued equally. When a culture values males more than females, the corresponding characteristics take on a value as well.

The following table lists some common ways dualities are expressed in the culture. As you read them, notice if you place more value on one quality than its counterpart. If you do, notice which one you feel has more merit.

Yin/Yang Characteristics

Male (Yang)	Female (Yin)
Sky	Earth
Heaven	Creation
Active	Receptive
Light	Dark
Good	Bad
Life	Death
Spirit	Body
Soul	Sexuality
Order	Chaos
Thought	Emotion
Right	Wrong
Cognitive knowing	Intuitive knowing
Competition	Co-operation
Civilization	Wilderness

Again, the characteristics themselves are of equal value. They are perceived to coexist as one, as two halves of a whole. In this way, life can be considered to contain both the sacred realm and the worldly as one whole. Order and chaos can be partners in a dance of creativity. Thought can not be divorced from emotion, and so on.

Deities found within cultures based on duality incorporate both aspects, too. Whether their deity was pictured as a female or a male, s/he contained principles associated with both genders.

Dualism: The Great Patriarchal Wound

When men are placed above women, as in the patriarchal structure, duality becomes dualism. Rather than seeing the dual nature of reality as partnership or complementary, it sees it as competitive—one being better than the other.

> ### Sophia's Wisdom
>
> Duality is wholeness; it doesn't think in terms of "either/or," as is common in Western thought. It thinks in inclusive terms such as "both/and." For example, human nature is *both* human *and* divine. Most indigenous spiritualities such as Native American, Australian Aboriginal, and African tribal, as well as Eastern philosophy and women's spirituality, are based in duality or holistic thought.

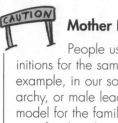

Mother Knows Best

People use different definitions for the same terms. For example, in our society, patriarchy, or male leadership is the model for the family. When the term *family values* is used, it does not necessarily refer to values that support women or children, it means upholding male leadership—sometimes at all costs. Ask what people mean when they use a term.

In dualism, the values associated with male became exclusive to him and more highly regarded than those associated with female. This thinking resulted in a split in the psyche that is the great wound of Western culture. We will discover how this wound is expressed in many ways throughout this book.

Patriarchal thinking perceives God as exclusively male, and consequently, male characteristics are considered more "Godlike." For the most part, being female means being excluded from the ruling or law-making parts of society. When a female gains rank in the male system, it is generally by using male principles; she is being accepted as being "like one of the guys." Just because a woman is in a leadership position does not necessarily mean that she is implementing feminine values.

Patriarchal leadership in our culture is largely the domain of Euro-American males. It's their worldview that has established law and order, and formed the basis for our cultural traditions. If you doubt that this is true, simply take a look at the cultural make-up of the Supreme Court, the Senate, Congress, and any religious institution. Women's spirituality understands that an exclusively male structure results in limited understanding. By failing to include women's values, and the values of other cultures, this structure is exclusive rather than inclusive.

Naturally Powerful

Feminist author and seminar leader Starhawk talks about two kinds of power: power *over* and power from *within*. Power over, as the name implies, is when a person or system imposes dominance over another. As we have seen, the patriarchal structure is based on having power *over* others.

Power from within is recognition that everything in creation is imbued with the spirit of the creator and has an innate power. In religion and spirituality, this innate power is referred to as God's presence or sacred presence in creation. Women's spirituality believes we are called to be in partnership with one another, with the world itself, and with the divine.

Jacob's Ladder to Sarah's Circles

Psychologist and pioneer in mind/body healing Joan Borysenko uses the "Climbing Jacob's Ladder" image to describe men's spirituality. She describes the way we have come to think of religion and spirituality in our culture by performance or accomplishing tasks—things we must ascend or transcend as a male model. She uses another image, "Walking Sarah's Circles," to describe the way women think of spirituality. Women find God in the center of the circle that encompasses all of creation. They connect to the sacred by connecting to their own center.

The circle is a good model to understand women's spirituality and to see that is not about "taking over," as many fear. Women's spirituality is not interested in simply reversing the societal structure we have now by placing women at the top of the ladder. It is important to make the distinction between just replacing the players and changing the game. Women's spirituality is about changing the game.

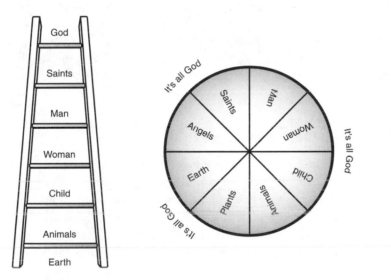

The ladder shows the hierarchical worldview. The circle shows a different model in which all parts of creation are shown in relationship to one another and all are necessary to make the circle complete.

The circle is a relational model for society. Where the hierarchical ladder imposes limited interaction between the groups, a circular model connects all the "kingdoms" at the center. Each part of creation is placed in equal position, and none is more important than another. In this paradigm, interdependence is recognized and wholeness is honored.

Liberation Spirituality: Changing the Game

Radical comes from the Latin *radix*, which means "root." To call for a radical transformation means to go to the roots or the foundational principles of an organization and restructure from that point. That is why women are insisting that the bottom-line organizational structure of society must be changed. That requires a shift in perception. They are recommending we shift to a partnership structure. They are not interested in merely placing more women and people of other cultures in the existing system. Women's

Wise Words

"Men have always detested women's gossip because they suspect the truth: Their measurements are being taken and compared."

—Erica Jong (1942–), best-selling contemporary novelist and essayist

spirituality is a voice for those who are working for the complete transformation of the religious and political structures—for organizing society according to equality and partnership.

The transformation begins with women having a transformed understanding of themselves. It means women seeing themselves as powerful in a culture that not only perceives them as morally inferior but also one that has often cast them in the role of evil. As women begin to create their own identity apart from the ones they have been assigned by society and culture, they are empowered to step forward into full equality with men—in a new model that is based in partnership. Women's spirituality focuses on lifting women up rather than trying to hold men down. It isn't the either/or approach of dualism; it is based in the holistic thinking of duality. The creator is the author of the power; everyone shares in it, and everyone has an equal share.

"I'd Like to See This in Some Other Colors, Please"

Women's spirituality began mostly among white, middle-class, educated females of Euro-American descent, and these women still make up most of the population of the movement. However, women's spirituality is becoming global, crossing national, cultural, racial, and economic boundaries. For the most part, it occurs in English-speaking countries. Since much of the information is passed through books and newsletters, as well as retreats and seminars that are mainly held in the United States, the language used is almost always English.

From the beginning of the movement, there has been a cultural gap between white women and women of color. This gap remains today, but many women believe it is closing. Women of color have challenged white women to expand their vision to include all forms of dominance, rather than just focusing on women's equality, which they believe has been the primary target for white women. Women of color have long maintained that the issue of working to gain position in a system that is racist forces them to make a choice between sexism and racism. We explore this in depth in Chapter 5, "Black Women's Spirituality and Womanist Theology."

Black women see race and gender as one and the same issue. Many white women working within women's spirituality agree with this position. However, the

Mother Knows Best

When women get together, it isn't always for the purpose of talking about men—only sometimes! Women's empowerment is the key focus in women's spirituality, and women spend most of their time talking about themselves! Sorry, guys.

experiences of many women of color have shown that there is a problem within the movement and that many women don't understand the full implications of what it means to go for the complete transformation of the system. In addition to linking these two very important parts of the problem, black women have identified a third aspect to be considered—the oppression of economics or class. Although there is still work to be done in mending the rift between black and white women, all informed women today understand and agree on the need to address economics and class.

Women's spirituality is maturing and being transformed as it grows. Thanks to the contributions of women of color, it is calling for the complete transformation that is necessary to end oppressive politics in all arenas. However, since there is no one establishing the rules for every group, feeding new information into the system—even important information such as this—takes time. There is no formal process in place. Information is passed through articles, books, and seminars. The educational focus within the movement is first and foremost on women educating themselves and each other. Hopefully the term women's spirituality won't always conjure up an all-white image.

Splendor in the Grass

Women's spirituality could be called a grassroots movement. That's a good image for it, because wherever it sprouts up, there is a mutual love of the earth. It is also grassroots because there is no central office, rulebook, membership forms, dues, or governing board. There is no religious doctrine, established belief system, written code of ethics, sacred writings, or any of the other things we have come to expect to be a part of religion.

In place of a written history, women's spirituality has an oral tradition; it shares a common story. The story is about remembering a time before patriarchy, when feminine principles were honored. When women gather, they tell their sacred story. They use books, most of which have been written over the past 30 or 40 years, in which archaeologists, historians, and other social scientists have reinterpreted old data as well as presented new data that increasingly support this story.

Serious scholarship is being developed to support the assertions that there was a time before patriarchy, a time when the world of the Near East and old Europe were once under a different organizing principle. They call this time the *matriarchy*, and we will look closely at it in Part 2, "Meeting Goddess," as we learn about women's history and the time of the goddess. But first, let's see where people from many different traditions who share common values are coming together.

> ### Sophia's Wisdom
>
> Whether the history is real or imagined, the result is the same: Women consistently building stronger self-esteem and renewing their spirit through sharing their story of a time of their power. In the process, they have raised enough questions to muddy the academic waters.

Meeting on Sacred Ground

A meeting ground for both political and spiritual feminists as well as a place where cross-cultural alliances are built is literally and figuratively sacred ground—it's the earth. Treatment of the earth and abuse of its resources is one area in which patriarchal insensitivity can be most profoundly witnessed. The modern Western economic structure, like all other aspects of the culture, is based on competition. Economics is the superlative measure in every business and industry, and it runs on competition. When these two giants come up against wise use of resources, environmental concerns give way to economics in every case. Women believe false religious beliefs, giving people dominance over nature, are paving the way for today's materialism that is threatening the global environment. For many women as well as our global neighbors, this is a primary concern.

The Holy Heresy: God Is

Women's spirituality is based on the principle of *immanence*, or God's presence in creation, rather than the principle of *transcendence*, which describes God's presence in heaven. Talking about God's presence in nature never fails to bring up issues of *pantheism*. Traditional religion defines pantheism as the belief that God is present totally in nature and considers belief in pantheism to be a false belief, or heresy. No law-abiding religious devotee wants to be accused of heresy, even in the twenty-first century.

Womanspeak

Immanence refers to God's presence in the creation. **Transcendence** refers to God's presence in the spirit world above and outside of creation. **Pantheism** is the belief that God is present wholly in nature.

The entire situation may very well be a confusion whose roots go back to the beginning of religious history and to that old bugger dualism we read about earlier. As the concept of monotheism (one God) was struggling to be born, it found itself up against the goddess cultures of the Near East, whose religion had many representations all based in the Divine Mother. The growing monotheism of the Near East was following a cultural pattern that seemed to be springing up all over the world at about the same time. It imaged God as only male, and in creating a monotheistic religious structure, the goddess cultures were annihilated.

Later, as Christianity was converting indigenous cultures, a similar situation arose. Not really understanding the holistic belief systems they were encountering, Christians considered these cultures *"idolaters."* Their "either/or" thinking couldn't comprehend that the Divine was *both* one *and* also many.

Time has shown that many of these cultures had highly developed religious systems centered in sacred relationships with the natural world. They understood the essential oneness of the creator and the creation and knew this presence took many forms.

This is where religion often gets into trouble—naming others' beliefs without really understanding them.

Womanspeak

Panentheism describes the belief that god is present both in creation and in a transcended way, too.

A new term has evolved to identify the belief in a sacred presence both in nature and transcended as well. The new term is panentheism. Panentheism refers to both immanence and transcendence, meaning God is present in creation but not limited just to creation. Again, these are the categories of traditional religion, not women's spirituality. A problem occurs every time one religion applies its categories to another religion or spiritual practice. This is how misunderstanding begins and what has resulted in many religious wars. The problem even with the term *panentheism* is that it still describes a "here and there," it still speaks from a dualistic understanding. However, for the time being, until the language is formed from a truly holistic understanding, it's going to have to suffice.

The issue of sacred presence is core to women's spirituality. If there is a clear line between women spiritualists and traditionalists, this is it. Perhaps a more appropriate way of stating God's presence for women's spirituality might be simply "God is."

Speaking New Language

Many women from traditional religion participate in women's spirituality where they gain a better understanding of themselves. Sometimes they continue to practice it along with their traditional religion. Sometimes you'll find women's spirituality inside religious traditions. However, it is usually identified as Jewish women's spirituality or Christian women's spirituality.

Wise Words

"For thousands of years, the incomprehensible mystery we call God has been presented as male. However, scripture provides many images of God: God as light, a woman searching for a lost coin, a shepherd, a bakerwoman, a rock, a wind, a woman giving birth, a pillar of fire, wisdom, a mother bird, and a midwife. To focus only on God as father or as masculine creates false limits, yet when female terms are used to describe the divine being, many people object. Considering God in other ways will open up new and rich perspectives of the sacred."

—Jean Morningstar, SNJM, artist and illustrator for *Prayers to She Who Is* (Crossroad, 1995)

In the Judeo-Christian and Islamic traditions, the female figure appears as Sophia, Shekinah, Lilith, Eve, and the Virgin Mary, although her position has been greatly reduced to accommodate the beliefs of these patriarchal religions. In order to get to the power of the mother figure, it is necessary to step outside the symbol system of your tradition and look at the material from a new perspective.

◆ Sophia material exists in fragments in the Hebrew Bible as The Wisdom of Solomon. Sophia, the embodiment of wisdom, is the feminine side of the masculine Godhead. She was almost completely written out of the texts.

◆ Shekinah appears in Jewish theology as God's presence in and throughout the world.

◆ Lilith appears in creation stories of some Hebraic traditions as Adam's first wife who left him rather than become submissive. Specifically, she refused to lie beneath him in sex. She is a relic of the Sumero-Babylonian Goddess Belit-ili of Jewish mythology.

◆ Eve is believed to be the first woman created. According to dualistic interpretations that have prevailed in the culture, she sinned and brought evil into the world.

◆ Virgin Mary is the human mother of the divine Christ. She is "all good," signified by her status as virgin. In dualism, she is often compared to Eve, who is "all bad."

Women's spirituality honors these women and also draws on religious symbols that predate them by many thousands of years, going back to the earliest time. The first symbol of a sacred presence was in the form of a woman known as goddess. It isn't necessary to worship her or to accept her as your religious symbol. However, in order to appreciate women's spirituality, you will want to look at her as who she is to those who honor her. When traditional women practice women's spirituality outside their tradition, they step into an ancient circle that has a spiritual history and its own set of symbols.

You'll meet the goddess and find out about how she is honored in Part 2, but first, let's read about the relationship between women's spirituality and traditional sources of authority. You'll also read more about the shift from matriarchy to patriarchy and perhaps discover that it isn't just a boy/girl thing.

The Least You Need to Know

◆ Women's spirituality is an emerging spiritual tradition rather than a religion, although it has been called both.

◆ Women's spirituality is spiritual, sociological, and political.

◆ Women's spirituality belongs to a liberation tradition sharing a common agenda of ending oppression and developing new models for society that reflect a value of spiritual and political equality.

◆ The primary symbol of women's spirituality is the goddess, who represents the sacred presence of the feminine in women and throughout creation.

Power, Authority, and a Group Hunch

In This Chapter

- ◆ All about power over and power from within
- ◆ Is there a there, there?
- ◆ Could a religious strike be in the cards?
- ◆ What's this thing called spiritual instinct?

A big difference between spirituality and religion is the understanding of power and authority. In this chapter you'll find out how women's spirituality handles these two principles. You'll also see areas in which this spirituality differs sharply from organized religion and find out if there's room for your traditional religious beliefs. You're going to hear about a tried-and-true method of moral discernment called spiritual instinct and learn how women are claiming it for themselves today.

Show Me the Power

The essential differences between goddess consciousness and patriarchal culture is how power is perceived and how that perception plays out in the society. The ancient cultures of the Great Mother were organized in the principle of equality; leadership was shared between men and women. These cultures were referred to as matriarchal. Later, society shifted to a patriarchal structure, which meant males ruled exclusively, and society became stratified. Those with power were on top; those over whom they had power were below. Currently, religion uses the patriarchal model. Changing the power paradigm is the bottom line agenda in women's spirituality.

A Spirituality of Partnership

Woman's spirituality is based in partnership. I first heard the term "partnership" used to describe a sacred relationship in graduate school in 1984, when I was studying religious education. The student body was mostly women. Our professors were complaining because so many of us were quoting Letty Russell almost exclusively in our papers. I remember one professor exclaiming in frustration, "What is all this about Letty Russell? There are 50 other books on the reading list … yet everyone uses Letty Russell!"

The answer was really quite clear when you think about it. First, Letty Russell was the only woman theologian on the reading list, and second, her concept of partnership made sense to our female sensibility. One woman went so far as to say, "It was the first time theology made any sense at all! Up to that point it had been an exercise in logic but never said anything that had *anything* to do with *anything!*" I don't know if I'd go that far, but I do agree that Dr. Russell made sense, and so do many of the women theologians writing today. They are putting words to many of the things women have known but weren't always able to articulate.

Russell talks about being in partnership with God and in partnership with one another. She goes on to say that the old way of one group of people interpreting religious truth and handing it down to others is no longer workable. She believes that no one person or group can interpret the meaning of the gospel for another person or group. Theology, biblical interpretation, religious doctrine, and spiritual principles must use the accumulated wisdom of all the people. Russell describes the new partnership as alive, full of *synergy*, *serendipity*, and *sharing*.

> **Sophia's Wisdom**
>
> Women's spirituality follows the principles of the old goddess traditions that were based on the equality principles of a partnership model. The later patriarchal societies were based on domination. Societies within patriarchy are organized according to a ranking system. People at the top have more power than those at the bottom. A matriarchy is based in shared power.

What Russell is advocating is a major shift in how theology is written and how power is perceived and used. The Western religious tradition is a patriarchy. Men are the religious leaders. In addition to being the guardians of religious truth, for 4,000 years they have exclusively held the power to decide what is important information to pass along, what would be discarded, and where to focus religion.

Leadership within traditional religion requires a certain level of education and also a particular kind of education. The end result does not reflect the experiences of the wider population, just the leaders. Russell, and others like her, are calling for a new model. The new model is for a moral voice of the people, rather than just the leaders. This would result in the collective wisdom being used as well as scripture to determine moral and religious principles.

> **Mother Knows Best**
>
> Gender isn't the issue! It's about values. Many men in the fields of religion and theology have the same worldview as women's spirituality. Likewise, not all women in religion are saying the same thing, either.

It's a Principle, Not a Gender!

Riane Eisler, scholar, feminist, and author of *The Chalice and the Blade* (1987), clarifies the position of many women when she describes the two systems as a *partnership* model and a *dominator* model. As Eisler points out, matriarchal and patriarchal tend to make it appear to be about being male or female and only further separates the genders. A woman can operate on a dominator model, and likewise, a man can operate according to partnership. Certainly many men as well as women believe in equality. It's a principle, not a gender.

> **Womanspeak**
>
> **Dominator** describes a hierarchical cultural model where one group of people has dominance over another group. **Partnership** describes a nonhierarchical model where all people are treated equally. Partnership extends to all relationships: God, nature, and people.

Omnipresence: Sacred Here, Now, and Always

Women's spirituality believes the creator is present in creation and the world is sacred. There are no levels to sacredness and no degrees of it. Nothing in creation has more of God in it than something else. The partnership, or *sacred*, model has no hierarchy.

God's immanence creates an essentially different relationship than God as transcendent, and that immanence is the basis for understanding partnership. When God is immanent, sacred presence is "here," now, in the material world. We are all already *saved*. Actually, the word "saved" wouldn't even be part of the vocabulary. You could substitute the word "sacred"—all are sacred. In the sacred worldview, power is perceived to be innate, God-given, and not dependent on any external source, set of beliefs, or practices.

The principle of transcendence places God outside and above the world—"out there." God is in heaven, and we are on earth. When God is perceived as transcendent, people as well as the natural world are not sacred, and they must fight against worldliness to become holy or sacred. The world becomes the enemy, something to conquer, rise above, or otherwise avoid at all costs.

In this model, "salvation" is located outside the self. It is something that must be acquired. You can become sacred through some particular action, such as a profession of faith, or by your good deeds, thereby assuring your connection to God. Again, you become sacred through something you must do; you are not created as sacred.

People who don't believe the same way aren't treated sacredly, nor is this sacred relationship extended to other parts of creation such as the animal and plant world, the air, water, or the earth itself. As a result, the "saved" group perceives itself as having more access to God than the "unsaved," and this gives the group's members more privilege, or higher rank. As a friend of mine says, "God help the unsaved!"

Women's spirituality sees power in the following ways:

◆ Power is God-given—it comes from God and is within all.

◆ God is immanent—God is present in creation, now.

◆ Sacred worldview—all are sacred (saved).

◆ Equality—expressed through partnership.

"Maybe There Really Isn't Any There, There"

Gertrude Stein made her famous remark as she visited Oakland, California, for the first time, saying, "There isn't any there, there." In repeating it, I extend my apologies to the people of Oakland. I have lived there and don't agree with her observation; however, the line works beautifully to illustrate the point I want to make. The statement, "There is no there, there," can also be applied to women's spirituality.

The idea of God's immanence is where most traditional theologians have trouble with women's spirituality and other earth-based religions that insist that God is here and all is sacred. Often traditionalists will go so far as to say God is both here (immanent) and there (transcendent), but can't be just here. I would like to invite you to explore this issue of *here* and *there* a little further. Those of you who have had enough can skip ahead to the next section. We'll pick you up later. Those who are interested, read on.

One thing about thinking outside the box is that you can explore ideas and sometimes even trip over a new one, or more likely a new twist on an old one. This happened to me the day I went out to the river. I was sitting under a tree, stirring a small bonfire, soaking up nature, and musing on this chapter and the realities of "here" and "there." I looked up into the branches over my head, and the idea came to me to climb the tree and go out on a limb, theologically speaking, that is. So being a tree climber from way back, that is exactly what I did. Here are the results.

Everyone seems to agree on the idea of God's *omnipresence*. I learned about it a long time ago in the *Baltimore Catechism*, that little brown book that contained all the answers for being a Catholic.

Question: "Where is God?"

Answer: "God is everywhere."

When we say that God is omnipresent, it means he is present in all places at the same time. God transcends time and place. It appears that it's in the comprehension of what that really means that things get murky. Omnipresent means just what it says—all present everywhere at the same time.

You can't have *omnipieces* or *omniplaces*. You can't have God present in your soul and not in your big toe, for instance, or present in you and not in me. Or for that matter, present in you and me and not in the branch over my head. God's presence is fully "here." So when you read the fine print on omnipresence, know there is no separation between the material world and the spiritual world. Maybe it's all really "here," now.

This led me to the question, "What if there isn't any 'there,' there?"

Be here, now? Isn't this what many religious and spiritual people have been saying all along? What if we *are* here, now? What if everything is *all here, now*, and our realization of that hinges on our ability to comprehend God's sacred presence—*here, now?* Maybe it's about awareness. Isn't this what the mystics in every tradition have been telling us? As they practice being still and going inside, they're able to open more levels of awareness, and they say they will eventually find God. They have a *mystical experience* that they describe as a *divine union*. I wonder what they mean?

Mother Knows Best _____

Women's spirituality doesn't challenge God. It challenges specific assumptions about God. For example, it challenges religious assumptions regarding God's gender, rules regarding who is saved and who is not, and the practice of thinking one's way to God. It also stands in resistance to interpretations that have been put on God and then imposed on others.

Womanspeak _____

Omnipresence describes the belief that God is present everywhere all at once.

A Rose by Any Other Name

As the poet said, "A rose by any other name would smell as sweet." What you call yourself isn't important to women's spirituality, either. The emphasis is on the nature of your *relationship* to creation—how you play your beliefs out in the world. This is characteristic of spirituality more than religion. *The essential religious or theological belief in women's spirituality is God's sacred presence here, everywhere, now.* This belief didn't disappear thousands of years ago when the culture shifted to a different model. It went underground, but there have been religious thinkers and "regular" people who have always thought this way.

Following is a list of some of the characteristics of religion and spirituality. If you think of it as a continuum rather than as oppositions, you'll find people who lean one way and others leaning another way. You might find it interesting to locate your place on the scale to see whether you lean more toward religion or spirituality.

> **Sophia's Wisdom**
>
> Women who practice women's spirituality use goddess as a symbol of their own sacred nature. She evokes a deep love and respect. Because this spirituality is based on partnership, the relationship between women and their goddess is different than how traditional religion relates to God. Women don't "worship" goddess like traditional religion's relationship with God; they love her.

Definite Beliefs	Individual Beliefs
Rules and laws	Ethics
Identifies as different	Seeks common ground
External authority	Internal authority
Regulates practice	Autonomous practice
Hierarchical	Partnership
Structured	Spontaneous
Exclusive	Inclusive
Truth	Mystery

The Voice of Authority: For Heaven's Snake!

The snake is a symbol of goddess's quality of renewal or regeneration as well as her wisdom. Snakes appear with goddess from the very earliest time and up into the Classic Greek period. Contemporary artist Judy Chicago combined thousands of years of this imagery into a composite form she calls the *Snake Goddess,* who has a place at the table as an honored guest in her famous multimedia work, *The Dinner Party* (1979). *The Dinner*

Party celebrates 1,000 women from the earliest images of the Great Mother to Georgia O'Keeffe and Virginia Woolf, each chosen to symbolize women's heroic struggle for freedom and dignity. The exhibit, a collaborate effort of many women, includes 39 place settings on a triangular banquet table 48 feet long on each side. The table runners were elaborately embroidered, and the whole exhibit sits on a tile floor cast just for it. In placing the snake at the table, Chicago reminds us that the snake "was the embodiment of psychic vision and oracular divination, both of which were traditionally considered to be part of women's magical powers." You can find more about Chicago and her famous exhibit, *The Dinner Party*, in Appendix C, "Resources."

The snake, a primary symbol of the goddess culture symbolizing self-generation, eternity, and wisdom.

Reconnecting to intuition is an important practice in women's spirituality as a means of reclaiming the women's oracular power. You'll learn all this in Chapter 19, "Spiritual Instinct." Now we'll discover more about women's moral authority, how it slithered away, and what they're doing to get it back.

Of Snakes and Snake Oil

In the Bible, "original sin" is symbolized by the image of a snake tricking a woman. Many women believe the choice of this image was not accidental. For thousands of years, women were believed to have gifts of prophecy and vision. This means

Womanspeak

Oracle refers to someone or something considered a source of knowledge, wisdom, or prophecy. Such information is received intuitively. **Divination** describes the methods or practice of foretelling the future or discovering the unknown through omens, oracles, or supernatural powers of prophecy or prediction. It is a premonition or feeling about something that is going to happen.

that they had the ability to discern "morality" within themselves. And in the early cultures, women were the guardians of the beliefs and ethics of the society.

Wise Words

"Eve is shown in the Bible as a temptress who not only sins herself but also lures her mate into sin. The first mother of our race seems a weak creature, possibly even evil. Women and men are both limited by cultural messages—men, that they must be perpetually in charge and powerful; women, that they must be endlessly nurturing. Men are as capable of nurturing as women are of wielding power."

—Patricia Monaghan, Ph.D., author and pioneer in the women's spirituality movement from her book, *The Goddess Companion: Daily Meditations on the Feminine Spirit* (Llewellyn Publications, 1999)

Judaism, Christianity, and Islam are based on the creation story of the Bible. (Genesis 3:1–24) The story uses a snake as a "trickster" or "the devil" to tempt Eve to eat of a certain tree God has forbidden her to eat from. In so doing, she falls into sin. She gets Adam to eat, too, and they suffer the consequences of their disobedience and lose their place in the Garden of Eden. The human race is believed to inherit this moral weakness in the form of "original sin."

Today there is a huge amount of disagreement among traditional scholars over the exact translation of this story and also how it is interpreted. Their findings may never completely agree on what was said and what was meant by the story. However, the understanding that is woven deep into our societal fabric has a major impact.

Sophia's Wisdom

In addition to there being two versions of the creation story in the Bible, biblical scholars and theologians from all religions are in great disagreement over the meaning of the two versions. New scholarship takes 20 years or more to get into the educational system, and then takes another generation to impart the new findings. We're about to approach the time when "new" biblical scholarship, which began in the late 1960s and 1970s, will begin impacting the general culture. When that happens, many of the things women have been saying will become part of mainstream religion.

In the popular culture version of the creation story, the snake was symbolically used as the vehicle by which Eve falls into error and commits "original sin." The snake, once the symbol of woman's gift of inner seeing or knowing, is turned against her. On the psychological and theological levels, this translates to her not being able to trust herself and also makes her untrustworthy. It paves the way for the core principle of patriarchal thought—women's innate moral weakness and the need for authority outside of the self.

Goddess and child, an early representation of a snake goddess from the late Neolithic period found in Crete.

(Artist: Susan Faulkner)

Feminist scholars and theologians both in and out of traditional religion have researched scripture and offer different interpretations of the creation story. Chapter 4, "Rethinking Religion," discusses this in greater detail, so here I'll just say that the new understanding goes a long way toward correcting errors of the past. However, many women question whether new interpretations can undo the thinking that's prevailed for so long that places women as the enemy and establishes males as authority.

Norma Rae, Where Are You?

Norma Rae is a young woman who helped unionize a plant in the South and secure better wages for the people who worked there. Sally Fields won an Oscar for her portrayal of Rae in the film version of the story. All of this is by way of introducing an interesting story about a women's spirituality group in Mississippi.

The group began as a Bible study group several years prior to my meeting with them. They were looking at new scholarship material about the Bible and applying the interpretations to scripture. The women had come to the conclusion that while the process had been meaningful, it required a lot of time and commitment. They believed that the "old"

ideas were so woven into our cultural fabric that they could not realistically be reworked. The overall tone of the group was one of great frustration and defeat.

When I asked the group what options they considered, they felt the images would have to change on a woman-to-woman basis; they compared the process to a slogan used by reading programs, "Each one teach one." Their slogan is "Each one reach one." They believe that women have always had a better grasp on spirituality and religion than they've taken credit for. "Women have been the laborers in the vineyard, and men have always been the management, yet women are the ones that keep religion in business!" is how one woman phrased it.

The group believes that the important role women play in religion would become more obvious if they would withdraw their support—just for a day—just long enough for them to realize the power they have. However, a "spiritual strike" is probably not going to happen, they admit.

In the words of one of the women, "If we can just change a woman's perception about herself and get her to see herself as powerful, the whole paradigm would eventually shift on its own. But if the past is any reflection on the future, it's going to be a slow process. You know we have the power; we've always had it. No one can take it away. It's not a matter of men understanding women's power; it's a matter of women understanding it!"

Calling for Common Sense

Many women practicing women's spirituality remain in their traditional religions and continue to use scripture as the source of their religious and spiritual teachings or moral authority. However, probably just as many women don't use it. When they don't use scripture as their authority and they don't follow any particular written rules, a couple of fair questions arise: "Where are they getting their information?" and "How do they know what's right and wrong?"

The source for spiritual guidance for many women in women's spirituality is *spiritual instinct*. These women feel that there's a quality for moral discernment within us that can be trusted. Developing one's ability to connect with this instinct is done by honing intuition. Spiritual instinct relies on personal reflection, followed by the common practice of sounding things out with your community.

Wise Words

"The more we look at the things around us with spiritually literate eyes, the more meanings we begin to find in them. It is no wonder that in ancient and modern rituals everyday things are used to signify important ideas. We can make our own readings of ceremonial objects through the spiritual practices of imagination, listening, and meaning."

—Frederic and Mary Ann Brussat, *Spiritual Literacy* (Simon & Schuster, 1996)

Women know they're naturally empathetic and sensitive to the needs of others, and they base their decisions on what they "know is right." They "know" it through what they describe as an inborn sense of right and wrong. Others say that while they work from a personal internal system, they also use an external measure. The external criterion they use is a simple one, the one most of us remember from childhood called The Golden Rule: "Do unto others as you would have done to you."

Women also refer to the Native American principle of *seven generations*. The principle of seven generations looks at the present situation for its affect to at least the next seven generations. The Native American's sense of interconnection knows that all actions have consequences that others must deal with. It says to look ahead as to how your decisions will affect your children, and your children's children, and their children's children, and so on for seven generations, and make the decision from there.

Women believe the spirit is one with the body, and just as we are born with other instincts such as our abilities to eat, walk, talk, seek shelter, and other natural functions, we have a spiritual instinct. They point to the fact that when it comes to determining right from wrong in a specific moment, a hard-and-fast rule doesn't always apply. Certainly many lawyers, judges, and others who are involved in determining degrees of accountability to the law would have to concur.

Sophia's Wisdom

In some circles, the only rule is, what goes around comes around—three times! There's a belief that whatever you do or even wish upon another comes back to you three times as strong. It keeps the prayer lines very clean!

Womanspeak

Seven generations refers to the Native American philosophy of making decisions with the understanding that they will impact the world in the future. Morality is determined by how it will affect seven generations of children.

A Group Hunch?

Comedienne Lily Tomlin's character Trudy makes her philosophical statement as she asks the question "What is reality anyway, but a group hunch?" That can also describe women's spirituality. Since it follows inner guidance and it includes others, women's spirituality is sort of a group hunch. Since we live in a culture that sees things from the male perspective, we often find ourselves needing a woman's viewpoint. How many times have you asked a friend to listen to what you're saying and give you feedback? Women's circles are important spiritual communities. They are sounding boards to clarify ideas and to get validation.

> **Wise Words**
>
> In her book, *The Spiral Dance: A Rebirth of the Ancient Religion of the Great Goddess* (Harper & Row, 1979), contemporary author, counselor, and seminar leader Starhawk defines community as "People to whom we can speak with passion without having the words catch in our throats. Somewhere we can be free."

Women's spirituality is building a tradition, and respect for the beliefs of others is an important principle. So if anyone is saying you have to believe certain things or have a particular image of the sacred, they are talking about something else, not women's spirituality. Women's spirituality is about finding out what you believe.

Generally speaking, women's spirituality is practiced in small groups of fairly like-minded people. If a person showed up with a view that directly opposed the group, the group would have to figure out a way to deal with it. There aren't any specific ways of handling dissension; it would probably be by consensus. Most women I spoke with shrugged off any concern, believing that it would be handled with common sense.

The Least You Need to Know

- Women's spirituality is based on understanding power as equal and God-given rather than unequal and acquired.
- Women's spirituality follows principles rather than rules. There is no doctrine or central governing board.
- It believes that the divine is present here, now, in this world, and is available for consultation.
- It believes in an inborn spiritual instinct that informs the individual about "right" and "wrong" behavior.
- Women's spirituality is a work in process.

Chapter 4

Rethinking Religion

In This Chapter

- ◆ Women theologians: doing it upside down
- ◆ Eco-feminism; *Super Natural Christians;* and Adam loses his manhood
- ◆ The inside skinny on Adam and Eve
- ◆ Can women's theology and traditional religion cohabitate?

Over the last quarter century, women scholars have compiled a body of work that forms the bones of women's spirituality. This scholarship gives footing to and strengthens the ideas generated by this spirituality. Their studies have resulted in feminist theory and feminist theology finding a place in colleges and universities throughout the country. Many of these theologians follow the lines established by classical or systematic theology, and others are using a new method of writing theology called process theology. It's written from the viewpoint of the people rather than the viewpoint of the hierarchical church. It calls the church into accountability, rather than the church calling the people into accountability.

Thealogy Isn't Misspelled

Over the last 25 years women have made enormous contributions to *theology* and religion through their scholarship. In addition, they have developed a new

Womanspeak

Theology is the study of religion. It uses cognitive reasoning, scripture, and tradition to determine the nature of God. **Thealogy** is the study of the divine feminine in the form of the Mother Goddess. It uses cognitive reasoning based on human experiences of the sacred to determine the nature of the sacred.

discipline called *thealogy*, the study of the female deity. Female Jewish scholars are devoting their efforts to developing new rituals that honor women, using inclusive language, developing female religious images, and creating a body of scholarship based in new biblical translations and interpretations. Christianity has seen an outpouring of new material written by women scholars who are basing their theologies on women's experiences. Like their Jewish colleagues, they, too, are reinterpreting scripture to correct the gender bias.

Give Me That Old-Time Theology

Today's women theologians belong to a tradition that goes back to the beginning of our country. Anne Hutchinson; abolitionists Sojourner Truth, Sarah Grimke, and Frances Willard of the Women's Christian Temperance Union; Elizabeth Cady Stanton; and other women throughout history were self-trained theologians who challenged Bible stories they found objectionable. Toward the end of the nineteenth century, theologian Elizabeth Cady Stanton, in a bold and courageous act of rebellion, published *The Woman's Bible*. Stanton was one of the first women to speak out against what she and others saw to be sexist interpretation of the scripture. Stanton saw that the biblical creation story was used to justify the economic and political subordination of women. She strongly advocated that offending scripture passages be reinterpreted or reconsidered as a source of revelation. You'll read more about Stanton in Chapter 12, "Our Foremothers," but first let's look at the process Stanton used in questioning authority.

Wise Words

"Through the ages, on all continents, people have worshiped the divine feminine. But for many centuries in our culture, the vision of a universal mother has been suppressed. There has been no great sky mother above us, no great earth mother on whose body we walk. There has been no goddess to whom we call out on dark nights when we, like lost children, yearn for her comforting presence."
—Patricia Monaghan, Ph.D., *The Goddess Companion* (Llewellyn Publications, 1999)

Playing the Social Equality Card

Theology begins with a question. The question is about God and what "the people of God" are called to do in any given situation. Theologians search scripture and look at how

scripture has been applied in the past. They
then determine what the correct response for
the people is. These early feminist theologians
approached from a different angle. They looked
at the Bible and how it had been used in the past
to hold women down and asked religious leaders
to show them how it reflected the central message
of God and Jesus Christ. In other words, they
called the conventional way of thinking into question. They approached theology questioning the
established order.

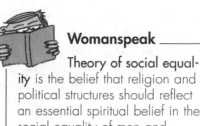

Womanspeak

**Theory of social equal-
ity** is the belief that religion and
political structures should reflect
an essential spiritual belief in the
social equality of men and
women and of all people.

These women believed the central teachings of Jesus were based on equality in society.
They began from the position that equality is a basic spiritual and religious right—God's
plan for creation. They approached theology through a certain perspective or belief. As
they read scripture from that basic assumption, they applied a *theory of social equality*. They
questioned things that did not match the basic teachings of Christ regarding social equality as recorded in the Bible.

Reforming Tradition: Keeping the Baby

Many women theologians remain within their religious traditions, working for change
from the inside. They know Judaism and Christianity need to be reformed, and they are
firmly committed to integrating women's stories, values, and experiences into religion.
They feel they can be most effective working from inside the systems and structures as
university professors, theologians, scholars, and teachers. These women can be called
reformers.

Firmly Rooted in Tradition

Reformers believe in the sacredness of the Bible
and that it contains the word of God, but they
don't believe it's the infallible source that traditionalists and evangelicals believe it to be.
Reformers approach religion from the critical
feminist perspective we talked about earlier, a
position that believes God's plan for creation is
for men and women to be equal. When biblical
text does not support this, they believe it should
be reinterpreted.

Womanspeak

Reformer describes feminists who position themselves
within their traditions. Reformers
firmly recognize that religion
needs a transformation, and they
believe it can best be accomplished working from the inside.

Reformers point to the fact that traditional religion is a repository of thousands of years of shared religious history, and it belongs to the people. They recognize the deep spiritual value of this material and, despite its patriarchal bias, they believe religion can be liberated from its oppressive practices. They draw on biblical themes of Exodus, Jesus as liberator, and the idea of a God who transcends all limitations, including sexuality. They turn to scriptural images of Shekinah and Mary.

Christian women point to the lifestyle of Jesus, referring to the central place women occupied in his ministry, the prominent role women played in witnessing Jesus' death, and the stories of the resurrection. Women remained with Jesus at the cross, and it is to women that the risen Christ first appeared. Women were the first preachers, directed by the risen Christ to go and tell the others. If this is not a direct ordination, Christian women maintain, then what could it be?

Jewish women point to the problems in the translation of the creation story and to the Zohar, one of the main texts of the religious movement of Judaism, the Kabbalah. An important aspect in this mystical teaching tells of the relationship between God and creation in which Shekinah, the female aspect of God's wisdom, plays a vital role.

Rosemary's Baby: Eco-Feminism

Rosemary Ruether is a reformist feminist theologian, Catholic theologian at Garrett Theological Seminary, author of 32 books, and pioneer in the eco-feminist movement. *Eco-feminism* is a term used to identify women who work to stop what they see as unchecked exploitation of women and the natural world. It is a particular branch of feminism that focuses its criticism on culture's domination of nature. They see all "-isms"— anti-Semitism, racism, classism, sexism—as aspects of the same oppression, one caused by the hierarchical ordering and stratification of the world.

Sophia's Wisdom

Eco-feminists are everywhere. They are inside traditional religions as practicing Jews, Hindus, Buddhists, and Christians. They share the idea of transforming religion from the inside. They work to eliminate patriarchy and institute new models of partnering. Others find a home in indigenous cultures such as Native American, whose beliefs and practices are based on a good relationship with the earth. Others are found in the Neo-Pagan movement and in modern-day Wicca. All work for environmental responsibility as a religious and spiritual mandate.

Ruether combines social activism and religious scholarship in her numerous books, articles, and lectures. Her book, *New Woman/New Earth: Sexist Ideologies and Human Liberation*

(Beacon Press, 1995), is a classic in the reformist tradition and has become the anthem of the eco-feminist movement. In it she analyzes Christian and Jewish thought, showing that male domination is deeply woven into their organization and structure.

Ruether maintains her position inside Christianity and stands firmly against the oppression of women found in traditional religion. Her specialty is in creating dialogue between groups holding opposing theologies. She cautions against the tendency to simply reverse the domination found in some of the radical groups. Like her predecessor Elizabeth Cady Stanton, Ruether urges women to think for themselves. She believes that there are ways traditional religion can be reinterpreted, and she encourages women to find these ways.

Reprieving Eve

Phyllis Trible, professor of sacred literature at Union Theological Seminary in New York, is a reformist who places herself in the middle between women who find no problem with women's place in the Bible and those who give scripture no authority at all. Trible considers the Bible a clearly patriarchal text; however, she believes it can be reclaimed as a spiritual source for women.

Trible maintains that centuries of interpretation have not actually told us the true story of Adam and Eve. She probes the issue by asking why woman should be considered second class and subordinate to man because of being created after he was? And she goes deeper, asking if humans should be subordinate to animals since Genesis 1:27 clearly says humans were created after animals were.

Trible goes on to say that the whole issue is beside the point because the first human, Adam, was not actually a male, anyway. The Hebrew term *'adham*, which was the source for the name "Adam," was a generic term for humankind. *'Adham* is a genderless term meaning "being created from the earth." According to Trible, man and woman begin as equals. Differentiation happens later, only as the female (*'ishshah*) is created does man emerge as (*'ish*). Sexuality is a simultaneous event for woman and man. Trible shows how the two genders are shown to be equal, inter-related, and interdependent.

Womanspeak

'Adham was a generic term for humankind (male and female), meaning "created from the earth." *'Ish* is the term applied to man as *'adham* was separated into two parts of a whole. *'Ishshah* is the term given to woman as *'adham* was separated into two parts.

Trible believes, as do many other theologians, that it's in the act of disobedience that women fall out of equality. It's in the disobedient state that man establishes his dominance. She concludes her discussion by saying that the oppression of women by men is not in accord with the ideal of creation; it does not give permission for a patriarchal culture; it stands in judgment of the culture.

Calling for Shekinah

Rita M. Gross received her Ph.D. from the University of Chicago, and she teaches, writes, and publishes in the area of women and religion. In the article, "Female God Language in a Jewish Context," published in *Womanspirit Rising* (Harper San Francisco, 1979), Gross uses the Kabbalah and the mystical tradition of Judaism as the basis of her discussion. She says that *galut*, meaning "exile," is a fundamental part of existence, and the primary cause of exile is the perceived separation of masculine and feminine in God.

 Wise Words

"She is a breath of power, a pure vision of glory, a reflection of eternal light, a spotless mirror of goodness. She is one, but she can do all things. She remains herself, but renews all things. Each generation she creates prophets and holy ones, for she is more beautiful than the sun or the stars, mightier than the earth itself, and she orders all things well."

—Wisdom 7:25–8:1

Gross calls for the reincorporation of Shekinah, God's female aspect. Just as God has been split in half in Western culture, the female half of creation is likewise in exile. Gross calls for a *tikkun*, or reparation, a *mitzvah*. Only when the female part of God has been reunited will women experience reparation and the world be restored to wholeness.

While Gross fully realizes that God is neither male nor female, she believes that female images for God must be reintroduced, and she uses female pronouns for God. All religious language is essentially metaphorical and is the only way that something so incomprehensible can be translated.

Gross reminds us that talking *to* God is what Judaism is all about, even more important than talking *about* God. In Jewish God language, the second person (spoken to) is far more important than the third person (spoken about). All language falls short in its attempt to relate to God and yet people need language for prayer. This challenge can be best met, Gross believes, by using female pronouns *in addition* to male pronouns. Changing noninclusive language is the first step in changing noninclusive images and to assuring full inclusion of Jewish women into Judaism. This is when the *galut* will end.

 Wise Words

"All religious language is really metaphor. God language does not really tell us about God, but it does tell us a considerable amount about those who use it."

—Rita M. Gross (1979)

Super, Natural Christians

Sallie McFague is one of the pioneers in feminist theology, calling for a new face and a new focus for Christianity. The new face is female, and the new focus is the earth. McFague is a professor of theology and former dean of Vanderbilt Divinity School. Her book, *Life Abundant: Rethinking Theology and Economy for a Planet in Peril* (Fortress Press, 2000), urges Christians to rethink themselves and their relationships with the natural world—specifically, to reconsider who they are in the bigger scheme of things.

McFague demystifies theology and invites readers to come up with one of their own. It isn't all that difficult, she says; it's about becoming conscious of how we live and work. She challenges the dominant American worldview, saying it is an outdated legacy built on eighteenth-century religious, philosophical, and economic theory that has turned into the gross materialism that is threatening the world ecology. The consumer culture is a market ideology that has become our way of life, our religion. She believes that North Americans are addicted to their consumer lifestyle and they are in denial of its consequences.

Mother Knows Best

Try recycling gifts, or regifting, as Elaine from *Seinfeld* used to call it. Gift-giving doesn't have to mean going to a store to buy something new each time. Most people already have too much stuff! Passing along a favorite book, some jewelry, or other things you have that you know your friend might like helps create a new consumer ethic.

McFague says that loving the earth isn't enough! People are going to have to make essential economic changes to make a significant difference in the ecological devastation we are currently wreaking on the earth. Americans are 20 percent of the world's population, and we are using 80 percent of the world's resources as if it were our divine right. McFague speaks for many who are seeking a simpler, saner life, not driven by greed. She addresses her message to the people rather than to the church hierarchy. By doing so, she is showing us where the real power for change rests. She is taking the liberation model one step farther than some of her contemporaries by focusing on the people and not the organizational church.

Religious Revolutionaries: Frying Other Fish

Another group of women writing theology is considered radical or revolutionary both in their treatment of the issues and in their approach to religion. Having assessed the mainstream religious thought and practice, they aren't sure that the present-day structures can be rescued from their deeply based patriarchal thought and language. These women have moved outside the traditional religious arenas and are finding new images and new forms for religion or spirituality—they are writing a new thealogy.

Thealogy is knowledge of the goddess. Thealogy is not just theology spelled with an "a." It is a comprehensive study of the religious systems of the Mother Goddess, and it includes a woman's self-knowledge and the knowledge of nature, the unified life force, history, and sciences in a feminine perspective. The goddess is an archetype. She exists within everyone's psyche. Feminists and thealogians believe that the suppression of Mother Goddess imagery as well as the life-affirming values associated with her have been the concerted effort associated with the rise to power of patriarchal religions. Thealogian and author Barbara G. Walker says that if we were free of the oppressive politics of patriarchal society and free to recognize the divine as an archetypal symbol, our unconscious mind would take us back to the Mother Goddess.

Becoming Post-Christian

Mary Daly was one of the first voices calling attention to the conditions inside traditional religion since Elizabeth Cady Stanton writing at the end of the nineteenth century. In her first book, *The Church and the Second Sex* (Beacon Press, 1968), Daly accuses the church of promoting the idea of women being inferior. She places responsibility on them for the worldwide oppression of women. Her writings show her gradual movement away from many of the Catholic Church's teachings, such as original sin, and her emergence as a self proclaimed *post-Christian*.

Womanspeak

Post-Christian is a term used by Mary Daly to describe her theological position, having moved through Christianity to her current position as post-Christian.

Wise Words

"There are and will be those who think I have gone overboard. Let them rest assured that this assessment is correct, probably beyond their wildest imagination, and that I will continue to do so."

—Mary Daly

Like her predecessor Stanton, Daly urges women to find their own beliefs. She created a feminist vocabulary reversing commonly used derogatory terms for women such as "shrew," "hag," and "spinster," turning them into words of praise. She adds to the growing lexicon in her book *Pure Lust: Elemental Feminist Philosophy* (Harper, 1984). And in 1987, along with Jane Caputi, she published *Webster's First New Intergalactic Wickedary of the English Language* (Harper).

Daly's philosophy is highly controversial and challenges even the most ardent feminists. Some praise Daly for completely breaking old forms and for not only rewriting theology but also rewriting language itself. Others find that she has gone too far, making her books difficult to read and reducing their impact, which feminists believe could be significant to their cause. One thing is certain, Daly will most likely continue to stir the waters and provide rich material for theological discussions both inside and outside religion.

Goddess Girls Just Gotta Have Fun!

Carol Christ is the first woman to receive a Ph.D. in theology from Yale University. She taught at Harvard Divinity School and Columbia University. Christ's book, *Rebirth of the Goddess: Finding Meaning in Feminist Spirituality* (Routledge, 1998), is the first systematic thealogy of the goddess. In it she presents her case that the shift from God to goddess heralds a transformation of Western theology, philosophy, and ethics. She believes it holds the promise of a new world order.

Christ talks about the growing numbers of women and men all over the world who are finding meaning in a new kind of spirituality that's based on the divine being female. It's a comprehensive guide to understanding the goddess spirituality movement, showing its principles, practices, and beliefs, contrasting goddess spirituality with Jewish, Christian, and feminist theologies.

Wise Words

"The image of God as male was at once the most obvious and most subtle sexist influence in religion. Nothing aroused the ire of male theologians or churchmen so much as the charge that traditional male language about God is sexist."

—Carol Christ (1979)

Christ challenges basic assumptions about our relationship with nature, about our history as a people, and about the goddess herself, answering common questions such as "Is she the female version of God?" "Is she out to take over?" "Is she 'out there' or in us?" "Is she one or many?" "Is she all about women's bodies and the exclusion of their minds?" "Is she Mother Nature?" "What color is she?" You'll find the answers to these questions in Chapter 6, "Trying on Goddess Slippers." Christ has moved outside Christianity and currently lives in Athens, Greece, where she teaches workshops and leads goddess pilgrimages to Crete.

Much of the feminist movement you've been reading about has focused on the works of white women. African American women rightly point out that when the word "woman" is used in our culture, it actually means "white woman," and they have withdrawn much of their energy from the movement. Black women have different experiences of the culture, a different history, and a different agenda. In the next chapter, we'll take a look at how African American women are creating a vital new approach they call womanist theology.

The Least You Need to Know

- ◆ Women's theology landed in America the same day the Pilgrims did.
- ◆ Women's theology approaches scripture and religious tradition from the belief that social equality is God's plan for creation.

◆ Women theologians and scholars have found many errors in biblical translation and interpretation, errors that build a strong case for feminist concerns.

◆ Some women theologians work for reform while remaining inside their traditions. Others have left traditional religion and are discovering new forms.

Chapter 5

Black Women's Spirituality and Womanist Theology

In This Chapter

- ◆ Getting out of God's way
- ◆ A committee of elders gives spiritual support
- ◆ Womanist theology
- ◆ Hospitality spirituality and prayer warriors

Black women bring a powerful and necessary perspective to the liberation struggle and to women's spirituality. Alice Walker's descriptive image of "womanist," in her book, *In Search of Our Mother's Gardens: Womanist Prose* (Harcourt and Brace, 1983), has given birth to a new theology called womanist theology. It is adding depth and breadth to the body of work known as liberation theology.

Womanists bring a different perspective to women's spirituality. Although all women share the common bond of being female, they come to the table with vastly different experiences of what that means. It's only as the differences are recognized and explored that the bonding can happen. Womanists add a deeper dimension and a broader scope to the women's movement.

Lord, Get Me Out of Your Way!

Annette Vanzant Williams is a 42-year-old African American woman who is married with two children. She is a deacon in the United Methodist Church, a position she describes as being in the eye of the paradox. As a deacon, her job is to connect the church and the world. The paradox is that as an African American deacon, she is an enigma in both arenas—church and world. Such a position might be uncomfortable to most people; however, Williams is sure of herself, sure of why she's there, and certain that she will receive the spiritual assistance she needs to be of service.

Despite the Evidence, God Is at Work!

Williams's working definition of spirituality is how we connect with God. For Williams the connection involves the combined disciplines of praying, reading scripture, and taking action. She is a liberationist. "Scripture and prayer always lead me to be an agent of change," she says. For her, political liberation and spiritual liberation are one and the same. This belief places her in the same theological camp as the likes of Sojourner Truth, Mary McLeod Bethune, and Martin Luther King Jr.

Sophia's Wisdom
Mary McLeod Bethune is one of the most influential women in history. Her parents and some of her siblings were born in slavery. Freed after the Civil War, she went on to become a renowned educator, civil and women's rights leader, advisor to U.S. presidents, government official, and humanitarian. She helped initiate the black pride movement in America, and her statement, "Look at me, I am black and I am beautiful," became its anthem.

The theme of tolerance keeps Williams on her knees these days. Her present spiritual challenge is to find tolerance in her heart for the intolerant. She fights against the temptation to use "being right as a banner," a polarizing position she sees many evangelical Christians take. "The real work is inside of ourselves, where we have to get to deeper and deeper levels of faith," she said. Williams believes "faith is in knowing God is at work in the world despite the evidence to the contrary; and watching the evidence change before your eyes."

"Waving a banner that says you're the *right side* of the issue creates separation, it isolates us from one another," says Williams. She understands God's kingdom as inclusive, and it's her job, as a Christian and as a deacon, to find the points of connection and build from there. "Love builds bridges. Sometimes it's a struggle to love someone who is saying the exact things that you're against, but that's the work."

Finding the Wiggle Room

In establishing connections, Williams approaches a situation with the assumption that everyone involved is trying to build a better world. "We just have different ideas on how to go about doing it." She has found that when she doesn't try to know all the answers and doesn't need to be right, good things can happen. An example of how that works happened recently at a professional conference where 1,000 people gathered, representing all different theologies. The issue on the table was regarding the church's position on ordination of homosexuals.

"I knew that my only hope of being a positive influence in the discussion was to be completely honest and humble," Williams said. "If I came on like I knew the answer and I needed to be right, that is, convince them they're wrong, I could not be a positive influence for change. I would get nowhere. I prayed, asking God to get me out of the way. I began from the position that I didn't know what God's will was on the issue of homosexuality. I admitted that while I had arrived at a different conclusion than they had, I was searching, too.

Mother Knows Best

Arguing doesn't change people's minds! Those who do conflict resolution know that the best way of working with controversy is to find a place where both sides agree and build from there.

"I don't pretend to know why people are the way they are, but I do know that they are created by God. I talked about how the church had met 200 years after slavery ended to seek reconciliation and repentance for not treating black people as equals, and that I felt these two issues were somehow related. In both incidences, people were trying to understand God's wishes. I just hoped that we would not be meeting 200 years from now to seek reconciliation and repentance for our treatment of gays.

"Many people in the group became open to reconsidering their stand. As a group we decided we had to pray and reflect harder before making a decision. I know that I was able to be useful in that situation because I was honest. I believe our job is to be faithful to what is true for us. It opens the space [and] creates some wiggle room, where dialogue can begin. That's our job. God does the transforming."

Aunt Henri's Committee of Elders

Williams draws on a rich spiritual legacy that comes from a long line of praying women and men in her family. Her mother was the secretary to the bishop of the Southwest Conference of the Methodist Church and regularly traveled eight hours from Wynnewood, Oklahoma, to Little Rock, Arkansas, with Williams and her younger sister asleep in the backseat of the car. Williams proudly recalls that she was baptized by three bishops!

Her spiritual inheritance includes a powerful group of elders summoned together by her Aunt Henrietta Beasley to guide and encourage Williams's religious development. Aunt Henri owned a recording studio in Oklahoma City, where a circle of friends regularly gathered. The group consisted of two doctors, a nurse, two school principals, and several teachers.

Under Aunt Henri's direction, they made an album of their prophetic hopes and dreams about Williams, who was less than a year old at the time. In what is an African tradition, Aunt Henri had recognized the gift within Williams and had already declared that she would become a minister. In their vision of her, Williams's elders saw a leader who would work to change the system. It was a vision they then helped shape.

Wise Words

"You may encounter many defeats, but you must not be defeated. In fact, the encountering may be the very experience which creates the vitality and the power to endure."

—Maya Angelou (1928–), celebrated poet, historian, and professor of American Studies at Wake Forest University, who was invited by President Clinton to compose and present a poem at his 1993 inauguration

Regarding black women's spirituality, Williams believes that today's women are drawing on the theology and spirituality of their grandmothers and mothers in a tradition that asks the question, "How does God call you to act?" She believes a lot of theological writing is done by contemporary authors such as Emilie Townes and Maya Angelou. In the black tradition, "theology isn't just an intellectual exercise, it's a direct, affirming, movement," Williams says. "Therefore, black women's spirituality is integrated into all aspects of their lives. It shows up in Tina Turner's performances, Marion Anderson's singing, Oprah's television ministry, and in the Olympic running of Marion Jones."

Williams talks about a growing body of work within the black church emerging under the name womanist theology. Womanist theology has given voice to black women and has identified the three-tiered oppression that is the unique reality of their experience: the prejudices of gender, race, and economics. We'll take a look at womanist theology and see how it has impacted the field of study called liberation theology and how it affects women's spirituality.

Those Audacious Women

When Alice Walker's book, *In Search of Our Mother's Gardens: Womanist Prose*, was published in 1983, it gave birth to a new religious symbol that would serve to unlock the door for many black women struggling with liberation. This symbol became the starting point for a new theology called womanist theology.

This new theology fills the void that existed between black liberation theology, written by black men in the 1960s and 1970s, and feminist theology, written about the same time by white women. Black liberation theology identifies *racism* as the oppressor, and white feminist theology identifies the oppression of sexism inherent in patriarchy.

The experience of black women, however, encompasses both; and in addition, their stories give witness to a third oppression, the oppressive economics of class difference.

Womanspeak _____

Womanist describes a woman who, according to Alice Walker, is " outrageous, audacious, courageous," and engages in "willful behavior." She wants to know more and in greater depth than is good for her.

Racism is the belief that the people of various races have different inherent qualities and that one's own cultural group is superior to another, accompanied by the ability of one group to have power over that group.

Womanist: A New Religious Symbol

Walker's new symbol describes both a colorful feminist and a feminist of color who is "... outrageous, audacious, courageous," and engages in "willful behavior." This behavior is further described by Walker as "wanting to know more and in greater depth than is good for one ...." In exploring this new symbol, Walker and black womanist theologians who are inspired by her image are identifying essential differences between how black women and white women approach the same goal of liberation.

Wise Words _____

"Daughter: Mama, why are we brown, pink, and yellow, and our cousins are white, beige, and black?

"Mother: Well, you know the colored race is just like a flower garden, with every color flower represented.

"Daughter: Mama, I'm walking to Canada, and I'm taking you and a bunch of slaves with me.

"Mother: It wouldn't be the first time."

—From Alice Walker's *In Search of Our Mother's Gardens: Womanist Prose* (Harcourt and Brace, 1983)

Womanist wisdom has been the source of discussion among women in the black community. As their stories are told, the scope of racism and feminism is enlarging—and a better understanding of the dynamic is emerging. We'll take a look at some basic differences between womanist theology and feminist theology that are being brought to light as the voices of black women inform theology, ethics, religious education, history, and other social sciences—womanist style.

Rooted in Africa

The black Christian church is a community from which African American women and men have drawn and continue to draw strength. The black church was the first place where slaves were able to gather together away from the eyes and ears of their masters— although it happened rarely. Black church offered at least a degree of safety, and it was a place slaves could experience themselves as a people through the eyes of God rather than through the eyes of their oppressor. Black churches were the center for many of the rebellions against slavery in the past and also in modern time. Black churches played a key role in the struggle for freedom during the civil rights movement of the 1960s and 1970s and continue to be a primary source of empowerment. White feminism is often directed at the church as a patriarchal institution that has contributed to the oppression of women. Black women's experience of church is different in a significant way for many women.

The modern-day black Christian church has its roots in African soil, which gives it an essentially different flavor than the white church that came out of Europe. European thinking was shaped by the Greek mind and influenced by Romans. It believed that the spirit and body are separate. Christianity quickly formed a ranking system in which some people are considered better than others. As Christianity was adapted by the Romans, it became militaristic and was spread across Europe. It became entwined with politics that reinforced its hierarchical ranking systems.

Christianity began in Africa and the Near East among people who had an integrated worldview. That is, they didn't perceive a separation between the world and spirituality. For them, the world was manifestation of spirit. As the slaves were reintroduced to Christianity through the European American slave owners, they heard its liberating message. They connected to Christianity as Jesus spoke it—telling of a nonhierarchical society in which all share in God's kingdom. It fused with their African tribal religion and transformed Christianity from its European experience, reconnecting it back to its African roots.

Brenda is an African American woman who attends church every Sunday, as she has all her life. She is politically savvy, a womanist, and involved in community action. Brenda talked about how her religion is the rock upon which she builds her life. Her church community is her family, her aunties and uncles. "Everything good that has happened for black people in this country has happened through prayer, through church, and by holding strong together. My problem is not with God or with my church," she says, "it is with a way of thinking and acting that is not in accord with anything remotely God-like. When a solution comes, as it has and as it most surely will again, it will come to us in prayer. I will be here with the others, praising God and listening."

Wise Words

"Christianity alone, adulterated, otherworldly, and disengaged from its most authentic implications—as it was usually presented to the slaves—could not have provided the slaves with all the resources they needed for the kind of resistance they expressed. It had to be enriched with the volatile ingredients of the African religious past and, most important of all, with the human yearning for freedom that found a channel for expression in the early black church of the South."

—Gayraud S. Wilmore, former dean of the Master of Divinity Program and professor of Afro-American Studies at New York Theological Seminary in his book, *Black Religion and Black Radicalism* (1983)

As one woman put it, "Sexism is alive and well in the African American church." However, the overall message has been one of liberation. Black Christianity is a transformed and transforming church. It has provided the spiritual support for black people to find their liberation. For the most part, it's doing what white women wish their church was doing.

White feminism builds a powerful case against patriarchal interpretation of scripture. However, many black women have a different relationship with the Bible. Black Christianity is what is referred to as a *prophetic church*, or a church based on the words of the prophets. Black Christians' struggle for equality and freedom is grounded in the biblical themes of exile and exodus, the image of the God of justice, the words of the prophets, and Jesus as liberator. Black Christians' interpretation of scripture is a transformed one.

Mother Knows Best

Tell it like it is—*for you!* Womanist theology and feminist thinking believe everyone's experience is valuable. As we hear each other's stories, we get a better understanding of ourselves, and a richer picture of the world emerges.

Solidarity: It's a Black Thing

Despite the fact that black men have sometimes moved ahead without black women, there is a profound sense of solidarity between men and women. Black women endured the oppression of slavery side-by-side with black men. They worked together in the fields and suffered the same consequences under the hands of their tormentors. The source of this oppression was the system that allowed owning slaves, not black men. They faced the continued oppression of racism together, and in their struggle for civil rights, they fought the same war against a common enemy. This is different from the experience of most white women, whose oppression came from within their own culture. The bond of trust between white women and white men was broken. Their oppression focused in gender, not race.

Womanist theologians do not back off from talking about the sexism between the men and women in the black culture. However, they know the issue is bigger than that. They tell us if we only look at an individual outbreak of oppressive politics, we don't go to the roots of it. At the root, all oppression comes from a system based on one group being better than another group. Whether it is because one group has the "right" God, the right skin color, the right gender, or the right amount of money isn't the point. You have to go below the surface; dig a little deeper and get to the thinking that creates the different situations.

For many black women, the home, like church, has been the place where family and friends gather in safety and can experience their culture. The preparation of food and gathering around the table are highly valued in the black culture. The mass exodus of white women leaving the home and abandoning the hearth in search of a higher place in a white male system isn't what black women want to do. They're more interested in transforming the entire structure than in seeking a better place within it.

> ### Wise Words
>
> "Meet the 'ism' brothers: rac- ism, sex-ism, age-ism, class-ism. They all come out of the idea that one part of creation is better than another part."
>
> —Luisah Teish, Priestess of Oshun in the Yorbu Lucumi (African) tra- dition, dancer, storyteller, teacher, and workshop leader; from her book, *Jambalaya: The Natural Woman's Book* (Harper and Row, 1985)

> ### Womanspeak
>
> **Hospitality spirituality** is a term derived from biblical tradi- tion that Westfield applies to the black women's tradition of com- ing together in their homes as community, sharing food and stories.

Hospitality Spirituality

Dr. Lynne Westfield, associate dean of religious educa- tion at Drew University, recently published a book called *Dear Sisters: A Womanist Practice of Hospitality* (Pilgrim Press, 2001), in which she identifies a particu- lar kind of black women's spirituality she calls *hospitality spirituality*. In it, she talks about the full-bodied Christianity of Africa, the tradition of prayer warriors, and hospitality.

Body and Soul

Westfield isn't sure whether women's spirituality is a product of nature or nurture, but she feels there's an inherently feminine aspect to all spirituality. "Spirituality engages an introspective, quieter, reflective part of us, aspects that are more cultivated in women than in men."

Westfield defines spirituality as "The awareness that the mind, body, and spirit are one; that we are spiritual beings in a body. Spirituality is God consciousness. It's the realization that we are connected to God, the ultimate spiritual being." For Westfield, spirituality can't be put into little boxes and marked "Sunday Only." She practices hers every day, in all aspects of her life, and sees her teaching job as a calling to ministry.

Westfield brings spiritual consciousness into her classroom in the way she relates to her students and in preparing the lesson. She teaches the whole student: mind, body, and spirit. While her spirituality also includes a formal practice of meditation and prayer, she feels that true spiritual attunement is practiced in our ongoing interactions in the world, through our relationships to our jobs, to our neighborhoods, to our families, and to our homes.

Knock, Knock, Knocking On Heaven's Door

There is a mystical tradition in the African American spirituality that Westfield describes as "ancient, supple, and very much alive." In what she describes as "a seamless relationship between heaven and earth, certain members of the community known as *prayer warriors* connect with the ancestors. They have special healing abilities that include receiving and transmitting spiritual information. The tradition is passed from one generation to the next by a prayer warrior recognizing the gift in another. The person then spends time alone, learning how her gift works, until she is ready to use it. Word goes out into the community, which then recognizes a new prayer warrior."

Womanspeak

Prayer warrior describes members of the church who have an ability to communicate with the ancestors and a particularly well-developed prayer life. It is considered a healing gift. Their abilities are recognized by the community, and their services are sought after.

Sophia's Wisdom

Westfield talks about a spiritual hunger that exists in many young people today—a hunger that leads them to many New Age practices. She points out that "Nothing is really new about New Age. These practices have existed since the beginning of time. There's a rich source for them within the black church."

A Night out with the Women

Black women have a particular kind of spirituality Westfield calls hospitality spirituality, a spirituality that arises when black women gather together around a kitchen table. Traditional hospitality includes host and stranger, meaning someone whose house is opened (host) to people who don't live there (strangers). Westfield describes black women's gatherings as stranger-to-stranger hospitality. Blacks often have no place they can really call home. Few black women own their own houses and so they often feel like strangers living on the landlord's property, knowing they could be moved out at any moment.

Safety is a rare commodity for black women. The racial memory of slavery remains with them. Shared stories that have come down through the ages recall the separation of families—children sold away while their mothers worked in the field—express an alienation so deep Sojourner Truth described it as a time when "None could hear me but Jesus."

Today, as they gather together around the table, black women share current stories. There is laughter, warmth, and, of course, food. In these moments they create a safe place for themselves, a sanctuary. Westfield describes these gatherings as essentially sacramental in nature. The women themselves would not consider the suppers as spiritual—they gather, they eat, they have fun, and they leave feeling refreshed and renewed in spirit. Westfield calls it a spontaneous kind of spirituality.

Roast Beef, Gravy, and Spiritual Awakening!

For the most part, Westfield worships on campus at the University Community. The congregation is totally politically correct: interdenominational; mixed race, gender, class, age, sexual orientation; and handicap friendly. When she worships in town, she attends black services, choosing her church by race and culture rather than by denomination. She prefers "low" church to "high" church. Low church has a less-formal liturgy, fewer hymns and anthems, and more gospel music. Westfield describes the preaching style as loose and free and sometimes takes up half of the two or more hours the service lasts.

> **CAUTION**
> **Mother Knows Best**
> Don't neglect your body! Taking care of the body is taking care of the soul. In women's spirituality, the spirit and body are one.

Westfield has had several spiritual awakenings, but the first one happened when she was a child. She remembers knowing that church was important but wondering why. She recalls one Sunday, as she was speculating on the "why" of church, that she fell asleep. She awakened (literally) during the sermon to hear the preacher using the metaphor "Jesus is the essence of life, like gravy on roast beef." In that moment, her question was answered! She says she got it, and it made perfect sense. She knew all about gravy on roast beef.

Westfield nourishes her spirit by getting massages and taking trips to a spa. However, the best place of renewal for her is her mother's kitchen table where her family and extended family gather to enjoy old family recipes, laughter, and conversation. Westfield says this is where she connects to "who I am, whose I am, and what I will become." On the third item, Westfield reports that she gets lots of help in the form of suggestions—many loved ones willing to share their wisdom! Another place of renewal is her work, where she feels she is living out her calling. In her words, "Liturgy means work of the people. Teaching is my liturgy."

Now that you've heard how and why women's spirituality came into being, in the next part of the book, you'll meet the goddess and learn why she is an important symbol.

The Least You Need to Know

- Faith means letting go of the need to be "right" and letting God into the picture to reveal a new truth.
- Womanist theology empowers black women to speak out and tell their stories.
- As black women speak out, they have added a new dimension to the struggle for liberation for all people.
- Hospitality spirituality is a way that black women gather to give one another support and encouragement and, at the same time, have a good time.

Part 2

Meeting Goddess

For 200,000 years of human history the female body dominated the formation of religion, politics, and artist expression. As the year moved through its cycles, nature sprouted, fruits ripened, and vegetation appeared to die. The spring brought new life, and the ancient theme of birth, death, and rebirth was wired into the human psyche.

Mother Earth incorporated the spiritual and religious essence of creation. Early goddess cultures understood the divine presence in the world. These cultures lived by the earth's cycles. They recognized their dependence on the earth for survival and expressed their gratitude for her generosity. In her honor, ceremonies and celebrations were created to honor the life-giving principles of the feminine. Many of these seasonal celebrations are at the heart of religious ceremonies today.

In the following chapters, you'll read about the how the goddess came down to us through history, emerging once again in modern time.

NO, GETTING IN TOUCH WITH MY INNER GODDESS DOES **NOT** MEAN I'LL BE DRESSING UP LIKE **WONDER WOMAN**!

Chapter 6

Trying on Goddess Slippers

In This Chapter

- ◆ The inside scoop on Goddess-land
- ◆ Is a matriarch just a patriarch wearing a dress?
- ◆ Were there really Amazons?
- ◆ Is the goddess a golden calf–type thing?

Sometime in the early 1970s a woman rolled over, propped herself up on one elbow, and snapped open a window shade in the consciousness of women all across the country. Shaking off thousands of years of sleep, she yawned and exclaimed, "I'm back!" Since that time, droves of women have been exploring ancient ruins, mythology, literature, and their collective memory to find out more about "her."

Who is she? Why is she so important to so many women? Is she real or merely Memorex? Does it matter? To answer these questions, and perhaps to raise a few more, in this chapter we'll take a look at the most interesting spiritual phenomenon of our time.

Rocking the Cradle of Civilization

Let's begin with a story. Since it goes back a very long time and has never been written down, there are several versions of the story in circulation.

You might have heard it told a bit differently than you'll hear this time. Stories are like that.

This is a story of the migration of people. It has caves and cave drawings, statues buried deep in the earth, pieces of broken pottery, and bones painted with red ochre. It has celebrations, dancing, art, music, and nights of lovemaking under the Turkish sky. Of course it has "bad times," too, great loss and death, and no real ending … yet!

The Black Mother of Africa

The hand that rocked the very first cradle of civilization was black. Our common beginnings have been traced back to Africa. Just as our physical life began there, so did our spiritual life and our earliest images of the sacred. That first image was of the Great Mother of Africa, known as the Black Goddess. She is believed to have originated in the rich and fertile Sahara Desert, where images of her have been found on cave walls. As climatic changes sent people in search of water and they began to move out from the Sahara, they carried images of their Great Mother of Africa with them.

Mitochondria DNA, *the original mother of Africa, by Noris Binet, courtesy of Martha Leigh Ferrell collection.*

Our story moves from Africa to Europe to the great cavern sanctuaries of France, where some of the very first people lived over 200,000 years ago. They followed the patterns of the seasons and saw that things died in the winter and then greened again in the spring.

They took this as a sign that the earth was in charge of birthing and rebirthing. Since females gave birth, they reasoned that the earth must also be female. She provided them with comfortable caves, wood for the fire, food, water, and beautiful flowers. All life flowed from her, and they wanted to honor her.

Goddess Guide

Images of the black Madonna have been found throughout Eastern Europe, Spain, France, and Italy. The Great Mother originated in Africa, and her images were carried throughout most of the world by migrating people and, later, through trading.

When someone died, the people prepared a grave. Pine boughs were cut to make a soft bed, and the body was painted with red ochre to symbolize the mother's blood that fed them in the womb (blood meant life). They carefully arranged the body in a fetal position so the Great Mother could keep it inside of her until time for its rebirth, and covered it with wild flowers from the field. When a little one died, they carved images of the mother's breast on the rock that would be placed over the grave so that the child's spirit would have plenty to eat and not be frightened.

The people carved statues of the Great Mother and placed them in niches near the hearth where she could watch over the family. They pictured her as big, with wide hips for birthing lots of babies. They liked to show her pregnant to remind the children where they came from. They grew crops, wove fabric, kept animals, and figured out how the sun, moon, and stars worked. They gathered huge stones together, made a calendar, and marked where the summer sun would shine on the longest day of the year. In the winter they danced and drew pictures of the dancers on the cave walls to celebrate life.

One day word began to spread about the approach of new tribes of people who rode horses and carried weapons. These others became known as warriors. They worshipped a different god who lived not in the earth but in the sky. A cold, dark shadow fell across the hearts of the people. The elders read the signs and saw their civilization was ending.

Goddess Guide

Western culture began in Crete. Greek religious rituals such as the Eleusinian mysteries as well as Greek mythology—which included Aphrodite, Athena, Demeter, Persephone, Artemis, and Hecate—became incorporated into the Greek pantheon and later expressed in the Roman culture. Greek Olympian games first appeared in Crete as sacred athletic events performed for the good of society.

A few small villages survived longer than any others. One was on the Anatolian plains of what is now Turkey, and one was on Crete. Anatolia was a rich and beautiful land where the town of Catal Huyuk was founded 8,500 years ago. The people who lived there were wild and wonderful. They had that glint in their eyes and romance in their hearts. Children were considered to belong to the mother, and property was thought of that way, too. With few or no restrictions on lovemaking, you can imagine what it was like out on the plains under a full moon.

And then there was the beautiful island of Crete. The society there would have been like a sparkling jewel in the crown of the goddess if she wore a crown, but she didn't. A crown would have been too politically incorrect for her. She believed in equality, loving all her children the same. (The mothers out there can probably relate.)

Wise Words

"From the minute the priest announced that I was the daughter of Oshun I began to think of myself in a different, more positive way. Oshun is the goddess of love, art, and sensuality. She is a temperamental coquette with much magic up her sleeve. She was the me I hid from the world."

—Luisah Teish

Yes, indeed, Crete was definitely the place to be in the Neolithic days. It was a "modern" city with paved roads, plumbing, and a mercantile fleet that sailed the seas trading wares. Most of the surrounding cultures lived under the new regime of the sky god. They had rigid social classes and warfare, and women were considered to be second-class citizens. In Crete, however, men and women continued to live in an equal relationship, and warfare was absent.

We're going to take a break in the story now and get caught up on some historical "facts." (Historical facts are actually stories with dates.) After that, we'll see how our story ends, if it does.

In the Beginning ... NaNa Buluku

According to Oshun priestess Luisah Teish, in African cosmology NaNa Buluku created the world. She is a deity with both male and female aspects who gave birth to twins, a woman called Mawu and a man known as Lisa. Mawu and Lisa together embody the principle of duality, showing how nature is composed of opposites that are really two sides of a whole. Teish teaches classes in African religion, and she tells about the time before colonization when Africans believed in a living universe she calls "continuous creation." Continuous creation describes the understanding that creation is still in process.

There is no image or gender for God in this tradition, according to Teish. The Yoruban people of West Africa believe that making an image creates a human limitation. Yoruban people cannot touch God, but he is known to them through nature. They talk about God in such descriptions as "Author of Day and Night" and "Discerner of Hearts." It was said that the Black Goddess carried a snake in her belly, signifying her nature contained both female and male. She was self-fertilizing.

Teish believes that it's important to explore female images of God to bring back balance, because the oppression of women has been on an erroneous assumption that the "Most High God is male." She talks about Oshun, Goddess of Love, who is reflected in the voluptuous river, with sweet water and beautiful stones. The people intuitively know she is female. If they observe a certain woman moves as if she carried the flow of the river in her hips, they might call her "Daughter of Oshun."

Woman's Words

"Oshun is brass and parrot feathers in a velvet skin. Oshun is white cowrie shells on black buttocks. Her eyes sparkle in the forest, like sun on the river. She is the wisdom of the forest. She is the wisdom of the river. Where doctors fail, she cures with fresh water. Where medicine fails, she cures with fresh water. She feeds the barren woman with honey, and her dry body swells up like a juicy coconut. Oh, how sweet, how sweet is the touch of a child's hand."

—Yoruban chant to Oshun from Patricia Monaghan's book, *The Goddess Companion* (Llewellyn Worldwide, 1999)

Matriarchies Are Not Patriarchies in Drag

Early evidence of goddess time in European history begins about 200,000 years ago at the dawn of civilization in the burial sites of what is now France. The first images of the Mother Goddess in human form in Europe appeared during Upper Paleolithic era (35,000–10,000 B.C.E.). Her ample figure, characterized by large hips, big belly, and big breasts, is often shown pregnant, telling of origins and life's abundance. The figures made of stone, bone, and clay were found in niches and hearths in cave dwellings and have come to be known as the "Venuses." She was seen as the primary creative force of the cosmos, and all life sprung from her womb. The symbol for this great mystery was the earth, and the earth's spirit was symbolized as the female body.

Honor of the Great Mother translated into power and social position for women. Society under her was called *matriarchal*. It operated under nonhierarchical principles, as opposed to hierarchical ranking. Often it is assumed that a matriarchy is a patriarchy turned upside down. This is not the case, however. In a matriarchy both men and women can lead. It is the style of leadership, which is based on service rather than privilege, that is different. Matriarchal social systems aren't rigidly stratified. Societies under the

Womanspeak

Matriarchy describes a society formed with feminine values; power is shared between women and men. In a **matrilineal** society, bloodlines are traced through the female, and property is inherited through female lineage.

goddess were most often *matrilineal*, too, which meant that property passed through the female side of the family.

Venus of Willendorf.
Upper Paleolithic, limestone,
archetypal female figure.
Circa 25,000 B.C.E. Europe.

(Artist: Susan Faulkner)

Differences Between Matriarchy and Patriarchy

Matriarchy	Patriarchy
Partnering	Male dominance
Equality	Stratified/hierarchical
Cooperative	Competitive
Inner authority	External laws
Spiritual principles	Religious institutions
Leadership by serving	Leadership as privilege

The Rise and Fall of the Goddess

The discovery of more recent civilizations provides a good picture of what early matriarchal societies actually looked like and how they functioned. Two of these societies were Catal Huyuk, located on the Anatolian plains of what is now Turkey, and the Greek island of Crete, considered to be the high point of goddess civilization. Archaeological studies of these cultures show how the goddess fell from power and how her images were appropriated into the surviving culture.

Life in Catal Huyuk: Just Another Day in Paradise

Catal Huyuk was a Neolithic city established somewhere around 8500 B.C.E. and occupied for over 800 years. Archaeologists have uncovered the remains of 12 layers or 12 different cities on the site. Religious art and symbols found there show a peaceful society. The location was chosen for its beauty, not for its ability of defense against attack. No evidence was discovered to lead to the conclusion that the people of these cultures were involved in warring.

Archaeologists study burial practices to determine how a society was structured. At Catal Huyuk, female graves were central; gifts buried with them as well as the size and position of housing shows a slight preference toward female ranking. Children were often buried with mothers but never with fathers, which indicates that lineage was passed through the female line.

The ancient religious themes of birth, death, and regeneration have been consistently expressed in religious imagery since the beginning of time, and the female has always been the primary symbol. The art at Catal Huyuk established a link between the archaic Mother Goddess cultures of prehistoric world and classical time. Mother Goddess imagery reappears in Christianity as the pregnant Mary. The Madonna and child venerated in the religious art of churches and homes all over the modern world are firmly rooted in the cultures and psyche of the people of Neolithic time.

Crete: Goddess's Last Stand

The Greek island of Crete was the seat of a highly developed civilization of 100,000 inhabitants that began in 6000 B.C.E., when Anatolian immigrants arrived, bringing their sacred goddess with them. The remains of Crete tell a story of great prosperity, peace, advancement of technologies, commerce, trade, art, music, and agriculture.

Over the next 4,000 years, the people of Crete developed technology in pottery-making, weaving, metallurgy, engraving, architecture, road-building, and sea-going trade. They had viaducts, pipes, fountains, and irrigation systems. The ready water supply as well as sanitation systems provided domestic conveniences that put them ahead of all the cultures around them.

Minoan Snake Goddess
from Knossos, Crete, c. 1600
B.C.E.

(Archeological Museum,
Herakleion)

Religion was expressed as a celebration of life and was the focal point of all aspects of the culture. Music, art, dance, processions, banquets, and games were all centered in religious celebrations. The sexes enjoyed equal status, which is shown by their clothing and their mutual participation in recreation.

According to author and historian Riane Eisler, power was seen as responsibility to the people, not as dominance over others. There were no battles depicted anywhere in the art found at Crete. There are no stories, monuments, or records boasting of the deeds of a ruler, and nowhere does any individual's name appear as a signature on a work of art.

The worship of the goddess survived late into history, falling to the Indo-European warrior tribes sometime between 2000 and 1600 B.C.E. An earthquake that occurred around 1400 B.C.E. destroyed Minoan culture, the goddess' last great stand, and brought the end to the matriarchal civilization.

Amazons: Sisters in Arms

Some of the most well-known and colorful legends of goddess time survive in the stories of the Amazon warrior women. They lived during the second and third millennia B.C.E. in North Africa, Anatolia, and the Black Sea, as well as Greece and all across Europe.

Contrary to popular belief, Amazons did not cut off their breasts to improve their archery skills—they didn't have to!

Amazon on Horseback, bronze stature found in Northern Greece, Circa 550 B.C.E., resides in the National Museum of Athens.

(Photograph courtesy of Amazon Subscriber Network; www.myrine.at/Amazons)

Stories of Amazons tell of exclusively female societies in which the women left only in the spring to mate and returned home to have their children. They taught their girls pride in womanhood, athletics, and martial arts to protect their independence. Their battle cries made men helpless, and their magic has inspired many legends. Greek soldiers believed there was no effective defense against them.

Goddess Guide

It's believed that Amazons were the first to tame horses, and they are pictured riding bareback across the great plans of Anatolia, displaying a red crescent that symbolized the Great Goddess of the Moon. This fierce warrior society arose to protect their beloved goddess and the matriarchal cultures against the invading patriarchy.

Amazons appeared among the Vikings as fleet commanders and war chieftains. Their presence both in reality and legend appears in cultures all over Europe, the Near East, and Northern Africa until the eighteenth century. Amazons have no doubt been romanticized and embellished, and it is difficult to distinguish the fact from the fiction regarding their stories. However, accounts of their battles have been documented as factual.

The Waning of the Goddess

The destruction of matriarchal culture in Crete ended the period of time when the mother was the primary religious symbol. She continued to be worshipped in Greece and later in Rome, however, in the words of author and artist Judy Chicago, "Greco-Roman goddesses paled beside their historic antecedents." As her images were absorbed into the Greco-Roman mythology, she who was "The First" became daughter and sister to the later gods. As the full-grown Athena sprang forth out of Zeus's head, women symbolically became a function of the male mind. Being born of the Great Mother makes sense to the imagination; being born of a man does not. To many it represents the distortion of the natural world that characterizes patriarchy.

The expanding Judeo-Christian tradition of monotheism eventually absorbed all deities into a single concept under a male godhead. Lest we think the goddess was overthrown lightly, Chicago reminds us in her book *The Dinner Party*, "At first the Jews, like many early peoples, worshipped both God and Goddess. It required six centuries for Yahweh to replace Ashtoreth as the primary Jewish deity, though for a long time their temples stood side by side. After Jewish patriarchs finally succeeded in destroying Goddess worship, women's former status gradually diminished."

Goddess: Appearing All over Town

The time span of the goddess was approximately 20,000 years, during which time she dominated cultures all over the world. The point in reconnecting to her is not to idealize the past, but to understand that there was a time when images of women as divine prevailed. Each period of history brings its challenges, and most likely the ancient world faced many of the same human issues as we do today. By bringing light to this period of time, women correct information that has been misinterpreted, overlooked, and destroyed. They work to create balance to 4,000 years of history in which the accomplishments of men have prevailed almost exclusively.

Faces and Facets of Goddess

The goddess appeared as different figures and names at different times and places; however, she is essentially the female spirit of the Great Mother. Here is a partial list of her titles and the great expanse over which she presided:

- **Ajysyt,** the "Milk Lake Mother," is revered as the goddess of birth in Siberia.
- **Ashtoreth** is the goddess of fertility and reproduction for the Hebrew people. She maintained her position side-by-side with the Hebrew God for 600 years.

Ishtar, in breast offering pose. Ishtar stood alongside Yahweh for hundreds of years. She is described in the Hebrew Bible in Jeremiah 44:19 as Queen of Heaven.

(Artist: Valerie Reynolds, age 8)

- **Atira** is "Mother Earth and Universal Mother" of the Plains Indians of North America. Life came from her and returned to her at death. Her symbol is an ear of corn.

- **Brigid** is the Irish fertility goddess who later appeared as St. Brigid, Bishop of Kildare. She is the patron of poetry, smithcraft, and healing.

- **Cerridwen** is the goddess of the moon and barley. She represents the cycle of life and death as the seasons of the year in Wales.

- **Changing Woman** represents a young girl's transition into womanhood for the Navajo people and brings honor to her new role.

- **Danu,** the goddess of plenty, gave birth to the Irish deities originally considered the universal mother in Celtic Ireland.

- **Gaea,** who sends the fruits from the soil to nourish the human race, was in charge of the life-death cycle in Greece.

- **Hathor** was the primary goddess of Egypt and the mother of the sun god Re. She watches over love, music, and dance.

- **Ilmatar** is the virgin daughter of air and a primary goddess of Finland. She was the creator of heaven and earth.

Lilith, Adam's first wife according to some Hebrew stories. She ran away rather than become subservient to him.

(Artist: Valerie Reynolds, age 8)

◆ **Omeciuatl** is called "The Lady of Our Substance." She is creator of the spirit of human life and source of all nourishment of the Meso-American people.

◆ **Quan Yin** is still honored today as the Chinese goddess of compassion and healing, watching over those who are heartsick as well as physically ill, especially mothers and children.

◆ **Shekhinah** is a female name given to wisdom in the Kabbalah, the mystical commentary on the first five books of the Hebrew Bible.

◆ **Spider Woman** spun and chanted the world into existence, giving the people the four directions. Her daughters set the sun, moon, and stars into existence. She made people from different colors of clay and connected us all to her with the thread of her web.

◆ **Tiamat** of Babylonia personified the primordial sea. She was killed by one of her sons, the god Marduk who broke her body into pieces and used them in the process of creation. The story foreshadows the coming of the male God.

◆ **White Buffalo Calf Woman** brought the sacred pipe to the Lakota people and gave them the creator's instructions on how to pray.

Need Help? Call 911-GODDESS!

Regardless of what you're facing, there is a goddess ready to reach out and give you a hand. Here is a partial and very brief index of women's endeavors and who takes care of what in Goddess-land.

Goddess Characteristics		
Art and Creativity	**Love**	**Power**
Athena	Hera (marriage)	Oya
Aphrodite	Xochquetzal (self-love)	Gaea
Brigid	Aphrodite (sensual love)	Artemis
Mothering	**Business and Politics**	**Healing**
Demeter (dedication)	Athena	Quan Yin
Yemaya (conception)	Oya	Mary
Juno (pregnancy)	Isis	Brigid
Mary (loss of child)		
Wisdom	**Death and Dying**	**Earth**
Shekhinah	Arianrhod	Artemis
Athena	Hecate	Gaea
Sarasvati	Cerridwen	Atira

The Rest of the Story

But wait! What about the rest of the story? Well, as you probably guessed, it isn't over yet. It appears that the goddess didn't die in the big earthquake in Crete. She was hit on the head with a huge rock and knocked unconscious, and she's been sleeping in the rubble ever since.

There is a tradition within women's spirituality of calling things into being by repeating their names and telling their stories. So as women gather together and do this, they believe they are awakening the Earth Mother consciousness inside themselves and bringing important principles back to life. They believe the goddess has something to say to the modern world about women and about the sacredness of the earth.

Women from many traditional religions honor the goddess as well as the god of their particular belief system and find no conflict in doing so. In the next chapter you'll read about the goddess as an important archetype and what that might mean to you.

The Least You Need to Know

♦ The goddess is the central symbol of women's spirituality, representing the divine presence within each of us and throughout creation.

♦ Matriarchy is not the reverse of patriarchy. It is built on female values, specifically shared power.

♦ For 200,000 years of human history societies were developed along female lineage and feminine principles. It has been only in the last 6,000 years that exclusive male rule has dominated.

♦ The ancient goddess cultures embodied equality between the sexes, deep respect for nature, and peaceful relationships. It was a time of great prosperity.

Chapter 7

Seeking Wholeness: Goddess as Archetype

In This Chapter

- What is an archetype?
- Would I know one if I saw one?
- Do I have one, and why would I want one?
- How the goddess can help you balance your checkbook

The goddess as archetype is an image that has endured through many cultural evolutions and continues to speak to women today. There are a number of possible meanings behind the current attraction many women feel today toward the goddess cultures of the ancient world. Are they foolishly digging up the past, or does this resurgence hold a plan for the future?

Archetypes: Creation's Blueprints

"What do you want to be when you grow up?" is a traditional opening line when talking with children. It's always interesting to hear what they come up with. One of my children wanted to be a mailman, and another wanted to be a Catholic priest. That was in the early 1960s, and both were girls, so, of course, they took other paths! However, women are now mail carriers, and

Episcopal priests can be female. Something helps move culture past its limitations. The "something" is referred to as an *archetype*.

Human Instruction Book

Archetypes can be compared to psychological templates. They are spiritual and psychological forces or impulses in the psyche. They manifest as universal personality types that can be recognized in all cultures. Psychoanalyst Carl Jung popularized the idea of archetypes. He believed that even if all the cultures of the world were destroyed, archetypes would appear to us in our dreams and visions and tell us how to re-create them again. Archetypes are the blueprints for creation. They hold the patterns for every created thing; they contain the instructions for being a human.

Jung called the archetypal realm the *collective unconscious*. He said it was the compilation of all the human experience of all time; it contains everything anyone has ever done or known. He believed we are born with archetypes in our psyche that help us know who we are, what we might become, and how to do things. We tap into this bank of information through our unconscious mind through our imagination and in our visions and dreams.

> **Sophia's Wisdom**
>
> Australian Aborigines see archetypal relationships expressed as "song lines" back to the original day of creation. They say that the universe was sung into existence and every form within it has its own particular song.

> **Womanspeak**
>
> **Collective unconscious** is a term used by psychologist Carl Jung to describe the inherited unconscious mind that contains memories, thoughts, and instincts common to all people.

Squeezing Through a Crack in Consciousness

Archetypes are awakened in us as we are exposed to models that reflect them. When we are exposed to very limited models, or no models at all, the very poverty of that experience creates a deep hunger or longing, and an archetype emerges from within us to move us along toward the wholeness our soul seeks. This may very well be the impetus behind the rise of the goddess archetype today. It's growing in our culture specifically because of the limitations that have been culturally imposed on women.

Since the end of the old goddess cultures more than 6,000 years ago until recently, the accepted roles for women have been restrictive. The only socially "approved" female archetype has been woman as wife and mother. And women are expected to be good in that role. When women sought employment outside the home in the world, they were expected to do so as caretakers, becoming "mothers at large." You can still see this reflected in the disproportionate number of women working as teachers, nurses, social workers, waitresses, and child-care specialists.

Like all archetypes, the "good girl" archetype has a flip side: the "bad girl." This is called the "virgin/whore" dilemma. The cultural definition of virgin means abstaining from sex, but in this case it is metaphorically used to include being a good wife. "Good" is defined by patriarchal values and usually means the woman is going by the (men's) rules and not causing anyone any trouble. Trouble is generally defined as questioning or disagreeing with the (men's) rules. And there you are, back where you started. Alice Walker talks about this when she describes a womanist as a woman who asks more questions than is good for her (see Chapter 5, "Black Women's Spirituality and Womanist Theology").

Wise Words

"From birth to 18 a girl needs good parents, from 18 to 35 she needs good looks, from 35 to 55 she needs a good personality, and from 55 on she needs cash."

—Sophie Tucker (1884–1945), vaudevillian and comedian known for her offbeat and slightly off-color remarks, who was called the "last of the red hot mamas"

New Girl in Town: Beyond Virgin and Whore

If you find yourself wondering what else there is besides good girl or bad girl, you will find you're in the company of many other women. So where's the shopping channel for archetypes you might be wondering? Well, the history or biography channels on cable television occasionally provide some. Amelia Earhart, Margaret Mead, and Eleanor Roosevelt are all examples of women who have broken through cultural norms. They are often known because of their breaks with tradition as well as the things they accomplished.

Literature is another source for models. Unfortunately, most literature follows the archetypal norms of the culture and provides limited images. If women are shown operating outside cultural tradition, they often are met with violence and death. Stories often reinforce restrictions rather than encouraging adventure and accomplishment. Think of the hundreds of movies you've seen in which a woman is being stalked or chased through the night, usually wearing only her underwear!

Wise Words

Martha Leigh, a young woman who describes herself as "just a rank and file woman who is fed up," expresses her rancor with the double standard by pointing out, "The week that Madonna's video [for] 'What It Feels Like for a Girl' was banned from MTV because of its purported violence against men, probably 300 women were shown being killed on TV and in the movies." Madonna's video pictured the singer driving in a car with her grandmother and running into a car filled with men.

"Myths and Legends for One Thousand, Please"

Besides being categories on *Jeopardy!* myths and legends are other places we can look for archetypal patterns. Unfortunately, school curricula don't include information about pre-patriarchal history and certainly not pre-patriarchal mythology. Yet despite the few numbers of role models provided by the generations before us, women continue to expand into new cultural territory.

Those who see beyond the images of any particular time are a culture's artists, writers, and philosophers. They're able to make the jump in consciousness necessary to connect to new archetypes. They are the ones who often birth the new archetype into consciousness for the culture. This is the collective window shade that snapped open in the late 1960s and 1970s, heralding the return of the goddess in the feminine psyche (see Chapter 6, "Trying on Goddess Slippers," for more about this awakening). Her awakening has sent many a woman scurrying to the bookshelves, dusting off old mythological stories, and looking at ruins here, there, and everywhere.

Writing a New Psychology

Jean Shinoda Bolen is one of the pioneers in reclaiming mythology as a source of archetypal images for women. Her book, *Goddesses in Every Woman: A New Psychology for Women* (Harper and Row, 1984), became a national best-seller shortly after being published. At the time, Dr. Bolen was a Jungian analyst and a clinical professor of psychiatry at the University of California, San Francisco. She realized the inherent problem in psychology that was based on a male model of the psyche. Since men and women have different experiences and different psychological processes—a fact that was not being taken into consideration—when women's behavior fell outside the very narrow parameters allowed by the male culture, it was labeled as pathological.

 Wise Words

"The goddess made the world with her needle. First she embroidered the moon, and then the shining stars, and then the fine sun and the warm clouds beneath. Then the wet pines in the forest, the pines with wild animals beneath, then the shining waves of the sea. The shining waves with fishes beneath. Thus the goddess embroidered the world. The world flowered from the swift needle of the goddess."

—Northern Russian folksong from Patricia Monaghan's *The Goddess Companion*

In her work, Dr. Bolen enlarges the scope of psychology and women's self-understanding as she explores the goddess archetypes of Greek culture. As she uncovers the essential natures of these ancient women, she shows how the information applies to women's lives in contemporary culture. As we rediscover these complex figures of yesteryear, today's parameters open and the world expands. Dr. Bolen draws from the goddesses of the Greek world because being a part of our common literary heritage, they are familiar to us. She divides them into three categories. The first category contains the virgin goddesses: Artemis, Athena, and Hestia. The second group contains the relational goddesses: Hera, Demeter, and Persephone. In the third category are the transformational goddesses: Aphrodite and Hecate.

Virgin: It's Autonomy, Not Anatomy

To begin with, the term *virgin* needs to be redefined for today's reader. In the pre-classical world, virgin did not refer to physical virginity but instead described a psychological state. Virgin represents the part of a woman's psyche that is not relationship oriented. It describes her *autonomy*, not her anatomy. It's the proactive component in her soul, her independent spirit.

A woman's virginal nature might manifest as a desire to achieve in the world, or it could lead her to a life of quiet contemplation. The point is that she is operating singularly in the world. A woman with this archetype does not seek validation from a man, from the culture, or from any source other than her own; she exists in a state of awareness of her natural wholeness. Three virgin goddesses of Greek mythology represent the range of this archetype: Artemis, Goddess of Nature; Athena, ruler over Culture, Wisdom, and Crafts; and Hestia, Keeper of the Sacred Fires and Temple.

Womanspeak

Virgin is a term used in the classical world to describe the psychological state of autonomy. **Autonomy** describes independence, self-government, personal independence, and the capacity to make moral decisions and act on them singularly.

Sophia's Wisdom

You can be married and still be a virgin. A virgin follows her own rules—not to prove anything, but simply because she must follow her own inner values, and live her truth. Even in marriage she will hold a part of herself in reserve, because a part of her psyche will always belong to only her and no one else. If you have ever longed to get away by yourself even for a weekend or need your own room, even though you're married, you are in touch with your virgin nature.

Not Tonight, Dear, I Have a Headache

Artemis is expressed as pure wild nature. In the old Greek world, her image was reflected in the untouched Arcadian forests of the Greek countryside where she ministered to the wild animals. There was a saying, "Where has Artemis not danced?" which refers to her all-pervading presence in the Greek psyche and Greek world. Artemis is depicted as a midwife in both the physical and spiritual senses. She is associated with the new moon, which is her virginal aspect. Artemis appears later in Roman mythology as Diana.

Goddess Guide

In the symbol of the new moon, Artemis is connected with two other goddesses: Selene of the full moon and Hecate, the old crone of the dying moon. The three of them create the trinity of virgin, mother, and crone. This theme, which is an archetype for a woman's life, is found throughout the old goddess stories.

When an Artemis woman enters into a relationship, and many do, she will find herself challenged by her independent nature. She will have to make an effort to allow herself enough vulnerability to be intimate with another and will probably always relish time alone and, in fact, need it to maintain her equilibrium. An Artemis woman can find happiness in a relationship, but only if she honors her Artemis needs.

Diana and the arch of the moon, 1933 by Rudolf Tegner. Rudolph Tegner Museum.

(Photograph © Maicar Förlag)

A Man's Woman

You've heard of a ladies' man? Well, Athena was a man's woman. In a contemporary society, she might go out for a drink after work with the guys without creating a scandal. She challenges female stereotypes by being a logical thinker, she remembers to stub all her checks (even the small ones), her checkbook is always balanced, and she keeps an even head in the heat of an emotional situation. Athena epitomizes wisdom, making clear, effective decisions in business, government, academic, military, or scientific realms. She stands in contrast to Artemis of the wilderness, because she is the architect of cities and culture. She protected Athens, which is named for her. She's a skilled weaver, too, in more ways than one. She was able to weave together two apparently different worlds—the world of business and politics and the world of arts and crafts.

Mother Knows Best

Check your facts! According to fragments of pre-patriarchal references collected in Charlene Spretnek's *Lost Goddesses of Early Greece* (Beacon Press, 1978), Athena existed prior to springing fully grown from the head of her famous father, Zeus, which was a later version of an existing story.

Athena is the largest indoor statue in the Western world. Located in the Parthenon in Nashville, Tennessee, Alan LeQuire's rendering of Athena stands 41 feet 10 inches tall.

(Photograph © Gary Layda)

Athena women defy a common stereotype of women: An Athena woman "thinks like a man." Today's Athena women can be found at the top of organizations, politics, education, scientific laboratories, or at the head of any public or domestic project. If you enjoy mathematics, science, grammar, research, or writing papers you've got Athena skills. If you pride yourself for being objective, logical, moderate, in good health, clear-minded, physically active, and practical you are reflecting Athena. Athena women are so comfortable with men that their challenge is to allow more women into their lives.

Keeping the Home Fires Burning

Hestia is keeper of the hearth and fire. She has no human form. Her essence might be expressed in the image of keeping the home fires burning, in which case, she is the sacred fire itself. Hestia is at the very center of home life, providing illumination, warmth, and heat for food in the physical sense, but even more so in the spiritual sense.

Hestia women seek quietness and often find that their home and homemaking offer the solitude they require. They find that household chores keep them centered and feeling harmonious. Hestia exists in the soul of life, rather than in the outwardly directed energy of Artemis or Athena. She is intuitive and sensitive and connects with others spiritually.

In contemporary time, a Hestia woman might be found in religious life, particularly in a contemplative order or in an Eastern religion deep in meditation. Outside the convent or ashram, she is the respected elder, the unmarried aunt whose detachment can be counted on for wisdom and guidance. She is a good counselor and truth-teller and can offer deep spiritual insight. She keeps the values for the tribe.

The Softer Side of Goddess

The three relational goddesses are Hera, Goddess of Marriage; Demeter, Mother and Goddess of Grain; and Persephone, Daughter and Queen of the Underworld. These three women represent traditional roles for women: wife, mother, and daughter. Their core identity and well-being are found in their relationship to someone else. Consequently, they need approval, love, and attention and are motivated by their desire to mate.

Hera: Marry Me and Take Me Away from All This!

In the pre-classical mythology, Hera represents the fruitful mother rather than a jealous wife. Woman scholars such as Charlene Spretnak have recovered many of these early stories. They present a different picture from later patriarchal tales, which tend to diminish the power of the goddess.

In the later versions, which are more familiar to today's reader, Hera was a beautiful woman who captured the eye of Zeus, the chief god. They married. After a time spent in blissful honeymooning, Zeus resumed his promiscuous bachelor ways, betraying Hera again and again. She responded with fits of jealous rage and vindictiveness, which she didn't direct at her errant husband but instead toward the women with whom he betrayed her.

Hera considered her marriage sacred and was humiliated by Zeus's actions. She felt dishonored because of his affairs and because he favored the children he fathered with other women. Her spite and rancor eventually became depression. Stories tell of her wandering to the ends of the earth and the sea, wrapped in darkness, isolation, and despair. However, she would allow herself to be coaxed back again and again to take her place at her husband's side.

Despite her problems and her faults, the Greeks loved Hera, and they celebrated with seasonal rituals. In the spring her beauty was honored as Hera the Maiden, and her virginity was restored in ritual baths. In the summer and autumn she was honored in sacramental weddings as the Perfected One and Fulfilled One. In the winter she became Hera the Widow, and her infamous fights with Zeus and her repeated disappearances and wanderings were acknowledged.

Wise Words

"Wherever the goddess was, beauty was. Beauty flowed out from her like water, like the light blue gown she wore, the gown that carried the sweet smell of her presence that hung as heavy as incense in the air. Beauty flowed from her, like her thick gold hair that spread out over her broad shoulders, beauty flowed out from her like light, radiating the brightness of lightning, beauty blazing through the world, wherever the goddess was."

—Homeric hymn to Demeter from Patricia Monaghan's *The Goddess Companion*

Hera's archetype embodies the ability to bond and be a loving and faithful wife despite the difficulties a marriage might bring. Hera epitomizes unconditional commitment. She fulfills her destiny through *sacred* marriage. It's marriage itself, not her husband, that satisfies her. However, as Hera's mythology shows, this absorption with a relationship at the expense of her self can bring depression and despair.

Demeter: Archetypal Jewish Mother

Demeter is the definitive mother figure, containing the archetypal form for nurturing, generosity, and motherhood. Her maternal instinct can be called on to assist with pregnancy; child-rearing; and physical, psychological, and spiritual nourishment to others. Demeter women are pictured in the Madonna and child image of Western art. They are also reflected in the "helping" professions such as nursing, teaching, social work, and counseling.

Demeter has been pictured with bundles of grain in her arms, because it was she who raised the crops and fed the people. Demeter women love preparing meals and feeding others. Demeter is like an earth mother goddess, solid, dependable, and grounded, with a truly giving nature. A Demeter woman naturally assumes the role of matriarch of her family structure and is the one who usually puts the family reunion together. In a work setting, she'll keep up with everyone's birthday, know the names of fellow workers' spouses and children, and organize the company picnic.

The Demeter archetype's challenge is to avoid becoming too smothery and to develop her self-worth independent of her children. The intensity of Demeter's relationship with her daughter, Persephone, was so powerful that it formed the basis of the Eleusinian mysteries that were enacted in Greece for more than 2,000 years.

Persephone: To Hell and Back

In the early stories, Persephone is a willing traveler to the Underworld. Like every child who must one day leave the safety of home and learn to navigate the world, she accompanies Hades to the Underworld. She masters it, gaining the skills to exist in "both" worlds, and returns to become a guide to the dead, not the victim of abduction and rape as she appears in later versions.

Persephone was Demeter's only child. She enjoyed a carefree girlhood gathering flowers and playing in the meadow with her friends until that fateful day, according to later stories, she was abducted by Hades and taken to the Underworld to be his unwilling wife. Demeter, grief-stricken with the loss of her beloved daughter, promptly created winter— shutting down all of nature until that time when her daughter would be returned to her.

Persephone was eventually rescued and brought home to Demeter. However, before leaving the Underworld, she ate six pomegranate seeds, causing her to have to return and spend half of each year there. It turns out that Persephone lied to Demeter, telling her that she was forced to eat the seeds when in fact she ate them willingly. In so doing, the line between her abduction and her willing participation is forever blurred.

Sophia's Wisdom
An archetype can be reflected to us through literature, the arts, or in the form a person we meet such as a really good mom, a smart businesswoman, or an athletic woman. Sometimes it will come through a series of dreams. It can show up as a quality we admire and want to develop, such as humor, bravery, loyalty, or a carefree attitude we admire. In spiritual language, this is our soul seeking its fullness, finding wholeness.

Persephone's dishonesty represents duality. She is both the eternal innocent maiden known as Kore and Queen of the Underworld. As the maiden Kore, she is compliant, passive, and at times even manipulative. In modern time she might be seen as coquettish, a people-pleaser, or a woman who resists growing up and taking responsibility for herself. However, in her duality there is a mastery that belies her immaturity. As Queen of the Underworld, Persephone masters the ability to live in both worlds.

Counselors and spiritual advisors can use her insight and skills in helping others. Persephone has survived abduction and rape and lived to become master of her fate. She can inspire and assist women in healing from similar wounds. She is the archetype for rebirth and our eternal ability to begin again.

The Goddess's Magical Side

The next two goddesses are both transformers. One is the Goddess of Love, Aphrodite, who embodies the impulse to create. She is behind all acts of creation—art, music, making babies. She charms and beguiles, illuminates and seduces—and keeps the wheel of life turning and reproducing. The other transformational goddess is the embodiment of wisdom and master of all the aspects of being a woman. She is wise old Hecate, also known as the old crone. She has seen it all and done most of it. She has learned life's lessons and is able to help other women through all the passages to their wisdom. She is also the one who takes you through your final passage of this lifetime into death. She is Shaman and High Priestess. Both of these feminine archetypes are extraordinarily powerful but are the least-understood female roles in today's culture.

Sex and the Single Woman

Aphrodite has inspired many a poet, artist, musician, and lover. Her singularly fixed goal is to consummate a relationship and create new life. She will do that through physical intercourse, bringing a new child into existence, or through the arts. She is present to all forms of creative work, influencing the world of philosophy, art, and music. Wherever the muse flies, she is. Everything is invigorated and charmed by her presence.

Have you ever been at a gathering and become completely entranced with someone, finding even the most ordinary remarks witty and clever while at the same time wondering what in the world was happening to you? You might even have been fantasizing about "after the party." If so, you and the object of your newly sprung affection were both being bathed in Aphrodite's golden light. Aphrodite is the one responsible when the "chemistry" heats up. She creates the powerful magnetism that will not be satisfied short of consummation.

Goddess Guide _____

Aphrodite probably pushes the patriarchal buttons more than all the other goddesses. She is passionately and intensely focused on her mission to create new life. In her unrelenting pursuit of her goal, she breaks the rules. She creates deep intimacy and extreme compassion spontaneously with the flutter of her eyelashes. She governs women's enjoyment of sexuality and sensuality and feels pleasure intensely—in or out of marriage. She falls in love easily and often but never for forever. She gets what she wants, giving pleasure in return, and when satisfied, moves on.

Aphrodite's transformational power is the power of love itself. She heals by opening our own hearts and connecting us to our deepest selves. It's Aphrodite who shines her golden light on those deep parts of us, causing us to fall in love with ourselves, transforming us in the process.

Coming Full Circle

Hecate, the crone of the dark moon, is the Goddess of Death. She commands respect and engenders terror! She guards the passage through which we must all go to reach eternity and regeneration. Hecate is sometimes shown wearing a long black robe and holding burning torches. On moonless nights she was believed to roam the earth with a pack of ghostly, baying hounds. She could be found standing at the triple crossroads with her pack of dogs as symbol of her function of choice. She helps women choose wisely.

Today, Hecate women are the most-feared and, simultaneously, most-respected women in culture. A Hecate woman is the post-menopausal woman who has come to grips with her self and her power. Having moved beyond the external beauty of the virgin and no longer childbearing like the mother, she has slipped the bonds of patriarchal control. Like the crone of the ancient world, such a woman is respected for her embodiment of wisdom and feared for the truth and clarity she brings to any situation.

Her image as she stands at the crossroads with her dogs and the need to placate her to assure safe passage translates to the family's invincible matriarch. Her council would be sought and her permission would be necessary for important events or contracts. She would have to be satisfied before a wedding or any other life ritual or passage could take place. Because Hecate has all power over heaven and hell, she is the High Priestess. Because she rules over death, she is the Shaman.

The Least You Need to Know

- Archetypes are like blueprints of the universal human characteristics, skills, and talents we are born with. They reside in our psyche or unconscious mind.

◆ Archetypes relate to instincts. They inspire and also assist in self-development. Whatever it is you want to create, there is an archetype available.

◆ The Western religious traditions compressed all the goddess archetypes into a monotheistic god who is male. As a result, many women do not find adequate female images or values reflected in that male god figure.

◆ Women's spirituality explores the mythological world to find a richer picture of the feminine that expresses women's spirit in a more complete way.

Chapter 8

Women's Altars: Seat of Power

In This Chapter

- Home altars and the women who build them
- Why women build altars
- What you need to know to build an altar
- How a home altar works with your tradition

Remember the rocks and shells you filled your pockets with when you were a kid? The pigeon feather or bit of turtle shell that was so fascinating you had to bring it home with you? As you held the item in your hand, you couldn't help but wonder how a bird flies or where the turtle went that used to occupy the shell. If you remembered to empty your treasures out of your pockets, they probably ended up on the dresser with your trading cards or hair clips. You probably looked at them every day and were devastated if they turned up missing. As you collected and displayed your treasures, you were connecting to an ancient tradition. You were assembling the rudiments of an altar.

Our Spiritual Umbilical Cord

When we think of an altar, most of us think of traditional altars found in churches, temples, or mosques. These formal altars are the exclusive territory of the priest or rabbi who uses them for official ceremonies. However, there is an ancient and widespread practice of altar-building that's inherently feminine. Since the beginning of time, women have built and maintained altars in their homes. Home altars are used as prayer and meditation centers and for ceremonies.

Altars make an intimate, personal spiritual statement and are remarkably similar in how they are built and function. We're going to explore the tradition of home altars and see how women of all religious and spiritual persuasions use them today. Whether you practice a traditional or nontraditional religion or are winging it, building a home altar creates a powerful spiritual center in your home.

Mirrors of the Soul

A home altar reflects the things you cherish. An altar works symbolically, giving form to what is sometimes very hard or even impossible to form in words. There are times when you might not be consciously aware of what you're attempting to express with your altar, or at least unaware of the impact it will have on you. Through the process of putting it together, bits of truth and wisdom begin to surface. Later, as you reflect over what you've gathered and placed in your altar, a deeper truth about yourself and the things you hold closest to your heart emerges.

Altar-building is an intuitive process, meaning it's a conversation between your unconscious and conscious minds that speaks what you feel, before you have time to think about it or come up with a verbal description. Your intuition loves to create symbols. Often it's through these symbols that we connect to one another at the deepest level. That is probably why receiving a flower from a loved one can be worth a thousand words.

 Wise Words _____

"Among all the women's altars I have seen, no two look exactly the same nor are used in exactly the same way. Each one represents the individuality of its maker; its conventional elements, candles and pictures of deities, for instance, are always wedded to a creative impulse. The home altar exists at the point of intersection between art and religion where the sacred is apprehended in a woman's imagined relationship with the Divine."

—Kay Turner, Ph.D. in folklore from the University of Texas and author of *Beautiful Necessity: The Art and Meaning of Women's Altars* (Thames and Hudson, 1999)

That Old Rascal, Authority!

Whenever the topic of altar-building comes up, so does the issue of authority. Two questions that are often asked are "By whose authority do you build it?" and "Whom are you building the altar to?" These are very pertinent questions, because they touch the absolute heart of women's spirituality. Unlike traditional religion, home altars or women's altars have no one to whom they must answer. Tradition itself backs the authority. Women seem to naturally know how to honor the sacred. When it comes to building altars, *you are the authority*.

To whom a woman builds her altar is a personal matter. There is a common understanding within women's spirituality that people are really all about the same business. We're all building our altars to the same *One*, who may be called by many names. Your altar is your sacred space. It's where you are in charge. You can build an altar to honor anyone or anything that's important to you: a grandmother, the goddess, Mary and the saints, or an ancestor. An altar can symbolize something you are praying about, wishing for, honoring, or letting go of.

Womanspeak

Old Rascal is a term used to identify a patriarch when he is interfering in women's business. You won't find this term in the dictionary; it's pure womanspeak. Use it 10 times and it's yours!

Here is an altar built in recognition of winter solstice. It incorporates the four elements—air, earth, fire, and water—in an artistically pleasing arrangement.

An altar might represent acknowledgement or praise, or it might be a way of asking for help with something you are struggling with. An altar begins with a desire to honor something that has meaning for you, and there's really no wrong way of going about it. Remember, it's instinctive. You know what you are doing, even if you don't "know" what you're doing.

Mother Knows Best

Regardless of how long it's been missing, or where your original tribe hails from, there is a tradition of building home altars hiding somewhere in your closet!

The Legacy: Grandmothers, Mothers, and Daughters

This female legacy of altar-building is often passed from grandmother to mother to daughter. Women have always built home altars as the center for religious ceremony in the house; they express devotion, offer protection, and provide a place to pray and meditate. Home altars are somewhere to go to seek council, ask for help, and receive healing. Altars are a tradition that is both ancient and very much alive today. The following sections share some stories that show how women use this ancient tradition today.

Dolores' Waiting-for-the-Baby Altar

Dolores is a young woman attorney of Latin descent who has built an altar to celebrate her pregnancy. She called her mother a short time ago to announce the arrival of a grandchild, and her mother's first response was, "Have you built your altar?" Dolores was pleased to be able to answer "Yes." In fact, Dolores told me, she would not have made the phone call if she hadn't already built it. Dolores grew up in a family where home altars were common. Her mothers, aunts, and grandmothers all had home altars, sometimes several going at the same time. Here is a look at Dolores's altar and how she will be using it.

Dolores placed her altar on the mantle of the fireplace in her old Victorian apartment on Green Street in San Francisco. The central piece is a statue of the Lady of Guadalupe. Across the Lady's belly is stretched a blue band, showing her pregnancy. There is a Bible, a rosary, and a small blanket arranged around the Lady. Dolores bought a book she will use as a journal to record her thoughts and feelings for the new child. She lights a candle, sits down by the window, and begins a letter to her baby.

> My Little Darling,
>
> Today your arrival was confirmed. I suspected it for several weeks, and now we know for sure. Your father and I are thrilled beyond belief. Soon I will be telling the family, and they will be eagerly awaiting your arrival, too. But for now, I want to spend a little time, just you and me, getting to know each another.
>
> I can't exactly feel you, but my breasts are very aware you are there. They began to ache about two weeks ago and that is how I first suspected you had made it from the other side. How was your journey? I get the feeling there will be lots of milk for you—not to worry.
>
> Today I am lighting a red candle for us. It seems to honor the blood that did not come this month. And red is the color of love. You must know that you are much loved. Each morning you and I will sit here and have our little talk. I will write things down in your book so you can read all about your auspicious beginnings.

We are under the protection of the Lady, and she knows all about these things. I am going to place this book on the altar now and go eat some breakfast. You must have a hearty appetite, because I am hungry all the time. Welcome to your new home, little one.

Love,

Mother

The Teddy Bear, the Cross, and a Stone

Women in all traditions are reconnecting to this bit of their sacred history. Here is an example of how a Protestant woman built and used her altar to help her at the time of her mother's death.

Pam, a Lutheran woman who lives in Chicago, began building her home altar after attending a workshop held at her church. Her altar is on the coffee table in the living room of her suburban home. She has placed a picture of her mother in the center, and around it are positioned various tokens that are reminders of their relationship: a cookbook, signifying times they spent together in the kitchen; her grandmother's pearls, connecting her to an important ancestor; seed packages, because they share a common love of gardening; a miniature teddy bear, which speaks of Pam's position as the child; and shells they gathered together last summer when spending time together at the beach. Pam has attached ribbons to her mother's picture and has woven them throughout the objects on the altar to represent what she calls the strands of DNA that connect her and her mother. There is also a cross, the Christian symbol of death, and a glass butterfly, to represent her belief in resurrection and afterlife. Between these two objects is a large stone. The stone represents the rolling back of the stone at the tomb, signifying Christ's resurrection. But it has also come to represent the heaviness in Pam's heart.

Pam's mother is fighting cancer. The outcome does not look good, and the family has begun to gather. Her mother's favorite prayer book is opened to the Psalms, and Pam reads one every night before going to bed. Glass containers hold candles that burn 24 hours a day. Pam keeps fresh flowers near her mother's bed at the hospital, and removes one flower from the arrangement to keep on her altar at home—again symbolizing their connection. Pam's intention is to acknowledge her gratitude for the strong bond she feels between her and her mother, as well as the women who came before them. Her intention is to ask for God's help in releasing her mother and strength to deal with the loss.

Mother Knows Best

Don't worry about what is sacred and what isn't when you build your altar. It's all sacred. Just follow your intuition and see what ends up on your altar—it might surprise you and teach you something new about yourself.

Wise Words

"Relationship with the Divine is a working relationship. Many women say that asking for healing and returning thanks is a labor that they perform joyously at their altars."

—Kay Turner, *Beautiful Necessity: The Art and Meaning of Women's Altars*

After her mother's passing, Pam was sitting at her altar when she realized that the stone had begun to capture her imagination. She found herself staring at it and sometimes holding it in her hand. It was speaking to her spirit in a slightly different way than it had before. Rather than symbolizing her mother's continued life in eternity, it now symbolized what Pam must overcome within herself so that she could experience her own resurrection—her life after her mother's death.

Pam asked a couple of her friends to accompany her to the nearby river to witness a ceremony she felt she must do. She held the rock as she spoke about her grief as well as her regrets. All relationships are complex; perhaps none is more complicated than the relationship of a mother and daughter. There were aspects of Pam and her mother's relationship that had been difficult for Pam, and some of the problems between them remained unresolved after her mother's death. Pam spoke of her willingness to let go, allowing the transformation to happen.

Goddess Guide

No doubt many of you have seen St. Christopher medals for cars and magnetized statues for dashboards. One woman who is on the road a lot for business keeps an altar in her car. She has rocks, feathers, and stones, along with a picture of her husband and kids, mounted to a piece of slate. There is a small candle, which although she doesn't light it, she likes the aesthetic, and it brings in the element fire. Her mobile altar keeps her from being lonely and feeling separated when she is far from home.

With the support of her friends, Pam dropped the stone into the water and watched it sink to the bottom. She said she physically felt the release in her heart, as if the stone had been lodged there and was now gone. In telling her story, Pam said that she continued to miss her mom and mourn her passing, but something had shifted. At the same time she felt loss, she also felt her mom's presence, "almost like she was right here," Pam said. She now laughs about the disagreements between them, recognizing their differences but no longer being threatened by them. She described her overall feeling as "a deep sense of freedom." She said, "I'm still her child, but I'm not the little girl. I'm a woman with my own ideas. I know my mom wants me to get on with my life, and do it the way I know is best. I can feel it!"

Yielding to a Greater Wisdom

Artists and writers often tell about how the piece they're working on begins to take over. They feel as though something bigger or greater than themselves is coming to form through them. They talk about not being aware of why they used a certain color or created a particular shape or where a phrase came from. When this happens, the artist has let go with her conscious mind and is creating from the depth of her unconscious—from instinct or intuition.

She is feeling her connections to the source, her spiritual links between "here" and "there," between the world of spirit and the material world. The process of building an altar likewise flows directly from these deep states of consciousness. This is the same place we enter during mystical experiences. It brings ideas, beliefs, and feelings that are rich with spiritual insight.

Mother Knows Best

When you take a stone from the ground, do it with consciousness. According to Native American beliefs, stones contain great wisdom and are the oldest living nation. When you want to use a stone for an altar, ask its permission first. It is a Native American custom to leave a tobacco offering in its place.

Allowing the Symbols to Speak

Once you have decided on what it is you want to acknowledge at your altar, begin to gather the objects to be placed on the altar that represent your intention. You do this mainly by *attraction*. Often during the process of gathering things for your altar, you'll find you're attracted to something that doesn't have a clear relationship to the big picture. The women I talked with all described how something "insisted" on being part of the altar even though they didn't know why, because it didn't seem to "fit." The beginning altar-builder may scorn such lack of logic and choose to maintain control of the gathering process. When this happens, you probably miss some of the intuitive "stuff," but your altar will still bring your intention or desire into form. It will express for you what you are intending to say; often much to your surprise, it will say it better than you thought you could.

It's March 21 in Alaska, and signs of spring are not easy to come by. My granddaughter, Valerie, and I are looking for signs of spring to build an altar in honor of the spring equinox. However, on the way home from the store this morning, we spotted a large eagle roosting in the top of a tree near my daughter's house. Robins are the traditional harbingers of spring "down South" in the "lower 48," but eagles scream its return in the far North.

Inspired by the eagle's message, Valerie and I set out to find something to put on the altar that would remind us that spring was coming. Not too far down the road we found shoots of wild pussy willows that had sprouted and grown up through the snow. Their small white buds were beginning to open. Valerie and I brought some of the pussy willows home and put them in a vase, adding some pine branches to show that while spring was coming, winter ruled the roost this day.

Pussy Willows, Pine, and Dog Biscuits

When we had finished gathering the things for our altar, we arranged them in a way that was both pleasing and meaningful to us. Like all forms of artistic expression, it's the contrast of light and dark, of like and unlike, that most engages our imagination. Altars work from the same principle. They're the place where things that appear on the surface to have no relationship come together and a new and deeper understanding of creation's interrelatedness emerges. We can find God in new and surprising ways. This is why our Alaskan spring altar ended up with pussy willows, pine branches, and dog biscuits!

It's a long way from our home in Tennessee to Alaska, and our visits to Valerie and her family are more rare than we'd like them to be. So we cram as much into each visit as possible, and everything we do together tends to take on mythological proportions. This visit was about home-baked dog biscuits, and we made batches and batches of them. Our plan was to deliver them to several of the neighbors as a goodwill gesture. They came to symbolize the relationship between grandchild, daughter, and grandmother, good neighboring, Valerie's desire to become a veterinarian, and just because we thought they should be there!

> **CAUTION**
> ### Mother Knows Best
> Regardless of your chosen path, you can represent your spiritual values with an altar. Whether you speak to Artemis, Yahweh, Buddha, Waken Tonka, Christ, Allah, or nature itself, the building of your altar reflects what is nearest and dearest to you. It's the personal expression of your spirit.

The Sacred and Secular

We've spoken in great detail about how women don't make a big distinction between the practical matters of everyday living and the sacred world of the hereafter. And we mean it! Here are a couple examples of what this principle looks like in action.

Finney's Altar and Sacred Footrest

As you enter the home of my friend Finney, you will encounter her coffee table in the middle of the room, which serves as her altar. It functions in all the ways we have just been talking about: It makes a statement about who she is and what symbol system she honors, it is used as the focus point in ceremonies, and it is also her personal altar.

Finney's altar is in a constant state of flux and flow. Today in the center, there is a pottery candelabra in the form of a circle of people holding hands. There is a bowl containing small slivers of dried ash, thorns from a tree in her yard, and oak twigs also from her yard. These symbolize her exploration into Celtic shamanism. Finney admits to being a bit too goal-oriented and wants to learn how to "hang out in the mystery of things and be comfortable there." She feels that since mystery is the domain of the shaman, and she is of Celtic descent, it just might work.

A bowl of colorful rocks sits in the center, because Finney likes to see the light bounce off them. There are some dried rose petals left over from a ceremony "because they look pretty." She added one more function to her altar that we haven't explored: footrest. It serves as a great place to prop her feet up when reading, grounding both her and the altar in the practicalities of everyday life. Finney is not given to sanctimony!

> **Mother Knows Best** ___
>
> Don't confuse sacred with sanctimonious. Women's spirituality is reverent but not stuffy. It's a chance to let your hair down and have some fun with your spiritual side. God probably gets bored with too much bowing and scraping!

From the description of Finney's altar, you can see that the objects you choose should be very personal. Liking the way something looks, smells, tastes, sounds, or feels is enough reason to put it on your altar. Likewise, not liking an object for any of these reasons is just cause for removal. Somehow women are able to close the gap between the everyday "stuff" and what is usually considered sacred. Finney's sacred footrest illustrates that point beautifully.

> **Goddess Guide** ___
>
> Women use the words *connection* and *relationship* again and again when describing spirituality. Altars are where these important spiritual concepts come to life. There, past, present, and future converge "now." At the altar, a woman can acknowledge the divine spiritual network that allows her to call on Sophia of the Hebrew scripture, along with Hestia, Goddess of the Hearth; the Virgin Mary, or her counterpart, Yemaya of the Seven African Powers; as well as the Ahpo Wi Chapi known by the Lakota people as Morning Star, or Maka, known as Mother Earth. All can be called with one breath.

Standing in the Eye of the Mystery

Annie just turned eight, and her favorite present was a new bicycle. Today she is setting out on her first trip all by herself. She will ride her bicycle down the street to play with her best friend, Celli. She's excited and grinning from ear to ear as she pedals down the driveway and turns into the street. She can hardly wait to show her friend the new bike.

About half-way down the block, something catches Annie's eye. She turns the bicycle sharply to take a closer look. She can hardly believe her eyes. There is a small nest lying on the ground beneath a tree. She gets off her bike and kneels down to examine it. Inside there is one tiny blue egg.

Ever so gently she picks up the nest, and cradling it in her hand, she carries it back to her bicycle. Despite the chilly temperature, she takes her sweatshirt off to pad her bicycle's basket as protection for the nest and its delicate contents. Annie turns her bike around and heads back home. She takes the nest inside to her room and places it on her dresser beside her bed. Before leaving again, she turns on a small lamp and covers the nest with a sweater. Later, after returning from her friend's house, she hurries upstairs to examine her find more closely.

Mother Knows Best

It can be your secret! No one has to know your altar is an altar. A simple and attractive arrangement using a plant, a shell, a candle, a beautiful rock, a photograph, and whatever else balances it out can be an altar. One woman has such an arrangement on her desk in a busy office many floors off the ground. She can look at it throughout the day and be reminded of what she feels is important.

Annie awakens many times during the night, checking on the egg's progress, feeling certain each time that she'll find a newly hatched bird. The next day her parents have a talk with her about how unlikely it is that the bird is still alive. In fact, it has begun to smell a little. Together the three of them carry the nest out to the backyard, where a small ceremony marks the occasion. Annie places the egg and the nest in the ground and marks the grave with a rock.

The casual observer might remark that this is a typical story about a child's curiosity. She might remember a similar time and a similar story from her own childhood. The casual observer would report the story the way it appeared to happen, and that's where the difference between the spiritual observer and the casual observer becomes clear. Our spiritual nature communicates with the unseen world. It goes beneath the surface of things to read what the events are portraying, what is being signified.

The spiritual observer would report that something very important had just happened. She would talk about how the child's imagination was captured, how she was stopped in her tracks and brought to her knees by the sight of the nest and the egg. She would say that as the child held her treasure, she was standing in the eye of the mystery, encountering existence itself. As the child radically altered her plans, abandoning her anticipated journey to her friend's house, she intuitively honored this great mystery. As she turned back toward home, she responded to a higher call, a spiritual instinct. When she placed the nest on her dresser, the spiritual observer would say she laid it on her altar.

The Least You Need to Know

- ◆ Women's altars have been around for more than 20,000 years, and they continue to exist in all cultures all over the world.

- ◆ You are the final authority in all aspects of building and using your home altar.

- ◆ Your altar has specific meaning to you; it imparts new revelations and symbolizes the things you hold most valuable.

- ◆ The practice of building a home altar exists in all religious traditions and complements the practice of traditional religion.

Ritual 101

In This Chapter

◆ What is a ritual?

◆ Turning a "ho-hum" ceremony into an "ah-ha" experience

◆ Can you participate in ceremonies and still have traditional beliefs?

◆ A blueprint for a ritual

There are many rituals that are part of our daily lives. Putting the kids to bed, for example, is a ritual. Mealtimes can be rituals, as can birthday parties, family reunions, and even a regular walk with a friend. Family rituals set patterns, reflect values, and show family members what is important. Spiritual rituals accomplish these goals, too, and have one additional intent: They are performed with the hope of gaining deeper insight. Rituals follow a process in which the use of symbols engages the imagination with the intent of bringing a new understanding, a change in how you think about something, a shift in consciousness.

Between You and Your Higher Power

The dictionary defines *ritual* as an established and prescribed pattern of observance; the performance of actions or procedures in a set ordered and ceremonial way; the reinforcement of social values. It describes *ceremony* as a formal event for the purpose of solemnizing something; forms of behavior that are observed on formal occasion; a polite gesture. Reading these definitions does not make rituals and ceremonies sound very creative or much like celebration. Yet rituals and ceremonies can be imaginative, creative, insightful, and transforming. What makes the difference?

Celebrating Your Spirit

When you have a specific belief, ideal, or "truth" you are seeking to reinforce through ritual, it becomes instruction or programming. This is not what we're going to do here. Women's spirituality is not about teaching or reinforcing a specific set of beliefs. It is about each woman who participates discovering more about herself, about how she imagines the divine, and about developing a relationship with God and with her own sense of the sacred. It works from the premise that you and your higher power can have a conversation without anyone running interference for you.

Rituals and ceremonies in women's spirituality are designed for the purpose of moving you beyond your conditioned mind and getting into some new brain cells that haven't been programmed, where you can have an authentic experience of connecting with your own truth. To do this you set the stage for a spontaneous engagement with the imagination in which a brand-new insight can emerge.

Mother Knows Best

Keep it simple! One of the quickest and easiest ceremonies can be simply giving "it" to your higher power, whatever "it" is. A tried-and-true ceremony popular in the 12-step recovery world is to write "it" down and put it in a small box called a God box. Once you put it in there, you can stop worrying about it; it's out of your hands, and in the hands of your higher power.

It's About Transformation

A ritual is an event or an experience created for a purpose. In women's spirituality the purpose of a ritual is for personal revelation and *transformation*.

Womanspeak

Transformation is a complete change to a more meaningful and helpful interpretation, understanding, or belief.

Rituals create a system or a structure that takes the participant through a process to engage spiritual imagination with the result of a new insight or understanding of one's self. Women's spirituality believes that the divine speaks to each of us. As a woman discovers her spiritual truth and shares it with the others, we all catch a bigger glimpse of the "one" we seek to know.

Sophia's Wisdom

You've probably been captured by a moonrise that demanded your attention or a summer day that simply refused to be ignored. These are ways that nature invites us into a spontaneous ceremony or ritual. You might find that you decide to call a friend to sit in the moonlight or break your routine to enjoy a walk outside on a beautiful day. As your intuition grows, you'll notice how often this happens.

Because the purpose of a ritual is to allow a new insight to emerge, you have to trust the process and trust that God, the goddess, holy spirit, or whoever you imagine being the source of revelation, knows how to inspire you. You are creating an opportunity for that to occur.

Rituals create experiences that awaken the imagination. The very word *imagination* implies that we begin to see something differently. As our established way of thinking is questioned, we open our minds just a bit, and new possibilities emerge. In that little space of time, a flash of insight can occur, giving us an opportunity to "rethink" and possibly come to a new understanding. This is what transformation means.

Spiritual Imagination: Ah-Ha! Not Ho-Hum!

Some people call this new insight divine inspiration or a message from God. Others consider it personal wisdom. The name isn't the most important part. Whatever you call it, this insight can get you over a stuck place in your thinking. You can talk all day "about" getting out of a stuck place and "about" changing your mind, but that doesn't do anything about actually changing it. In order for it to change, you have to get out of the left hemisphere and move over to the right one where new ideas come from. The imagination is located in the right hemisphere. That's also where dreams originate, and most important, that's traditionally been where God has spoken to people.

The right hemisphere is where mystics and those who meditate regularly go to experience the divine. It is the land of the shaman, spiritual healers, intuitives, philosophers, artists, writers, dancers, athletes, and gardeners. It is that quiet, still place inside where you can go and come back feeling as though you've spent a week on the beach. Women's rituals are designed to take you on an inner journey where you will free yourself from the limitation that you place on God's possibilities for you.

Wise Words

Although Albert Einstein (1879–1955), scientist and philosopher best known for his theory of relativity, is definitely not a woman, he speaks with a wise woman's heart when he says "Imagination is more important than knowledge."

Wise Words

"Imagery is a process that invokes and uses the senses: vision, audition, smell, taste, the senses of movement, position, and touch. It's the communication mechanism between perception, emotion, and bodily change. A major cause of both health and sickness, the image is the world's oldest and greatest healing resource."

—Jeanne Achterberg, Ph.D., professor of psychology at the Institute of Transpersonal Psychology in Menlo Park, California, and author of *Imagery in Healing Shamanism and Modern Medicine* (Shambala, 1985)

Without engaging the imagination, rituals and ceremonies are flat. They become tedious and serve to reinforce the "same ol', same ol'," creating a ho-hum experience rather than an ah-ha one. Women's ceremonies are designed to take the lid off potential and put the celebration back into ceremony.

What a Ritual *Isn't* About

A ritual is an intentional process designed for the purpose of bringing the participants to a new awareness within themselves. Women's rituals do not have *specific* agendas in mind as part of their purpose, but they set the stage so that the people who are participating have an opportunity to discover something about themselves. That's an important characteristic of this spirituality in all ways. The practice is not about transmitting a particular dogma or way of thinking. Quite the opposite. Its about presenting opportunities for a woman to discover her own beliefs.

We have already talked a bit about what women's spirituality is *not* about, which should clear up any worries on what might be going on during a ritual. It isn't about doing bad things to chickens, hexing your old school principal, or extracting additional child support. There's a general rule that can always stand repeating, something to keep in mind when you approach a ceremony: Do not participate when you don't know the people and aren't clear about what the purpose is. This isn't just a spiritual principle by any means; it's common sense. The same rule can be applied to getting into poker games or the backseat of someone's car.

Structure Marries Spontaneity

If you are new to the idea of creating ritual, it's helpful to find someone with experience to help get you started. There are also good references in Appendix C, "Resources." It is not as difficult as it first appears to be, but there are a lot of components to the process, and they can seem intimidating to the beginner. Someone described it as a bit like herding cats. You can begin by letting go of any worry that you'll do something terribly wrong. You can also spend time learning about the different parts to the art of ritual before beginning to practice. There is a creative balance between structure and spontaneity that allows a ritual to have enough room to breath without completely dissolving into the ethers or holding it so tight that you choke it to death. You are aiming for the middle ground. If you don't make it the first time, fear not. Remember that this is an art form, and hosting a ritual is a bit like performing on stage.

Allowing the Spirit to Speak

There are ways of structuring a ritual that will help you create an atmosphere where discovery will be the likely result. However, like creating an altar, spiritual ceremonies follow customs rather than rules, and you are always the final authority on what gets celebrated and how it is done. You'll find that there is an intuitive logic used in constructing a ritual. It needs structure, but it shouldn't become rigid or repetitious, which would defeat the purpose—to engage the imagination and *allow* a transformation to happen.

While we're on the subject of *allow*, let's talk a bit about it as a spiritual principle. Because most of us have not had very many opportunities to discover what we think or feel about something without having to sort through a lot of other people's ideas or interpretations, allowing is not one of the concepts we are well practiced in. Allowing takes a high degree of awareness to assist others in a transformational process without thinking you have to give them new ideas.

As you will hear over and over again, women's spirituality is about learning how to trust yourself, your intuition, and your natural sense of the spiritual. Everyone has a different inner process. While we are laying out the framework for a successful ritual here, you can experiment with it until it works right for you.

> **Sophia's Wisdom**
>
> Theater has its roots in religious ceremony, and the shaman heals by engaging the imagination of the people. As you practice, you'll learn how imagery and symbols evoke the imagination, and you will master the art. Your ritual will become like a fine weaving. The different parts will begin to function together to create an experience that reflects the intention and the occasion.

Creative Chaos

If the form ends up making everyone uncomfortable, like they're afraid of doing something wrong, you've gone too far and the form is too rigid. If it gets all disconnected and vague, it has wandered too far off course. If it's boring, it may be too repetitious or does

Womanspeak

Chaos refers to the state of unbounded space and formless matter that is believed to have existed before the creation of the universe. Here it refers to the relationship of unboundedness or letting go of our structured thoughts so that something new can be created.

not allow the participants to contribute. You have to be willing to make some mistakes to be able to make the adjustments that work for you and for your group. When you do, you find that you develop a natural sense of the sacred.

Effective rituals have both form and spontaneity. A bit of form gives spontaneity a place to depart from and helps keep things from feeling totally chaotic. Remember, however, that there is always an element of *chaos* involved with a transformational ceremony. There's always a time when the ritual takes an unexpected turn. A good leader is one who can recognize the "magic" and give it some room while still keeping things on track. Obviously it takes practice. That's one of the values of working with the same group of people. You find your rhythm and the group's beat, too.

We suggest that you invite two or three other women who might want to learn about the process of creating rituals to join you right from the beginning. This way, you build the structure together, and you will all fit into it. Coming together to explore is a spiritual process in itself. You'll be surprised at all that gets stirred up as you begin your project. Give yourselves plenty of time and space to process as you go, and allow it to unfold.

Sacred Time and Space

A ceremony always begins with an intention or focus. It can be as simple as an exploring ritual. We have suggested some themes in the next chapter that you might find helpful. You might begin to explore your beliefs about spirituality, your relationships with each other, or what brought you to this place. You can include any number of people, but we recommend beginning with three to five. Generally people sit in a circle either on the floor with cushions or in chairs. The circle doesn't have to be exact; casually sitting around your living room is fine. Take the phone off the hook, and ask guests to turn off beepers and cell phones or leave them in another room. Put a "Do Not Disturb" sign on the door. You are the guardian of the time and space.

Setting the Stage: Ambiance Counts

Ambiance refers to mood and tone. You want to stimulate the imagination, and the best way into the imagination is through the senses. That is why candlelight, soft music, flowers, the smell and taste of good food, the feel of table linen, beautiful china, the clink of glasses, and deep, meaningful conversation with someone you enjoy being with creates magic. How many people have fallen in love in just such a setting?

Your ceremony or ritual works the same way, although it can be a lot easier on your credit card—it isn't necessary to spend a lot of money to create the ambiance you want. Just remember to engage the senses. Nature does the rest. For example, holding a seashell in your hands, closing your eyes and feeling its roughness and smoothness, opening your eyes and looking closely at the colors, and holding it up to your ear and hearing the ocean all evoke the senses and take you into your imagination. Add candlelight, the smell of incense, and some very soft music, and you have all you need to be transported to wherever your imagination takes you.

Womanspeak

Ambiance refers to the atmosphere or mood of a place.

Goddess Guide

When setting the stage for ceremony, make sure you stimulate all the senses. Have color, smell, sound, touch, and taste. The senses take you into your imagination, and that is where you want to go for your ritual. That's where you'll have a new experience.

Putting the Sacred in Sacred Space

Create an altar in the center of the circle. It can be very simple or elaborate, depending on what you like. We'll use a simple one with the elements and the four directions as our example (shown in the following figure). The elements are a neutral or universal symbol, meaning they can be effective within every belief system. We are all living together on the earth, and the elements honor that truth.

Looking at the altar figure, you can see how the intersection of the four directions creates a center point. This is an ancient ceremonial pattern. It places you at the center of the universe. That in itself is an interesting point to ponder. As well as being in the center, the four directions connect us to the bigger universe; they create relationship. As we've been learning, women's spirituality honors paradox. You always look at opposites. You notice what it feels like to bring the focus into yourself as center of the center. And you feel what it is like to expand out into the farthest reaches of space and what it means to be in a relationship with the universe.

Place each element in its respective corner within the circle, and place flowers, fruit, or other natural items in the middle. Use seasonal items to connect you to your natural world. In women's spirituality God speaks through nature—it is a source of revelation.

Wise Words

"We tend to think of things outside and separate from ourselves. But when we read the world spiritually, we discover that things often set us on pathways, which lead us back to the meaningfulness of our lives. Things house our feelings, memories, and connections with others both living and dead."

—Frederick and Mary Ann Brussat, *Spiritual Literacy*

The four directions and placement of the elements.

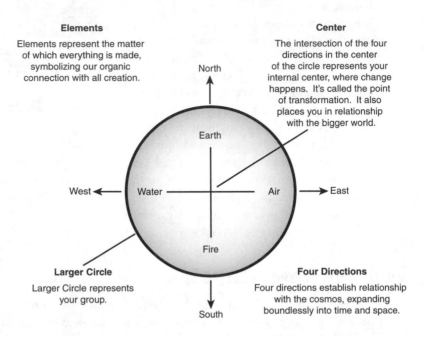

Ceremonial Centering Altar

Elements
Elements represent the matter of which everything is made, symbolizing our organic connection with all creation.

Center
The intersection of the four directions in the center of the circle represents your internal center, where change happens. It's called the point of transformation. It also places you in relationship with the bigger world.

North

Earth

West ← Water — Air → East

Fire

Larger Circle
Larger Circle represents your group.

Four Directions
Four directions establish relationship with the cosmos, expanding boundlessly into time and space.

South

You can ask participants to bring a personal item to place in the center of the altar. Ask them to say a bit about what the piece they brought means to them. It is amazing how quickly the symbolic mind begins to connect things. If the folks in your group are goddess gals, you can put an image of her in the center. Otherwise, stay neutral with nature.

Purifying and Grounding

Ceremonies begin with a purification to help participants release the tension and worry of the day so that their attention can be focused in the present time and on the process. It is part of how the sacred space is created; it lets people know that something important is going to happen in this place.

Burning sage, cedar, or sweet grass—or a mixture of all three—is a way of purifying before a ceremony. This is also called smudging. You can buy the ingredients in a health food store, along with a container such as a shell to put them in. Light a few pieces of the mixture. "Wash" your hands and face in the smoke, and brush it all over yourself.

Next comes a grounding exercise. Grounding gets you focused in the here and now in the most literal sense by bringing your awareness to the earth beneath you. Your mind can't stay at the office while you are imagining your "roots" in the earth right where you are. It's also a good idea for you to spend time getting grounded before your ceremony guests arrive.

A simple grounding exercise can be to close your eyes. Imagine putting down roots into the earth below you. Imagine the roots going right through the floor and into the earth beneath you. Take a moment to notice what the earth feels like to you. Is it hard or soft? damp or dry? sandy or rocky? warm or cold? When you feel your roots have gone down deep enough, let the problems of the day drain away. Let them go down into the earth, where they can be transformed. When that has happened, begin to draw energy up through your roots into your belly. After about six deep belly breaths, open your eyes.

The Heart of the Ceremony

Now you are ready to approach the heart of the ritual. You may have noticed how you felt a gradual disconnection from the outside world and its commitments and a growing connection to your inner world. Your focus and careful attention to detail as you set your intention, prepare the room, gather the things for the altar quiets your mind and builds expectation. Your brain knows that something magical is going to happen. It's your sense of expectancy that builds the power and makes the transformation.

Casting the Circle

The circle symbolically establishes a boundary between the participants and the "rest of the world." Your circle suspends time and space to create a sanctuary where the ordinary world does not intrude. You can do this by meditating in silence for a few minutes, by having everyone imagine a circle of light around the group, or by honoring the four directions.

After you decide the theme for your gathering (check the next chapter for some ideas), there are some general guidelines for working with groups that will be helpful as you form your circle. The leader acts as facilitator, making sure everybody who wants to talk gets a chance to, also to keep the focus and keep things moving along. Most women I know can do at least three things at the same time, so this won't be hard! Two hours is about long enough for a ritual. It can be done in less time, but I recommend not going longer than that. After the invocation, observe a moment or two of silence, followed by a *brief* check-in.

Goddess Guide

There are imaginative and effective ways of checking in that will avoid long, detailed accounts of the week's activities, which you want to avoid because it will break the focus. Here is one I have used for groups in a variety of settings that always works. Ask everyone to close their eyes and relax by taking a few more deep breaths. Ask "If you were an animal right now, what kind would you be? Where do you live? (Pause) What do you eat? (Pause) What is it like in your world? (Pause)." Now ask everyone to come back into the circle to check in. Ask each person to tell what kind of animal she imagined and what it feels like to be that animal. You can substitute animal with flower, tree, body of water, or time of year. This keeps people in their imagination and lets them check in emotionally.

Using a Kindergarten Mind

Next, you will lead the group through a process you have designed that has a connection to the time of year your ritual takes place. When you begin to design your process, think like a kindergarten teacher. Old, familiar rituals like arranging fall leaves or planting seeds in a milk carton really work well. The easier and simpler the exercise, the deeper it will go!

A spring ritual I attended recently used flowers and other greenery gathered from the yard and field to make a crown. You can use inexpensive wire from the flower shop, lace, scraps of material, net, or anything else you might imagine weaving into a garland of flowers. We worked outside on the patio, talking and laughing. Rituals don't have to be "serious" to be spiritual. In fact, laughter is a sign you have engaged your imagination. Later on, when you start connecting the ritual to life, you'll go much deeper, but, again, the spirit of women's rituals can be light, knowing they go deep when they need to.

When we finished with our crown, we went back inside into our circle. The leader asked us to take a few minutes of reflection to discover what it was that we were signifying by our crown. As we went around the circle, each woman told what she was crowning herself queen of. It is amazing how such an apparently simple exercise evoked such deep responses.

Sophia's Wisdom
The subconscious mind speaks the language of image. Our images tell us what picture of ourselves we are going to project into the world. Deep structural changes happen when we change the image. Ritual is one of the ways we can get to the subconscious level and change the image. As the image changes, we change how we perceive ourselves, and the impression we project into the world changes.

One woman declared herself the "Queen of Arts." She is struggling to create an identity for herself as a professional artist. As she crowned herself, we all bowed in recognition of her new status. Another woman declared herself "Queen for a Day." She has been over-working and realized how exhausted she was. She also realized she had been taking herself way too seriously. As she crowned herself, we draped a scarf over her shoulders and gave her a yardstick to hold. Someone asked what she was going to declare as Queen for the Day? She declared that next Saturday was a complete day off. She was going to stay in bed all day and read, order pizza, and take naps. We cheered.

In both situations, women were making significant changes in their lives, and they were doing it imaginatively and creatively. Changes made like this go to the subconscious mind, where they take root and have the best chance of actually bringing you the transformation you are looking for.

Tying Up Loose Ends

A ritual needs a formal way of closing. One way is to be silent for a few minutes and have the leader go back through the elements, thanking them for their presence and presents:

- We thank the earth for providing our bed and rest.
- We thank the water for quenching our thirst.
- We thank the fire for brightness and warmth.
- We thank the air for the life it brings.
- We thank each other for the gift of friendship.

Mother Knows Best

Don't let the focus drift off without a formal process of closing. It is good form for all meetings, especially for working spiritually.

Some groups like to drum, chant, or sing at the end of the ceremony. Others hold hands for a minute. Others pass a hug around the circle. It is also nice to have some cookies and tea or something light to eat after your ceremony. This is the kind of thing to decide with your group. Some groups have elaborate covered-dish get-togethers, and others prefer to keep the focus on the ceremony. It's up to you.

That is the nuts and bolts of structuring a ritual. In the next chapter you'll read about themes for honoring the cycles and seasons of nature and also how to celebrate important events in your life.

The Least You Need to Know

◆ The women's rituals and ceremonies performed today are contemporary versions that follow patterns of ancient ceremonies.

◆ A ritual has structure and form balanced with a spontaneity by which it creates an experience that brings spiritual insight. The "experience" is a spontaneous response and can't be planned.

◆ Ritual is not a place where dogma or belief is transmitted; however, it does serve to reinforce principles such as respect for the earth, equality, and respect for individuals' beliefs.

◆ It is helpful to work with one or two others as you plan your ceremony. You can share leading different parts, but it's good to have one person who holds the whole thing together.

Chapter

10

Nature's Themes

In This Chapter

- ◆ Why women love the moon
- ◆ The truth behind moon time madness
- ◆ Cyclical and seasonal wisdom
- ◆ Avoiding the winter blahs

Women's ceremonies honor life's everyday encounters and bring insight and strength to our lives. Nature itself provides universal patterns that can be the source of deep spiritual wisdom. You can use the spiritual teachings of the moon as it moves through its lunar cycle, and you can use moon energy in your rituals. The wheel of the year is the basis for the spiritual celebrations of many earth religions and is also the foundation for the liturgical calendar used by traditional religions today.

That Ol' Devil Moon in the Sky

The moon is an ancient feminine form that has always called for a ceremony, even if that ceremony is only walking outside your apartment to watch it rise over the city. The moon has inspired songwriters, lovers, and just about every-one who has ever been out underneath it. As the moon goes through it cycle of waxing and waning, it reminds us of our life cycle and is particularly feminine because of its connection to woman's reproductive cycle. So if the moon is your thing, here are some ways you can use it to create a reflection for a ritual.

Lunar Reflections

The three phases of the moon have been a symbol for women's life cycles since the beginning of time (see Chapter 7, "Seeking Wholeness: Goddess as Archetype"). The new moon corresponds to the young woman, or maiden. The full moon symbolizes the fruition and the fullness of the reproductive years, whether that is accomplished through childbirth or other creative work. As the moon wanes, we are put in touch with our own aging process that is always associated with gaining wisdom. As the moon completely disappears and the sky looks dark and empty, we contemplate death. Not to worry, however, as the new moon soon appears in the sky, and we are shown the ongoing cycles of nature and that our own rebirth is inevitable. The moon was one of the first spiritual symbols that told people of the cyclical and regenerative journey of the spirit.

> ### Sophia's Wisdom
>
> Every body of water on Earth feels the gravitational pull of the moon. We can see it most easily in the tides. You, too, are a "body" of water—water makes up 78 percent of your physical body. As the moon goes through its cycle of waxing and waning, you feel it in your body.

Here we see the three phases of the moon: new, full, and waning. They are symbolically related to women's lives: maiden, mother, and crone.

Each phase of the moon has a different energetic pattern that relates to different spiritual principles. Before you start to use the moon, it might be interesting to spend a month keeping up with its different phases, noticing how they affect you physically and emotionally. These reflections show how the moon's different aspects translate into spiritual principles.

New Moon on the Rise

The primary message of the new moon is the spirit's ability to continuously be reborn. If you are meeting under a new moon, some ways you might use this energy are ...

◆ To initiate a new project. This is the time to begin something new in your life.

◆ To recognize your virginal nature, the part of you that might be a bit of a loner. It could be your private side or even your childlike side.

◆ To recognize the rising of a new awareness inside yourself. Maybe you can't quite identify what is brewing inside you, but you feel something new stirring around. This is a bit like the very first days of pregnancy, when you have the feeling of new life inside you, but who this new child will be is very much a mystery.

◆ To honor your ability to begin again. We are constantly faced with having to pick up and begin again. This aspect of the moon will give you support when you are facing one of those "Here I go again!" times.

Goddess Guide

In ancient cultures all over the world, the moon took precedence over the sun in its importance in people's imagination. The Egyptians called the moon the "Mother of the Universe" because of its connection to the female reproductive cycle. Upper Egypt honored her by calling itself the "Land of the Moon," where the moon was the "Eternal Great Mother." The Sioux Indians called the moon "The Old Woman Who Never Dies." The Iroquois called her "The Eternal One." Ancient calendars were based on the moon rather than the sun, and the moon still governs the planting and harvesting times in many agricultural cultures—including our own *Farmer's Almanac*.

Complete Lunacy!

The primary principle of the full moon shows our spirit in wholeness, magnificence, and richness. It is the mother's belly full with new life. Here's how you might use the full moon as the focus for your ceremony:

◆ To recognize the fullness of your life.

◆ To energize something you have been working on toward fulfillment.

◆ To wish for something in your life.

◆ To experience the wholeness of your spirit.

The Dark Side of the Moon

The waning moon brings wisdom and foreshadows our eventual death. If the moon is waning as you gather, the intentions might involve …

◆ To let go of a belief, feeling, or behavior you don't want in your life anymore.

◆ To explore your beliefs about your aging and death.

◆ To assist you in finding the hidden aspects of a situation.

◆ To explore your shadow side—something about yourself that you keep hidden.

Moon Struck

A moon ceremony hopefully will include going outside and being under the moon's light for at least part of the evening. Maybe the ceremony could follow watching the moonrise or drumming or dancing outside in the moonlight. However, given weather's fickle nature, and factoring in the complications of city living, you can always do a moon ceremony right in your living room.

> **Mother Knows Best**
>
> Don't think that the moon is only a symbol in ancient religions. Even in modern time the moon plays an important part in one of the biggest Christian feasts. Easter is determined by the full moon following the spring equinox and sets the schedule for the liturgical year.

Moon Talk

In a moon meditation ritual, each person has a new white candle (they can bring one or you can provide them). The leader will ask everyone to lean back, get comfortable, and prepare to go on a journey. When everyone is relaxed, the leader begins a short, guided journey to explore the moon. To open the imagination, suggest that each woman create a magical way of going to the moon. Imagine what the temperature is like. What does the moon feel like to your feet? Are there any noises up there? What can you see when you look up? When you look down? Find a comfortable place to sit on the moon, and allow yourself to be quiet for a few minutes.

Slowly read some questions you have formed from the preceding suggestions. For example ...

◆ The moon is full tonight. Are there areas in your life that are particularly full? What are they? Are there places that are not full ... maybe even empty? You don't have to do anything about anything right now, just let the awareness be there.

◆ Is there something in your life about which you would like to experience fulfillment? Are you willing to have that fulfillment?

◆ Is there something you have been secretly wishing for? Something you haven't dared to talk about, yet? See if you are willing to wish for it now. The moon is in its fullness, and it reminds us of wholeness. How are you experiencing wholeness in your life right now?

Work slowly, allowing time between questions. Participants don't have to respond to all of the reflections; they may find that one or two are enough. When you are asking open ended questions like these, any one question can begin a whole inner process. Less is definitely more.

Moon Wisdom

At the end of the meditation, spend a few minutes with journals making any notations to be explored later. Take turns going around the circle and ask each person to light her candle and share something that she realized during the meditation. For example, if fullness was the focus, each woman might talk about specific things about which she is feeling grateful or fulfilled. As she finishes, have her place her candle in the center of the circle to symbolize the full moon. Let each person talk for about 5 minutes, remembering that it is hard to pay good attention much longer than 40 minutes at a time.

If your group is too big to accommodate sharing in a reasonable time frame, break into small groups of three and take turns. Each women's sharing generally sparks more insight in others. It's helpful to make notes in a journal rather than having a general discussion, but you can arrange it in any way that works for your group. It's good practice to keep the attention on the person who is sharing. This means avoid letting her comments take you into your process. You will remember the insights you get when listening and can share them when it's your turn. You can imagine how messy it can get if everyone takes each comment and runs with it, and it takes the focus off the one who's talking.

Goddess Guide

In planning a ritual, remember not to make it too busy or too full. When you are working deep, as you do when you engage the imagination, it's better to have lots of space in the program. Sometimes one question can spark a whole evening's worth of meditation and insight.

The Wheel of the Year Goes 'Round, 'Round, 'Round

Observing the changing seasons seem to naturally catch our imagination, signaling what's happening in our internal world and grounding spirituality in the here and now. The custom of honoring life by honoring the earth's seasons is a practice shared by many traditions. Many Jewish feasts were set by nature's calendar, and nature is the basis for the liturgical calendar followed by many Christian denominations. When feasts were established by traditional religion, they were based on the organic spirituality that was already implanted deeply in the hearts and minds of the people.

Sophia's Wisdom

We are drawing our example from the Celtic calendar of old Europe. Notice how many of these ancient feasts are part of our holiday traditions and are celebrated as religious feasts. Feasts sitting opposite one another represent dual aspects of a spiritual principle. For example, the darkness of winter sits opposite summer's light. February 2, a time of initiation is opposite the first harvest on August 1, when we begin to reap what we have sown. Beltane or May Day, the celebration of life, sits opposite Halloween and the time of death.

Mother Nature's seasonal feasts and festivals show the spirit of the earth calendar. The year begins at Halloween, but you don't have to wait to start at the beginning—begin where you are. Rather than just lasting one day, the holidays last six weeks, creating a spiritual focus for the season.

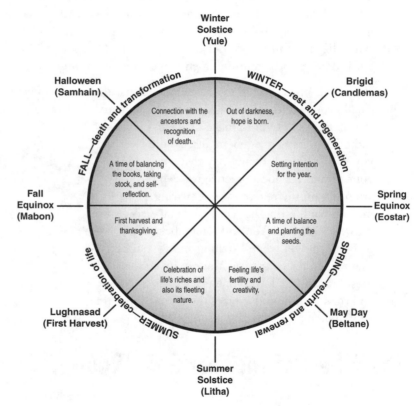

A Long Winter's Nap

The winter solstice (December 20 through 23) honors the darkest moment—and at the same time, it marks the moment when the light begins its return, thus its dual aspect expresses both despair and hope. From now on, the nights will grow shorter, but you will be experiencing darkness for at least three more months. Winter's task is self-care, and themes for this holiday include ways we can rest and regenerate.

Questions for reflection are: What renews you? What are the fears that arise at this time of year? From where do you draw your hope? Activities for a ritual to nourish the body, mind, and spirit include making bath salts, essential oils, or scented candles. Things to consider as you go into the winter might include sharing something you've just read at a book exchange, or having a soup exchange, each person bringing a favorite soup to share. Make plans to get together once a week for dinner and a movie. Reminder: Use lots of candles or colored holiday lights.

Goddess Guide

Candlemas day is also the Festival of Lights and celebrates Bridget of Kildare, sometimes called Bride. She is the Celtic goddess of fire, the hearth, fields, poetry, and childbirth. She also gives blessings to women who are about to marry. Women still invoke her name on their wedding days when they are referred to as "bride."

According to legend, Bridget would visit and bless homes on this day. If the sun was seen, winter was over, but if the sun was hidden behind clouds, winter was still to come. This old tradition is still with us in the form of Groundhog Day. When the groundhog comes out of his den, if he sees his shadow, he goes back in again for six more weeks. Older pagan names for Candlemas include Imbolc and Oimelc. Oimelc meaning "milk of ewes" and Imbolc translates as "in the belly," pertaining to the earth.

The feast of the Celtic goddess Bridget (February 2) occurs midway through the winter. It honors the return of the light. Metaphorically it reminds you that the infant sun that was "born" at the winter solstice is now six weeks old and its presence is becoming more obvious. The days are growing longer, lifting the spirit. You might even begin to look at seed catalogs and plan your garden.

The spiritual theme is about planting a new virtue. Topics for reflection are: What spiritual seed are you planting this year? What do you hope to cultivate within yourself? What gets stirred up inside of you as you till the field? What are some weeds (old ways of thinking) that will have to go? A planting ritual using small milk cartons for flowerpots is fun. As you place your seed in the dirt, you are symbolically planting your spiritual garden.

It's a Spring Thing!

The spring equinox (March 20 through 23) celebrates the earth coming back to life! It is a joyful time. Promise and possibility are pushing their way up through the soil. This is the time to check on the intention you planted at the Brigit ritual. Is there anything holding you back … anything you need to "push through" in order to grow into the person you want to be?

Spring's spiritual theme is rebirth. Reflection questions: What is coming alive within you? Is it getting enough water and sunshine to grow? Is there anything blocking it from sprouting? If so, you might ask for help in removing it from your path. Is there anything you can do to help your spirit feel more joyful? Make paper chains and bind your wrists together. Say out loud what it is that you are breaking through in your life, and then break the chains and free yourself!

Mother Knows Best

May was a month of sexual freedom in Europe up into the sixteenth century. Wedding vows were suspended, and couples were free to enjoy a sexual romp with whomever they wanted. The elders believed that it relieved sexual tension and made fidelity the other eleven months out of the year workable.

May Day (April 30 or May 1) celebrates creativity, love, fertility; it honors the dance of life. The fields are sown, the birds are tweeting, and the bees are buzzing! You know the rest! Couples have traditionally made love in the fields to encourage the crops to grow. (At least that was their story!)

May Day's spiritual principle is fecundity. Questions for reflection: What is your relationship with your creativity? Are you giving your creative side enough time to just "be"? We are always creating, what you are creating? What attitude are you cultivating? Is there something keeping you from seeing your current situation creatively? Do you want to change that attitude? Sleep outside on the ground tonight. Make love with someone or with yourself.

Let the Good Times Roll!

The summer solstice (June 20 through 23) is the longest day of the year. You have planted your spiritual seeds, and they are growing. This is a time for celebration. We are reminded that tonight begins the decline that will take us back into the darkness. Even in its fullness, life is fleeting. Grab the moment and celebrate!

A spiritual principle for summer is to take time to enjoy your life. Questions for reflection: Are you too busy to enjoy life as it passes? If you weren't too busy, what would you like to do for fun? Do you resist the natural rhythms, holding on to people, ideas, attitudes, or behaviors, rather than letting life move through you? This is a time for opening your arms wide and accepting the fullness of life and celebrating the richness. Go on a picnic!

The first harvest (August 1) celebrates the first cutting of the fields. It corresponds to Thanksgiving, and it's a time of communion. If you have been attentive, the garden is producing, and the fields are ready to be reaped. It is a time to share the bounty with friends.

Wise Words _____

"Much of religion has lost its sense of celebration because it disconnected itself from the lives of the people and from the earth itself. Yet everything we are and everything we celebrate has a direct connection to the earth and to her cycles and season."

—Janet Marine (1935–), poet and artist who travels in her motor home and lives in Hesperia, California

The spiritual principle of this holiday, sometimes called Lughnasad, is gratitude. Questions for reflection are: How can we doubt that we are cared for? What are the things for which you are the most grateful? Take a drive through the countryside and see the fields in their fullest. Look at the bales of hay stacked there like huge loaves of bread. Visit your local farmer's market and bring home fresh fruits and vegetables for a meal with friends, and don't forget to include fresh flowers. As you eat the food, you are partaking in its life force. In the spirit of Lughnasad, the corn king dies so that the people may live. Become aware of the gifts the earth gives.

As the Days Dwindle Down

The fall equinox (September 20 through 23) again celebrates a time of balance between day and night before moving into the darkness of winter. This is a time of thanksgiving for the fullness of summer and an opportunity to take stock of your reserves. Many people find their energy begins to decrease at this time of year. As you look at nature, you see it is shutting down. It's time for you to slow down, too.

The spiritual principle is reflection. Questions for reflections: Go back over the intention you set on Bridget's feast. How is your plan progressing? We are about to till the soil and let it rest for the winter. Do you need to rest, too? Do you need to let go of anything that is in your way? You can give it to the earth and let it mulch into new soil.

Halloween (October 31) marks the end of the year in the earth cycle, and likewise the beginning of the New Year. However, the new cannot be born until the old one dies. Halloween honors death. It is when the ancestors are remembered. It corresponds to All Hallow's Eve, the night before the feast called All Saints Day in Christianity.

The spirituality of this feast is about death and the regeneration that follows it. Reflections for Halloween might include: Sharing stories with a friend about someone you have known who has died. As you talk about this person, notice how he or she is still alive in your life. This is a good time to be more conscious of your life. Write your epitaph and you will see what you would most like to be remembered for. Are you being true to this ideal?

Sophia's Wisdom

The Celts celebrated the New Year on November 1, when the sun god was taken prisoner by Samhain, the Lord of the Dead and Prince of Darkness. On this night it was believed that the veil between the living and dead was at its thinnest. Samhain rallied the dead who would take different forms, with the bad spirits taking the form of animals—the most evil becoming cats. After the crops were harvested and stored for the long winter, cooking fires in homes were extinguished. Druids, the Celtic priests, would meet in their sacred oak groves where they lit new ceremonial fires. As they danced around them, the season of the sun passed and the season of darkness began. Each family took embers home to start their new cooking fires. These fires kept the homes warm and free from evil spirits.

You've just seen how the cycle of the moon and the wheel of the year move us through the seasons creating an organic spirituality and natural themes for meditation and ceremony. Next we'll see how the events of our lives and life passages provide opportunities for growth and rich substance for spiritual celebrations and rituals.

The Least You Need to Know

◆ Over thousands of years, nature has laid a pattern for spiritual celebrations. These ancient themes have been woven into the psyche of the people.

◆ When spirituality is connected to the earth through the cycles and seasons of nature, it comes alive.

◆ Earth rituals can be inclusive of all beliefs and don't conflict with traditional religious services. In fact, many religious celebrations were taken from the earth calendar.

◆ Rituals have the power to operate at deep levels and help us come to resolution about life's events.

11

Passages to Power

In This Chapter

- ◆ Marking life passages
- ◆ Ending 6,000 years of menstrual taboos
- ◆ Awkward situations call for rituals, too
- ◆ When a marriage ends
- ◆ Grabbing the power of growing *old!*

Women have always created rituals to assist them on their life journeys. Often these were intimate rituals, done in secret and kept as mysteries. Circumstances change over time and from culture to culture; however, a woman's life follows a universal pattern. We don't have the details of those ancient rituals, but we know the ceremonies built power, honored passages, invoked the gods and goddesses for special assistance, and provided an opportunity to share lives.

Women today are tapping into this rich spiritual reserve to mark the important events of their lives, to bring them support and strength to deal with life's adversities, as well as to celebrate the good stuff. The ancient themes of maiden, mother, and crone represent the passages in women's lives.

It's a Girl Thing!

Nothing is as cloaked in mystery, imbued with power, surrounded by fear, and laden with taboos as a woman's menstrual period. It has been both upheld as sacred and as a source of banishment. Can this completely natural function that lies at the core of being a woman be reclaimed from thousands of years of negative enculturation? We'll hear from women who have taken back their power by creating rituals of empowerment for themselves and their daughters. Often all the participants—mothers, daughters, and grandmothers—are transformed in the process.

> **Goddess Guide** _____
>
> Author, researcher, and noted feminist Barbara G. Walker tells us that menstrual blood was once referred to as "sacred red wine" in Greece, and menstrual blood of Mother Goddess was considered holy for its healing properties. The Norse god Thor was reputed to have reached the land of enlightenment and eternal life by bathing in a river of menstrual blood flowing from the primal mothers who once ruled the ancient world. Egyptian pharaohs became divine by drinking the blood of Isis, and Celtic kings assured their immortality by ingesting the "red mead" of Mab, the fairy Queen. Tribal people believed menstrual blood contained the soul of future generations, which was one reason why they had matrilineal societies.

The female body and all its reproductive functions were honored in matriarchal society. As the world shifted from matriarchal to patriarchal values, the power associated with women's blood posed a serious threat to cultures built on the idea of male power. Menstrual blood came to be considered dangerous and unclean, and even became the source of tremendous fear. Menstrual taboos were established by Hebrew scripture and became part of the religious heritage of Christian writers and theologians as well.

In some Jewish and Islamic traditions today, women are forbidden to pray during their menses. In Christianity, restrictions put on women's participation as priests and ministers is based on menstrual taboos. It's clear to see that this old idea has not died; it continues to play a part in the structure of Western religion and in the larger world culture as well.

Breaking Taboos

Women today struggle with unpacking thousands of years of cultural baggage surrounding this natural process. As they redefine themselves spiritually, they are interested in providing the next generation with a better way of becoming a woman than most of them experienced. Some of the essential questions women ask in the process of self-reflection on their coming of age include …

- How did you first hear about menstrual periods?
- Who told you?
- What happened the day you first got yours?
- What reaction did the people in your family have?
- How could it have been handled better?

Diane decided to break the menstrual taboo in her family by inviting her daughter and a group of her friends along with Diane's friends for a weekend getaway at a cabin the woods. She told them to come with their questions about sex and that no topic would be off limits. What teenager could resist such an offer? They all knew in advance what the topic would be, but no one knew the impact it would have.

Mother Knows Best

In perhaps one of the most outrageous statements about menstruation, Pliny, author and administrator of Rome in the first century, stated that it could do everything from blight crops to rust iron and bronze. Thank you, Pliny.

Declaring Goddess Day

The first night was filled with good food, music, and dancing. Saturday was spent on the lake, enjoying the water and fresh air. Saturday night dinner was cooked outside and was followed sitting around a campfire. It was well after dark before the subject came up, and nature provided the moment. One of the girls, Cynthia, started her period, and it took off from there. Diane brought out pillows and a quilt and made a comfortable place for Cynthia on the chaise lounge. Diane began talking about what the ideal situation might be like if women were supported and honored during this time.

Drawing on stories she had heard about Native American moon lodges, Diane talked about how a woman's body follows the cycles of the moon and has times of great creativity and times of regeneration. She talked about the importance of being aware of your body and following its energy. Pretty soon everyone was really into it, telling stories and asking questions. They decided to create a ritual in which Cynthia would be honored, with her consent. They brainstormed for suggestions, and here are some of the things they came up with.

Cynthia passed on the herbal tea, preferring a cold drink instead. A couple of the girls began brushing and braiding Cynthia's hair. Two of the women began rubbing her feet. They talked about taking time out to rest at least the first day or two of their cycles. One of the women suggested a dream journal as several had talked about the vivid dreams that accompany their periods. They talked about mild exercise and yoga postures that help relieve menstrual tension.

Wise Words _____

"Woman is the seed containing the potential for the growth of new life. Her feminine nature is cyclic, corresponding to the cycles of the moon. The intuitive power within her grows toward fulfillment from the beginning of the cycle until ovulation, then wanes toward introspection from ovulation to menstruation. In this intimate process, shared by every woman, no matter what her color, she gives to herself the opportunity to be born again."

—Noris Binet, Ph.D., author, seminar leader, and teacher, in her book, *Women on the Inner Journey* (James C. Winston Publishing, 1994)

Menstrual taboos were set straight, and every area of sex and sexuality was explored. The night ended with the girls grabbing their sleeping bags and forming a dream circle around the fire. Diane believes the girls benefited from hearing what the women had to say. She and her daughter have declared the first day of their cycles Goddess Day! If they want to take time off from school or work, they can. The choice is up to them. The main thing is that the girls were given some positive attitudes about their cycles and how their bodies work and the fact that they have choices. If they feel like taking a day off, they don't have to see it as dysfunctional; they can do it because it's a good idea. And they have women they can openly talk with about sex.

Motherhood: More Than a Hallmark Moment

Becoming a mother is acknowledged through baby showers, visits from friends, gifts, and often a ceremony at church. However, none of these things really addresses the spirituality of motherhood, and they don't primarily focus on the woman as the central figure in what is probably the most important relationship in our collective human story. From conception to birth, motherhood is pretty much ignored in traditional religion. Most women agree that the situation deserves a blessing. Today, women meet and talk about how to create a spirituality that honors this very important event.

Honoring Pregnancy

Three months into Caroline's pregnancy, she and her husband, Frank, made their announcement. They invited family and friends for a dinner at which time they shared their good news. In addition to the traditional declaration, they asked Caroline's grandmother to bless the new mother and child. They had spoken with her in advance to make sure she was comfortable with the request. Caroline's grandmother was comfortable and honored. She offered her blessing and presented Caroline with a beautiful shawl to wear over her shoulders during her pregnancy. Others volunteered to bring dinner to the house and make sure Frank took a night out when he felt like he needed it. The focus stayed on the couple during the pregnancy, not on the new baby.

For a variety of reasons, not all pregnancies end with a happy birth. Miscarriages, abortions, and stillbirths have a lasting effect on a woman's body and psyche. Women's spirituality supports a woman having control over her body. Regardless of whether an individual agrees or disagrees with the decision being made, women's spirituality reaches beyond judgment to offer support.

What happens when the pregnancy terminates prematurely? Miscarriages may be acknowledged by those most intimately involved but not with ritual that identifies the loss at the spiritual level. A woman is often left to grieve alone. While her mate may be supportive, it usually takes the experience of another woman to understand the significance a miscarriage can have.

> **Mother Knows Best**
>
> Ceremonies aren't everybody's cup of tea. Don't insist that your friends or family members participate in ceremonies if that would make them uncomfortable. If something is important to you but your family isn't the place to have it honored, you can always find others who will fill the roles for you.

> **Sophia's Wisdom**
>
> Some churches offer funeral rites for a loss that takes place after a certain point in the pregnancy, but usually not in the early stages. Many women have found healing in acknowledging a conception has happened; a spirit has incarnated even if only for a short time. For many, a naming ceremony and releasing the soul are two important aspects to healing. This can be done simply and privately between the mother and father or with a few close friends.

What about when a pregnancy is intentionally terminated? Abortion often needs to be acknowledged in the same way as a miscarriage. Having a ceremony witnessed by others in which a woman spiritually understands the choice she has made establishes her authority and the responsibility of her decision. Such a ceremony heals emotional scars and feelings of guilt that can last a lifetime.

Placing Your Child with Another

Although the process of giving a child up for adoption is not as secretive as it once was, it is not always talked about openly. Women who have faced this very difficult situation

Mother Knows Best

Don't underestimate the power of ceremony. Ceremonies work directly on the unconscious mind. The physical body, as well as the emotions and the spirit, are all influenced through ritual. Women who have been unable to get pregnant have conceived after performing a ceremony.

often go through it alone or with a few close friends, but it is not recognized with the sensitivity that it demands.

A ceremony can bring support and spiritual understanding to the mother and child as well as all who will be involved in raising the child. Whether or not the mother and child will be together in the physical sense, there is a physical, emotional, and spiritual relationship that continues between the two of them throughout their lives. Having a process by which this relationship is recognized brings meaning and peace to a potentially devastating situation.

When a Marriage Doesn't Make It

More than 50 percent of marriages today end in divorce, yet there is no established ritual or ceremony by which to give spiritual support to the resulting brokenness. Often entire families are left to handle overwhelming difficulties of redefinition and restructuring with no spiritual help. Creating a ritual gives the family a spiritual resource and new identity for life after divorce.

Building a New Family Structure

Nancy and Bill married 14 years ago and have 3 children. Two years ago their marriage began to falter and ended in divorce. Despite this fact, they will remain lifelong partners as parents. In addition to working out the everyday dynamics of parenting from two different locations, they will go through many life passages together. It is important for all the members of the family to be able to see how they still remain a family in many ways.

Working with a counselor, they began redefining themselves as a family in process long before the finalizing of the divorce. Bill and Nancy participated in conflict-resolution classes and learned how to communicate without going through the children. The children eventually realized that their parents would continue to be their parents regardless of where they lived.

Staying in Communication

In a ceremony designed by the whole family, they enacted the coming changes, showing how they would physically separate but remain connected in important ways. They lit candles to signify the warmth that would always be there as a family, and they created a

ceremony using a ball of twine, physical movement, and time to feel the emotions as they arose.

The ability to stay in communication was of
prime importance. The family sat on the floor in
a circle. Using a ball of twine to represent lines
of communication and connections that would
remain, they passed it back and forth across the
circle as each member shared his and her concerns. They wove a web that represented their
relationship that would be there forever. Bill and
Nancy gave the children phones, and they talked about how they would always be able to
reach each other. They also established times for getting together as a group in the future,
during which they could redefine their commitments, acknowledge changes, and communicate concerns and feelings. The ritual showed them that they were still connected in
many ways.

> **Sophia's Wisdom**
>
> Using ceremony to assist in
> divorce does not increase its
> occurrence; it greatly reduces the
> damages that can incur during a
> divorce. Giving spiritual assis-
> tance leaves the way open for
> reconciliation.

Enjoying a Twanda Moment!

In the film version of Fanny Flagg's book, *Fried Green Tomatoes*, the culture got a whole
new image of what it meant to be a menopausal woman. When the character played by
Kathy Bates is "aced" out of a parking place by two young girls who laugh about her
being so slow, she responds with, "Yes, but I am richer and have more insurance than you
do" and rear-ends their car. It seems that every woman of a certain age could relate to
hormonal rage!

Jo's Revenge of the Wise Woman

The passage from menopausal to post-menopausal is not always a smooth one, so why
aren't women more celebrative when they finally get there and things smooth out?
Women say that as men age, they are seen as handsome, stately, and wise. As a woman
ages, she is seen as old and useless. Some women feel it's time to claim the power of this
passage. Jo Searles, recently retired professor of English and women's studies at Penn
State, now concentrates on writings and rituals for her newfound territory. She lectures on
Hecate, facilitates "Rise Up and Call Her Name Workshops," and mentors Baby Crones.
Here she shares her passage to wisdom (from "New Wrinkles in Old Skins," *Of a Like
Mind*, XIV:3,25):

"I had met the Wise Crone, and She was me. No more would I apologize for my
responses or my age. I owned them; they owned me. Finally. Acknowledgement of and
recognition for my own experience, my 'wise blood,' the ability, based on years of cyclical

events, to separate shit from sincerity, secular from sacred. With that, Goddess surfaced, and—hallelujah—came Old Woman. Not just 'older'; OLD. The Triple Goddess is *triple*, not double. To be complete, She must contain the Crone, whose function is not to bring only death, but to continue the cycle into transformation and rebirth. Yes, She is ancient. Yes, She is wrinkled. But on her, wrinkles look great. Spider Mother spins in a frenzy, silver hair flying in the wind. Kali the Destroyer dances. Her skull-adorned way through the flux of death and life, equally ecstatic about both. And Destroyer Medusa grimaces dangerously at those who would deny Her wisdom and power."

Wise Words

"We women in our 60s and 70s are now in foreign territory. We're on the cutting edge, with the state of the art, taking risks and having adventures. We're where few women have gone before, exploring a wizened, gray landscape long despised and neglected by our culture—at least until now, when more and more souls will of necessity follow our lead, death being the only alternative."

—Jo Searles, Ph.D., retired professor and full-time wise woman

Stepping Into Power: Rene's Croning

A tradition is evolving in the women's spirituality community in which women are meeting together, claiming the power of their wisdom, and creating a new identity for themselves through a ritual they call "*croning*." In the ceremonies they design, they are declaring themselves "wise women" by claiming the spiritual wisdom that is acquired only by a lifelong process of gathering experience. Here is a ceremony one woman designed to make her transition intentional and powerful.

In designing a ceremony, Rene wanted to acknowledge the end of her reproductive years, acknowledge her continued sexuality, claim her wisdom, and declare the next period of time as hers. A comprehensive reframe, no doubt! Here's how she accomplished it in a croning ceremony.

Womanspeak

Crone comes from Rhea Kronia, who was "Mother of Time" in the ancient world, according to Barbara G. Walker. It is also associated with Coronis, a carrion crow, because in mythology, crones were often associated with death.

Rene invited friends to celebrate her fifty-fifth birthday at a rented house at a Florida beach. She asked each one to bring something from nature as a symbol to represent her relationship with Rene. The women then took turns placing a symbol on the altar and saying a few words about how they knew Rene. As the women in the circle spoke and as the symbols were placed in the center, some things about Rene's spirit became obvious. Nothing else had to happen to make the point Rene wanted to make: She was a woman of many facets, and there was no reason to expect that would change as she stepped into her next role.

To honor her new role, Rene had built an archway that led from the front deck onto the patio to the beach. Holding red roses in her arms, she walked through the archway and down to the water's edge. One by one she tossed the roses into the surf, signifying the end of her monthly cycle.

Her arms were now open and empty. She faced the ocean and welcomed the ever-creating *Yemaja* to be with her as she entered this new time in her life. She stripped naked and went into the water, inviting her guests to join her in what turned out to be a spontaneous initiation and baptism. A fire had been made on the beach, and as they huddled around it, Rene gave each of her guests a white rose. She talked about some of her hopes and dreams for this next phase of her life. They went back into the house and played records from the early 1960s and danced for a long time.

> **Mother Knows Best**
>
> Not every woman celebrates entering her wisdom time at the same age. It generally is some time after menopause, but it's up to each woman to decide when she feels she is a wise elder and is ready for the ritual.

> **Womanspeak**
>
> **Yemaja** is one of the African Orisha (gods and goddesses). She encompasses the enormous creative spirit of the ocean.

As you can see, rituals are very much like regular celebrations in our lives. The difference is that rituals use symbols to connect to deeper meanings. Women who participate in spiritual rituals say it has shown them how everything in life has spiritual significance and that there is spiritual help available to us to deal with all aspects of life.

The Least You Need to Know

- Rituals rework negative images from the culture and support women in claiming their power.
- You can create a ritual to help you through anything in your life.
- Rituals work on the unconscious mind as well as the conscious mind. The results continue to unfold for a long time after the ritual.
- Spiritual rituals and ceremonies have been part of the human story since the beginning—they're wired into your brain. Your intuition will tell you when and how to hold one.

Part 3

Continuing the Legacy: Inside the Organization

Women's spirituality is focused very much in the world and in the lives of the people. One of its key characteristics is the connection to the world and the commitment to issues of justice. As you look back over our history as a nation, you will find that it was women who powered the social, political, and educational changes, broadening the American dream to include all the people. Then as now, women bring an understanding of relationships to their professions and understand that for any religious vision to be accomplished in the world, the children must be fed and educated, the sick must be cared for, and the earth, as sustainer of life, must be respected. Women have always understood that social justice is a spiritual mandate.

In this part, we will look at our common history as women and learn how some of our foremothers overcame societal restrictions to make powerful changes within religion and in the larger society. They left a rich legacy, and we'll see how women are continuing this work from within religious traditions today.

I DON'T KNOW, MARGE. I'VE CONNECTED WITH MY INNER WISDOM AND IT **STILL** TELLS ME TO BAP THOSE FOLKS WITH **15 ITEMS** IN THE **TEN-OR-LESS** AISLE RIGHT OVER THE HEAD.

12

Our Foremothers

In This Chapter

- ◆ Women's spirituality of social equality
- ◆ Bold escapes and daring rescue missions
- ◆ Women leading the fight against slavery
- ◆ Winning the right to vote

It has long been said that if you find a piece of writing or work of art whose creator is listed as "Unknown," a woman created it. Anonymity has very much characterized women's contributions to the world. The women's movement of the 1960s and 1970s went a long way toward recovering our unsung heroes and shining a light on women's important historic and religious contributions. Hopefully, tomorrow's daughters won't have to dig quite as deep to find themselves as the generations before them have had to.

In attempting to follow their faith and answer God's call, women overcame enormous blocks to find ways of being of service and to spearhead many of the important social changes that are part of our national and religious history. This chapter presents the stories of six women whose lives and work have been absolutely elemental in bringing justice into our American society. There are hundreds more who deserve to be mentioned, and I urge you to use this discussion as merely the beginning of a much larger study.

Freedom and Justice for All

Two movements dominate the social/political/religious terrain in the 1800s—the abolition of slavery and women's right to vote. Four women leaders, two black and two white, saw how these issues were linked, and their lives intersected at this crucial time in history. Their understanding, passion, and tenacity has yet to be matched—they are giants.

Sojourner Truth: "Ain't I a Woman?"

In 1797 Isabella Bett was born the second youngest of the 12 children of Elizabeth and James Bett. She was born a slave and would never learn to read or write, yet she would become a great orator and one of the most powerful women of her time. Her childhood was spent on the New York farm of a wealthy Dutchman, and her first language was Dutch. At age nine she was sold to an English-speaking family in Kingston, New York, and was later sold two more times, ending up at the hands of John Dumont of New Paltz, New York, where she was treated cruelly. But her master was unable to break her strong spirit.

Bett married and gave birth to five children. When the state of New York began freeing slaves within its jurisdiction, Bett's master promised to release her on July 4, 1826. Three months later, when she realized her owner was not going to keep his word, she set out on foot, carrying her youngest child in her arms. She found refuge with a family who kept her safe until her liberation was secured. However, one of her children had been sold into slavery in Alabama despite the New York law banning this traffic.

Bett's first act as a free woman was to recover her son, which she did with the help of her Quaker friends. She brought her son home, discovering he had suffered permanent injury from beatings received at the hands of his slave master. More than ever, Bett was firmly resolved to do everything she could to abolish the evil of slavery.

> **" " Wise Words** _____
>
> "Women's liberationists, white and black, will always be at odds with one another as long as our ideal of liberation is based on having the power, which men have. For that power denies unity, denies common connections, and is inherently divisive."
> —Bell Hooks (1952–), author, scholar, and Distinguished Professor of English at City College in New York, in *Ain't I a Woman* (South End Press, 1981)

Isabella took the name Sojourner because she traveled around the countryside; she added Truth to signify the word of God she preached. In her travels, Sojourner heard about the women's rights movement and attended her first convention in 1850, where she met and became closely associated with Lucretia Mott, Elizabeth Cady Stanton, Susan B. Anthony, and other leaders in the rising movement.

Later, at a women's rights convention in Akron, Ohio, Sojourner became angry with white male ministers denying women's claim to equal rights. When white women in the audience failed to challenge them, she spoke up. She specifically responded to one man's charge that females were helpless and needed to be looked after by men by pulling up her sleeve to show her powerful arm and asking her famous question: "Ain't I a woman?"

 Wise Words

"Look at me! Look at my arm! I have ploughed, and planted, and gathered into barns and no man could head me! And a'n't I a woman? I could work as much and eat as much as a man—when I could get it—and bear de lash as well! And a'n't I a woman? I have borne thirteen chilern and seen 'em mos' all sold off to slavery, and when I cried out with my mother's grief, none but Jesus heard me! And a'n't I a woman?"

—Sojourner Truth (1851)

Truth settled in Battle Creek, Michigan, gathered her family around her, and continued her work for abolition. During the Civil War she was invited to Washington, D.C., by President Lincoln, where she remained throughout the war, helping with integration by teaching and assisting freed slaves find jobs.

After the war, Truth turned her efforts toward women's rights. Referring to the wording of the proposed 14th and 15th Amendments, Truth strongly maintained that if women were not given the same rights, they would end up being subjugated to black men. For the next 30 years, she traveled the country speaking out against slavery, advocating for women's rights, women's suffrage, and temperance. She became a leading figure in all four of the major reform movements of her time: abolition of slavery, women's rights, women's suffrage, and temperance. Sojourner Truth died on November 26, 1883, in Battle Creek, Michigan, one of history's most auspicious freedom fighters.

Harriet Tubman: In the Tradition of Moses

Harriet Tubman's grandparents had come to America from Africa in chains. Tubman lived to escape slavery, conduct numerous daring rescue missions on the Underground Railway—in which she brought 300 slaves to freedom—served as a spy in the Civil War, was a nurse, and became a leader in the causes of women's rights and social reform. Tubman epitomizes the indomitable spirit of her people and of women.

She was born on a plantation in Maryland in 1820. As a young woman, she heard rumors that she and others might be sold south, and she boldly made her break for freedom. She no sooner reached her destination in Philadelphia than she set out to rescue others. In a series of daring missions she brought her family north. For the next decade she made more than 15 trips, leading 300 slaves to freedom.

Wise Words

"I gain strength, courage, and confidence by every experience in which I must stop and look fear in the face … I say to myself, I've lived through this and can take the next thing that comes along …. We must do the things we think we cannot do."

—Eleanor Roosevelt (1884–1962), one of the best known and much loved first ladies, wife of Franklin D. Roosevelt; she was instrumental in her husband's administration and worked tirelessly on social causes

Her daring exploits, sharp ingenuity, and fierce determination earned Tubman fame but didn't deter her from her mission. She devised codes and communicated instructions to her escapees by song. Grateful survivors tell of the depth of her commitment as she held a gun to their head and gave them the choices of dying right there on the spot, going back in slavery … or getting up and continuing!

Sophia's Wisdom

There is a story of a close encounter in a railway station with a former owner whom Tubman feared would surely recognize her. She upset several crates of chickens and escaped in a cloud of feathers and commotion. She continually outsmarted her would-be captors. In their frustration, they put a $40,000 price on her head, yet they still failed to catch her.

During the Civil War, Tubman went to Beaufort, South Carolina, where she nursed wounded soldiers, taught skills to the newly freed slaves, and served as a spy and scout, leading reconnaissance missions behind enemy lines to gather information for Union raids. After the war, she went home and devoted the rest of her life to helping others. She cared for her aging parents, raised funds for schools, helped destitute orphans, and founded a home for dispossessed blacks.

Tubman saw racial liberation and women's rights as parts of a whole. She supported the movement for women's suffrage and served as a delegate to the first national convention of the Federation of Afro-American Women in 1896. She was the guest of honor at the New England Women's Suffrage Association in 1897.

This remarkable woman died at her home in Auburn, New York, on March 10, 1913, at the age of 93. In 1886 Sarah Bradford gave Tubman the epitaph by which she is remembered—*Harriet Tubman: The Moses of Her People.*

The Gospel According to Stanton

Elizabeth Cady Stanton was born on November 12, 1815, in New York, on the other side of the tracks from her two contemporaries, Truth and Tubman. She was a pioneer feminist, theologian, author, and lecturer who shared the spirit of liberation with them.

Stanton became one of the most radical feminists of her day, going further than anyone had before in declaring women's rights, publicly demanding suffrage for women. She soon met Susan B. Anthony, and the two became allies for the next 50 years, fighting together for women's rights.

Stanton wrote *The Woman's Bible*, a translation and critique specifically aimed at exposing the contradictions in scripture, particularly regarding women's place in creation. She hoped to inspire women to question theological teachings that held them in subservience. When she published the first volume, it outraged even the most ardent feminists, who considered it sacrilegious and feared it would damage the cause. The clergy, not surprisingly, declared it a work of Satan. Then, as now, controversy works wonders in the marketplace, and her book became a best-seller. It was the topic of the day, and her intention of urging women to think about theology was a success.

> ### Sophia's Wisdom
>
> Stanton and Lucretia Mott had met years earlier in London, where they attempted to attend an anti-slavery conference and were refused admission because of being female. Their subsequent discussions on the nature of oppression led to the first women's rights convention in the country, held at the Wesleyan Methodist Chapel in Seneca Falls, New York, in 1848.

 Wise Words _____

"From the inauguration of the movement for woman's emancipation the Bible has been used to hold her in the 'divinely ordained sphere,' prescribed in the Old and New Testaments. The canon and civil law; church and state; priests and legislators; all political parties and religious denominations have alike taught that woman was made after man. Creeds, codes, Scriptures and statutes are all based on this idea. The fashions, forms, ceremonies and customs of society, church ordinances and discipline all grow out of this idea."

—Elizabeth Cady Stanton, *The Woman's Bible* (1895)

Stanton urged women to reject anything that held them back and to question any religious or political doctrines they interpreted to be harmful to women. She died in New York City on October 26, 1902, at the age of 87, a rebel and leader to the end.

Susan B. Anthony Gets the Vote

Susan Brownell Anthony was born on February 15, 1820, in Adams, Massachusetts. As a young woman, she joined the temperance movement, founding the Woman's New York State Temperance Society. Like her contemporaries Truth, Tubman, and Stanton, Anthony was also active in the abolitionist movement.

> **Wise Words** _____
>
> "I should like to see our young people face with enjoyment the fact that they are going to have to go along uncharted paths. I should like them to be filled with confidence at meeting new challenges. Whether or not they have made the world they live in, the young must learn to be at home in it, to be familiar with it. They must understand its history, its peoples, their customs and ideas and problems and aspirations … the world cannot be understood from a single point of view."
>
> —Eleanor Roosevelt

It was the women's movement, however, that caught most of Anthony's attention, and she became one of the most famous women's rights activists of the nineteenth century. She met Elizabeth Cady Stanton in 1850, and they joined forces, becoming an impressive pair of activists. Anthony worked to secure an expansion of the Married Woman's Property Act in New York and petitioned the United States Congress for women's suffrage.

The two women did not abandon the abolitionist cause, however. During the Civil War, they formed the National Woman's Loyal League to gather signatures for a petition insisting on the emancipation of all slaves in the United States. Lincoln's Emancipation Proclamation freed slaves in the states that were at war with the Union only. Both Anthony and Stanton opposed the 14th and 15th Amendments because the language was worded to exclude women from gaining the vote. In withdrawing support from black male suffrage, Anthony and Stanton positioned themselves in the same camp as black abolitionist and feminist Sojourner Truth, who likewise questioned the wisdom of the amendments. However, a 20-year split in the movement resulted from their action, and it is still the basis of disagreement between black and white women today.

Anthony founded the National Women Suffrage Association; owned the *Revolution*, a women's rights newspaper; and was president of the national American Woman Suffrage Association. The 19th Amendment, guaranteeing women's right to vote, is often referred to as the Susan B. Anthony Amendment. Anthony died in her home in Rochester, New York, on March 13, 1906. In 1979, when her likeness appeared on a dollar coin, she became the first woman to be honored on United States currency.

The Next Wave

The women you have just read about fought to establish basic rights guaranteed by the United States Constitution and the Bill of Rights. They paved the way for women of the next century to build social systems to level the playing field for women and minorities. The next two women you'll read about established educational facilities for women and secured women's rights to control their bodies.

Educating the Spirit: Mary McLeod Bethune

On July 10, 1875, in Mayesville, South Carolina, Patsy and Samuel McLeod, both former slaves, gave birth to the fifteenth of their 17 children, Mary McLeod Bethune, who would become one of the most influential women of the twentieth century. They quickly recognized her extraordinary intelligence, and she began her education at the Mayesville Presbyterian Mission for Negroes. From there, Bethune earned a scholarship to continue her studies at Scotia Seminary for Negro Girls in Concord, North Carolina, graduating at the top of her class.

Bethune had a dream of going to Africa as a missionary, but she was ironically turned down because of her race. She made the decision to go back home and work with blacks. She began teaching, gathering experience in her field for the next nine years. In 1904 she opened her own school, the Daytona Normal and Industrial Institute for girls. With Bethune's hand at the helm all the way, the school quickly grew from 5 to 300 students.

Wise Words

"The future belongs to those who believe in the beauty of their dreams."

—Eleanor Roosevelt

Bethune was a skilled executive, bringing together diverse segments of society. She garnered support from other black leaders, wealthy and influential white women, Proctor and Gamble Manufacturing Company, and the Methodist Church to assure the school's development. Her school later merged with the coeducational Cookman Institute of Jacksonville, Florida, and it became an accredited junior college. Bethune-Cookman College went on to become a four-year institution, awarding its first Bachelor of Science degrees in education in 1943.

Wise Words

Eleanor Roosevelt reminds us: "Do not stop thinking of life as an adventure. You have no security unless you live bravely, excitingly, imaginatively; unless you can choose a challenge rather than competence."

In addition to her contributions as an educator, Bethune became the president of the National Association of Colored Women, the most prestigious position in the country for a black woman. Feeling the association's vision was too small, she went on to found the National Council of Negro Women (NCNW), an organization she headed for the next 14 years. By the time she stepped down, there were 22 national professional and occupational groups under the NCNW's wing. The organization created a powerful lobby, speaking out against lynching and job discrimination and in support of public housing and social welfare programs.

> **Sophia's Wisdom**
>
> During World War II, Bethune continued her fight for equality for black women, focusing her efforts on the newly developed Women's Army Auxiliary Corps (WAAC), assuring their acceptance into the ranks. She went on to persuade World War II Army officials to designate nearly 10 percent of the places in the WAAC's first officer candidate class for black Americans. In 1945 Bethune became an assistant to the secretary of war, helping in the selection of prospective female officers in the renamed Women's Army Corps (WAC).

President Roosevelt and First Lady Eleanor Roosevelt placed Bethune in the position of unofficial advisor on race-relations. She organized more than 100 individual black advisors into what was unofficially called the Black Cabinet and officially known as the Federal Council on Negro Affairs. She presided over two historic national black conferences held in Washington in which recommendations were made on government policies. As a special representative of the State Department, in 1943 Bethune was invited to attend the conference that established the United Nations. She remained in the capacity of advisor on race issues for Presidents Truman and Eisenhower.

Throughout her career, Bethune held a bold vision, and she thought comprehensively. She always saw how pieces fit together, how organizations are formed, and how power is built. In her later years, she established the Mary McLeod Bethune Foundation, promoting an international movement with the purpose of uniting people behind a set of universal values. She received a Medal of Honor and Merit from Haiti and the Star of Africa Award from Liberia. Bethune died in her home in Daytona Beach, Florida, on May 18, 1955, at the age of 81, one of the most influential women of her time.

The Woman Rebel: Margaret Sanger

It would be difficult to imagine how our lives as women would be today without Margaret Sanger's important contribution. She was born in Corning, New York, on September 14, 1879, one of the 11 children of Irish American Anne Purcell and Michael Higgins.

Despite the poverty of her early life, Sanger was able to get through two years of college before lack of finances forced her to drop out to take a teaching position. Shortly afterward her mother died, and Sanger returned home to take care of the younger children, while pursuing further training in nursing. She married at age 23 and had three children. The marriage ended in divorce. She remarried later but kept Sanger's name.

Wise Words

"We are not interested in the possibilities of defeat."

—Queen Victoria (1819–1901), who took the throne of England at age 18 and reigned for 64 years, giving her name to an era of history

Sanger worked as a home nurse, serving the poorest of New York City. Every day she witnessed the ravages of unlimited childbearing that many of the women endured. Too many pregnancies, doctors withholding birth control, and the carnage of self-induced abortions drove Sanger to her life's work, getting birth control information into the hands of women. She felt that her nursing career was merely putting a bandage on a much bigger wound. Believing that if women were ever going to achieve any degree of autonomy, they must gain control over reproduction, Sanger left her nursing career to enter the world of social change.

She began dispensing birth control information in her publication, *The Woman Rebel*, in violation of the law, which referred to it as "obscene" and "indecent." She was soon arrested. Sanger escaped to Europe, but not before circulating 100,000 copies of her guideline for contraceptive use. She came home to New York the following year to stand trial. However, her daughter died suddenly, and the public demanded sympathy for Sanger; the court responded by dropping the charges.

Sanger forged ahead, opening America's first birth control clinic in Brooklyn, New York, in 1917, only to be arrested again. This time she served 30 days in a workhouse for violating obscenity laws—with no sympathy from the court!

However, the Superior Court of New York had opened the door a crack when they included a specific exemption for physicians prescribing contraceptive devices for married women to protect them from diseases. Sanger slipped through the crack by reframing birth control as a medical issue. She founded the American Birth Control League (ABCL) in 1921 and the National Committee on Federal Legislation for Birth Control in 1931.

In 1923, with the help of a female physician, the door that began to open with a tiny crack, swung wide open as women entered the first birth control clinic in the United States with a doctor on duty. It was called the Birth Control Research Bureau in New York City. Sanger's work took on a global dimension when she organized the World Population Conference in Geneva and the International Contraception Conference in Zurich, focusing her efforts on women in India and Japan.

Sanger died on September 6, 1966, in Tucson, Arizona, having secured women's rights to family planning.

Sophia's Wisdom

The United States Supreme Court eventually held that the law could not interfere with public health by banning the mailing of contraceptive information and materials to medical doctors. However, many state courts weakened this ruling by limiting its application to only currently existing cases and patients in danger of dying. In so doing, it refused to protect the rights of clinics. It wasn't until 1972 that birth control information and devices became a formally settled constitutional issue.

The Least You Need to Know

- Women understand social inequality as a spiritual and religious issue. Their spirituality calls them to address the social realities of their society.

- The leaders of the abolition and suffrage movements fought the issues on both fronts. They were focused on creating justice in the society.

- After the basic rights for women were secured, the next wave of feminist leaders began building educational systems and the right for women to control their bodies.

- Today's women who continue to work for justice and equality as spiritual rights do so from a strong historic platform—standing on the shoulders of the giants.

13

How Jewish Women Do It

In This Chapter

- ◆ Monotheism enters the picture
- ◆ Doing away with original sin
- ◆ Meet three Jewish goddesses
- ◆ Discover the secret mystical teaching of Judaism

Judaism is the oldest of the major religions of the Western world. Many say the greatest gift of the Jewish people is the idea of monotheism—one God for all people. Judaism also gave the world the Hebrew Bible, its rich spiritual history. The Hebrew Bible stands by itself as a religious text and also is foundational to understanding Christianity. Judaism has a more holistic understanding of sexuality than is the cultural norm in the United States. This almost always translates to better treatment of women and a better relationship between men and women.

Judaism has contributed a major work to the Western mystical tradition in the *Kabbalah*. The Kabbalah contains universal truths collected over the ages. Its wisdom was not written down for thousands of years; the teaching was transmitted only through individual instruction with a master. Today women and men study this masterpiece of spiritual teaching to discover and impart its wisdom to the modern world.

The Jewish Story

Judaism is one of the oldest major living religions, its origins dating to the dawn of the second millennium B.C.E. in the Fertile Crescent of the Middle East among the nomadic tribes who lived there. It developed the idea of a single God, taking the polytheism of tribal people and fusing it into the single Godhead of the Judeo/Christian Bible—a personal God who is actively involved in the lives of the people.

Love of the Law and the Law of Love

Judaism is a religion of law and the Bible. The Talmud is the collection of ancient Jewish writings that makes up the basis of Jewish religious law. While the word *law* often conjures up a feeling of being restricted, in Judaism, you can substitute the word *love*, because the law represents God's loving care for the people. In an ongoing process, God's word is reflected upon and applied to life. Religious duties are especially emphasized in connection with the family and the welfare of society. Jews hold the following ideals in high regard:

- Truth
- Justice
- Humility
- Faithfulness
- Loving-kindness

In the Hebrew world, the generic name for God was El. He is referred to as ...

- El Shaddai, which means God of the Mountains or God Almighty.
- Elyon, which means God Most High.
- El Olam, which means God Everlasting.
- Elohim, which means God.

There are several branches within Judaism that are different expressions of the one Jewish religion. They are not to be confused with denominations.

♦ Orthodox, dating back to the days of the Talmud (second to fifth centuries)

♦ Conservative, which rose out of nineteenth-century Germany

♦ Reform, the most recent expression modified and adapted to Western culture

Reform Judaism includes a variety of interpretations of God and provides the spiritual home for religious humanists, mystics, and naturalists. In the Reform view, humans are in partnership with the divine. People are seen to be basically good, although education enables them to reach their full potential. Jews do not believe in original sin. People sin in their social actions when they don't go by the established religious laws and ethics. Sin is always being reinterpreted as part of a dynamic religious system that adapts to every age. Jews maintain that if a religious tradition or understanding clashes with justice, the religious law must be reinterpreted.

Women: Separate but *Not* Equal!

There are differences in translation and interpretation of biblical texts in Judaism. Most Jewish scholars agree that humans were created as a dual gender and were later separated into male and female—two equal parts of the whole. The difference between the genders is reflected in various religious practices or demands required of men but not of women. This is said to be in respect of women's highly developed spirituality, not because she isn't worthy. Women are separate but not unequal in the practice of the Jewish religion. A woman's obligations are different and are valued as much as a man's obligations. Both man and woman were created in the image of God.

There are many negative statements in the Talmud, however, and women Judaism scholars struggle to redefine scripture without the accumulation of cultural bias. For example, women have been described as lazy, jealous, vain, gluttonous, prone to gossip, and particularly subject to the occult and witchcraft. Although it may be because of men's propensity to lust rather than women's lesser status, men are warned against associating with women. Women are discouraged from higher education because it might conflict with their primary duties as wives and mothers. As is often the case, there is a world of difference between practice and theory within the religion.

History has shown that the rights of women in traditional Judaism were much greater than they were in the rest of Western civilization until this century. Women could buy, sell, and own property and hold their own contracts long before these rights were granted to women in America.

Mother Knows Best

Regardless of what the Talmud says, you have only to look at history to find that Jewish women have taken an active role in the society. Don't forget, Gloria Steinem is Jewish!

Going All the Way in America

Jewish settlers arrived in America as early as the mid-seventeenth century, but it wasn't until the late nineteenth century that they emigrated in large numbers to escape persecution in Eastern Europe. Often women were sent ahead to find work. Jewish women's roles were limited compared to the men's roles. Their primary responsibilities were in the home—meals and education of the children in religion. Passing the religion and traditions to the next generation was and still is an important part of Jewish life. Education and scholarship is, likewise, an important value, but until quite recently it was reserved for men only. Jewish women were not considered full members of the congregation, and they were separated from the men during worship.

In 1854 Temple Emmanuel in New York City led the way in abolishing the women's gallery, which began a gradual inclusion of women in all aspects of education and worship. However, it would be more than 100 years until a woman rabbi would be ordained. Sally Jane Priesand of the Reform branch of Judaism was ordained on June 3, 1972, becoming the first female rabbi in the United States. The Reconstructionist branch of Judaism ordained its first female rabbi, Sandy Eisenberg Sasso, in 1974, and the Conservative branch ordained Amy Eilberg in 1985. The Orthodox branch does not ordain women. The presence of women as religious leaders has begun to change the face of Judaism by creating new rituals and ceremonies that allow females greater participation. The issues they have brought before their congregations follow a similar form to the social issues Christian women bring to their religion—social justice, world peace, and working with AIDS.

> **Sophia's Wisdom**
>
> Hadassah is the Hebrew name for Queen Ester and also for the Women's Zionist Organization of America, the largest Jewish women's organization in the world. The organization was founded by Henrietta Szold, a scholar and women's rights activist. Education is an important focus in everything Hadassah does.

The Heart of Judaism: Education, Music, and Family

Singer and songwriter Janis Ian was raised Jewish in a black Baptist neighborhood in New Jersey. She compares her experiences there to the twentieth-century philosopher Jean-Paul Sartre's remark, "The Jew is defined by the other." "Judaism is who I am both as a person and as a musician. Music is a major part of the Jewish experience—music and food! Music is intrinsic to holy days—prayers are sung. Many of my melodies have a definite Jewish flavor to them."

Ian' parents and grandparents spoke Yiddish and Hebrew. She describes them as traditional Reform Jews. Reform Judaism is shaped by the American democratic culture;

women have an equal place in the religion. Ian said it would be difficult to separate women's spirituality from the religion. "Judaism is very much about women's values. A woman is the head of the home, and the whole religion functions to support and protect the family structure. If a woman stayed at home, as was the norm until 30 years ago, she often administrated the business and family finances. In contemporary Reform Judaism, women have full access to education."

Lively conversations are part of the family dinner ritual. Children are encouraged to think and reason. There are no easy answers, and reevaluation goes on constantly. The phrase, "Yes, but …" characterizes these discussions. Ian uses the example that "school girls prefer to date the smartest boy in the class rather that the best looking."

> **Wise Words**
>
> "A foundational social ethic in my upbringing was that the strong care for the weak. There is a Jewish axiom that says Judaism can be reduced to one rule or law: 'Do not do to others what you don't want done to you. All the rest is a commentary on that basic belief.'"
>
> —Janis Ian

"Music, art, and social awareness are considered foundational to the educational process. Good deeds in the community are expected, because you are supposed to do it, not to get a reward. God isn't in the reward business." Ian thinks of God as "kind of like a supervisor in the sky. Even though I refer to God as a 'he,' God is genderless. He oversees things and helps out when you get too far off track. Other than that, we're on our own. Life works by free will. God allows you to find your own way, and all things are possible."

J.A.P.: Jewish American Priestesses

Because Judaism existed for hundreds of years along with the goddess religions of the Middle and Near East, it has a strong feminine side built into it. This is often reflected in Jewish women's self-confidence and their awareness of their goddess side. While you have probably heard the slang expression *Jewish American Princess*, referring to Jewish women, we are transforming that into *Priestess*. Three Jewish American Priestesses prominent in today's public arena express different approaches to feminism and embody different goddess energies.

Gloria Steinem, E.V. (Ever Virgin)

Remember that being a virgin is a state of mind, not a physical state. Despite her recent marriage, Gloria Steinem is of the virgin goddess tradition. She combines Artemis and Athena, with a touch of Aphrodite for sheer class.

> **Wise Words**
>
> "If the shoe doesn't fit, must we change the foot?"
>
> —Gloria Steinem

Mother Knows Best

When asked why she was a feminist, Gloria Steinem replied, "If you're a woman, the only alternative is being a masochist."

Sophia's Wisdom

In 1972 the revolutionary *Ms* magazine hit newsstands with Steinem as a founding editor. The magazine was published for 20 years before it closed down for a brief time in December 1989. It reopened in July 1990 with Steinem as an advising editor. Steinem has published four books and considers writing as her mainstay.

Perhaps no one epitomizes the modern-day women's liberation movement better than Gloria Steinem. Born on March 25, 1934, in Toledo, Ohio, she comes by her revolutionary spirit naturally, because she is the granddaughter of Pauline Steinem, 1908 delegate to the International Council of Women and president of the Ohio Woman's Suffrage Association.

Steinem gained fame as a writer when she secretly entered the "Playboy bunny" world as an undercover reporter. She was invited onboard as a contributing editor for *New York* magazine at the time of its founding in 1968. It was there that she began her column, "The City Politic." Her journalism career led her to a meeting of Redstockings, a New York City feminist organization. As a result, she entered the women's rights movement, where her involvement has become legendary. She was a co-founder and board member of the Women's Action Alliance, a founding member of Coalition of Labor Union Women, and a member of the National Women's Political Caucus National Advisory Committee.

Clearing Ground for a New Vision

Judith Plaskow, professor of religious studies at Manhattan College in New York, lectures widely on feminist theology, particularly Jewish feminist theology. Plaskow co-edited (with Carol Christ) *Womanspirit Rising: A Feminist Reader in Religion* in 1979, which has become a classic anthology of the writings of contemporary feminist theologians. Dr. Plaskow sees her job as shaking up complacent attitudes and fostering a critical consciousness among her students and those who attend her lectures or read her books. She encourages women to reflect critically on both the political and religious traditions, hoping to create more just social and religious institutions in the future. She believes the purpose of this critique is to clear ground for new vision.

Dr. Plaskow calls on the classical model of Jewish religious reflection called a Midrash, which describes the process of questioning gaps or contradictions in biblical texts, in an effort to correct injustices. She points out that although women appear both often and powerfully in the texts of Jewish scripture, their stories are always told from the male perspective. A question she brings to the story of Isaac, for example, is how did Sarah feel? A feminist Midrash, according to Plaskow, finds Sarah refusing Abraham's choice.

Plaskow sees the internal struggles of Judaism such as those engaged by feminists as also fitting into a larger context. She looks at the Jewish instruction to be kind to strangers and uses this to remind Jewish men not to turn Jewish women into strangers by excluding them from stories, prayers, and rituals. She further explores how this particular teaching works when it is turned outward to other cultures—specifically the Middle East. "If women's stories are missing, who else's stories are missing, too? If the teaching of kindness to strangers is taken seriously, can Jews oppress Palestinians?" she asks of her audience.

In developing a model or symbol for feminism, Plaskow and Christ went to the old Jewish legend of Lilith, Adam's first wife. Lilith was created equal to Adam but found she couldn't live with him and took flight. This left her in exile. As the myth continued to develop, Lilith, symbolic of the isolated woman, is received into a community of women. They begin to share stories and create what the two authors describe as the "yeah, yeah" experience that happens when one woman's story connects with another's and sisterhood is born, an early version of consciousness-raising. Using Lilith as the basis of their work, Plaskow and Christ developed a transforming thealogical process of coming together and sharing stories. Judith draws on Athena, because she uses logic to bring deeper logic to ancient Jewish teachings, and Hestia, because she is the fire around which women gather in community.

Goddess Guide

Joan Rivers embodies three goddesses: Demeter, Aphrodite, and Hecate. She is Demeter, the definitive mother, as she appears on television with her daughter, Melissa. Her Aphrodite aspect draws to her the "beautiful" people—the glitz and glamour of Hollywood is her arena. She is Hecate, because she stands at the crossroads where all must pass with her tongue sharpened to a fine edge. She tells it like it is.

God, Sex, and Women

Rabbi Shoni Labowitz is a Venus-Aphrodite woman with Hestia's fire burning at her center. In her work as a feminist scholar, writer, teacher, and rabbi, Labowitz has respiritualized sexuality, reestablishing its connection to both the sacred realm and to our bodies. She does so by exploring the stories of the women in the Hebrew Bible and the Kabbalah, the mystical tradition of Judaism you'll read more about later in this chapter.

Labowitz looks at eight women of the scripture with a feminist perspective, uncovering meanings that have been lost for a long time. She reveals their passion, confidence, and sexuality, and shows how women today can benefit from these wise women.

Labowitz believes Eve was not blindsided by the snake but rather encouraged. All growth requires a death. In stepping forward into life, Eve would find her sexuality and her divinity and with it, the inevitable loss of innocence. Life calls us forward; it isn't always safe and secure, yet we must move on. Eve takes the risk, and as she does, she fears she has lost her connection with the Divine. She must trust that she will find her goddess self within. Eve illustrates women's sense of adventure and also women as spiritual teachers and leaders. She awakens Adam to join her in the ultimate act of faith—life.

Unlocking the Mysteries

As the Hebrew Scriptures are Judaism's gift to Western religion, the Kabbalah is its gift to the Western mystical tradition. The Kabbalah is a book of teachings whose exact origins are not known. Like all mystical material, it is surrounded by mystique. Some sources say it was conveyed to Adam and Eve after their fall, as a spiritual map to be followed, showing how to return to God. Other sources claim Moses received it on Mt. Sinai. Most sources trace its origins to Egypt and tell us it was handed down through the ages by oral tradition, thus making the exact lineage of the teachings difficult to determine. It is part of a larger mystical tradition found in many different cultures. The Kabbalah is a philosophical system and was reserved for people of highly advanced spiritually. It relates core teachings about the nature of existence, our deep purpose, and where we go when we complete our current incarnations.

Kabbalah and Western Mysticism

The Kabbalah is an esoteric, mystical teaching of Judaism. It has gained popularity within women's spirituality because it draws on traditions of the ancient world, some of which are based on goddess images. It illustrates the divine presence within creation and our common journey as humans to return to the source. The word *kabbalah* means "Qibel," "to receive." It was an oral tradition transmitted only between teacher and student. This could mean that the teachings were too sacred or subtle to be written down or, quite possibly, too heretical.

The Kabbalah belongs to the Western mystery tradition; it is a rich mixture of spiritual teaching drawing on ancient Egyptian Mysteries, Pythagorean mathematics, the work of Plato and Aristotle, Eastern Paganism, Greek teaching, astrology, Goddess spirituality, and Gnosticism. In other words, it draws on the entire body of philosophical and religious thinking of history. It was first written down by a mystic, Rabbi Shimon, sometime after 70 C.E. It was hidden in a cave and not rediscovered until the Middle Ages.

The Kabbalah isn't an exclusive teaching; it is part of a body of spiritual or mystical writings that belong to all time and all people. Its particular importance lies in the fact that it offers a contemporary teaching with deep historic roots that supports a different worldview from mainstream Western thought, yet is Western based. It supports universal truths found in Eastern *mysticism* and in the teachings of many Native Americans and other indigenous peoples.

Womanspeak

Mysticism is not focused on religious morality, theology, law, or dogma, but on the experience of the divine.

The Tree of Life

The Kabbalah uses the Tree of Life as its framework. It describes 10 spiritual qualities and activities of the divine. Each of the 10 teachings offers lessons that build on one another, creating a spiritual chart or diagram. The 10 teachings operate on two levels. They address the "cosmic picture," referring to our questions about the meaning of the universe, and they also provide guidance for our everyday life, or the "small picture," helping us get through the day.

The Tree of Life shows the highly interactive composition of creation. Everything we do resonates throughout and affects the entire universe, up to and including the creator. Likewise, divine presence is everywhere, touching and affecting all.

Sophia's Wisdom
Like many beliefs of Judaism, the area of mysticism is open to personal interpretation. Some traditional Jews take mysticism very seriously. Other traditional Jews take it with a grain of salt. It is reported that a prominent Orthodox Jew recently said on the topic of mysticism: "It's nonsense, but it's Jewish nonsense, and the study of anything Jewish, even nonsense, is worthwhile."

The Tree of Life, showing the names of the teachings. The Kabbalah includes feminine aspects of divine and is a popular resource for many women.

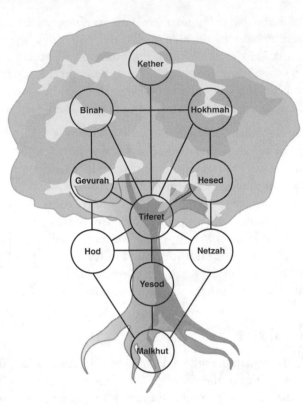

The 10 spiritual qualities and activities of the divine as described in the Tree of Life are as follows:

1. Kether—Crown
2. Hokhmah—Wisdom
3. Binah—Intuition and Understanding
4. Hesed—Divine Mercy and Love
5. Gevurah—Judgment and Strength
6. Tiferet—Beauty and Glory
7. Netzah—Victory and Power
8. Hod—Majesty
9. Yesod—Foundation
10. Malkhut—the Kingdom (describes the Divine Shekhinah the feminine indwelling of the Divine)

The Least You Need to Know

♦ Three of Judaism's contributions to the Western religious tradition are (1) the concept of monotheism—one God over all people; (2) the Hebrew Bible; and (3) the Kabbalah.

♦ In Judaism women scholars are correcting mistakes in translation and interpretations of scriptural text that have caused problems for women over the years.

♦ Jewish women have enjoyed respect and freedoms that were not part of the mainstream culture until recently.

♦ The study of the Kabbalah is of interest to women because it is one of the few teachings of Western religion and spirituality that uses female images for the divine.

Chapter 14

Common Roots and Shared Heritage

In This Chapter

- ◆ Catholics and Protestants—kissing cousins
- ◆ Women were there in the beginning
- ◆ The underground feminist movement
- ◆ Meet a holistic mystic
- ◆ My other car is a broomstick

Jewish, Protestant, and Catholic theologians and scholars are working together to correct many of the errors in biblical translations and interpretations that have been used for thousands of years to keep women out of leadership positions in religion. In the struggle to gain full partnership in their faith traditions, Protestant and Catholic women go to the same sources. They go to the stories of the early Christian movement. Christian women share common stories with the women in the ministry of Jesus, the lives of the martyrs and saints, the development of the mystical tradition, and the devastating witch-hunts of Europe and America. Their cultural heritage continues to be a vital part of women's spiritual identity today.

Lilies of the Same Field

For 1,500 years, the Christians of the Western world shared the same history. In the early part of the sixteenth century, Martin Luther had his famous falling out with Catholicism, initiating the Protestant revolt, and the Lutheran church was born. Only a few years later, Henry VIII in a similar move instituted the Church of England, declaring himself its head. Within the next few decades all across Europe, similar breaks were happening, and Protestantism was in full swing. The differences between Catholicism and Protestantism have been well documented, and often these differences have been a source of separation among Christians.

This is not as true for women as it is for men. As women of all faiths struggle to achieve equal status in their various churches, they are far more likely than their male counterparts to overlook theological differences and work together on what they feel is important. In doing that, they draw on their lengthy and rich history together. This particularly true when you go back to the beginning of their common journey.

In the Beginning ... Women Were There

Christianity is based on the teachings of a Jewish rabbi, Jesus of Nazareth, believed by his followers to be the son of God. He lived and taught in the Near East. His message conflicted with both the religion and the politics of the Roman world and eventually resulted in his arrest and conviction of treason. He was put to death on a cross, according to the Roman custom of the time. Three days later his followers believe he rose from the dead and walked again among them. Christians believe he is the *Messiah*, in fulfillment of the Hebrew Scriptures. Jews, however, do not believe Jesus is the Messiah, and they still await the Messiah's arrival.

Christianity began as a small sect within Judaism. The separation between the emerging religion and its Jewish parent became final about 70 years after the death of Jesus. For many years, the Jewish people had resisted the growing oppression of the Romans. In 70 C.E. the Romans crushed a rebellion in Jerusalem that resulted in the destruction of the Jewish temple. The destruction of the temple caused the Jewish religion to close its ranks, to pull in and tighten its circle. As Judaism tightened control on its people, fringe groups, such as the one called Christianity, were considered heretical and were pushed outside of the circle. This is when Christianity began to develop as a separate religion from its Jewish parent.

It was about this time that the term *Catholic* was given to the nascent church. Catholic means "universal" and was used to describe the core message of Christianity—that it is a religion for everyone—Jew, gentile, woman,

Womanspeak

Messiah means an anointed king who will lead the Jews back to the land of Israel and establish justice in the world.

man, rich, poor. During his lifetime, Jesus gathered a community of men and women around him, and they later formed the basis of the new religion called Christianity.

Biblical history shows that women were central to the ministry of Jesus, present in the intimate gatherings of his followers and in the public arenas as well. This was against the norm within the culture and time in which these events were happening. Accounts say women remained at the foot of the cross until Jesus' death, and it was to women that the risen Christ first appeared. Women continued to take an active role in the emerging church, spreading the teachings of their founder, side by side with the men.

Mother Knows Best

Jesus challenged the traditional role of women in society. Shortly after his death, however, his followers began to revert to the societal norm. As the church grew from small communities to a larger unified structure, it became hierarchical rather than communal, and women were relegated to lesser positions. This does not reflect the character of the early communities in which Jesus lived and taught.

Women such as Mary Magdalene, Priscilla, Aquila, Mary, Martha, and early Christian martyrs such as Perpetua, Agatha, Agnes, and Lucy tell of the strong faith and bravery of women as well as men. Today, as women seek full empowerment in the church, they point to scriptural references that show women's integral involvement in the early church.

Christians were persecuted by the Roman Empire for the first 300 years, and millions were killed because of their faith. In 313 C.E., the Roman emperor and great military leader Constantine made Christianity legal, thus ending its status as an "underground" church. Constantine also gave the early church its structure, which was essentially a military model with power centralized under one leader. The suppression of women was already a practice, and it was at this time that the practice became institutionalized. For the next 2,000 years, women have shared in the struggle to be free of this domination that has characterized both the church and the culture.

Sophia's Wisdom

As the New Testament was developed, scriptures that would be accepted into the Bible and those that would be left out were decided on. Women scholars point out that men made these decisions, and during this editing process, women's roles were greatly reduced—even written out of the text. However, a few references remain. Phoebe, a woman in the early church, is called a deaconess in the New Testament. Romans 16:1–4, written about 57 to 58 C.E., says "But I commend to you Phoebe, our sister, who is in the ministry of the church at Cenchrae, that you may receive her in the Lord as becomes saints, and that you may assist her in whatever business she may have need of you. For she too has assisted many including myself. Greet Prisca and Aquila, my helpers in Christ Jesus, who for my life have risked their own necks."

Mother of God or Goddess in Residence?

Women's Christian history begins with Mary, the Mother of Jesus. Mary was a young Jewish girl who was engaged to be married when her life took a sudden and totally unexpected turn. An angel appeared to her and asked if she would consent to becoming the mother of the Messiah. Mary consented and was made pregnant by the Holy Spirit. Her intended, Joseph, was visited by an angel in a dream and told to stay with her despite her unexplained pregnancy. Sometime late in the pregnancy, they traveled to Bethlehem to register for a census. Unable to find room anywhere else, the couple took refuge in a stable, probably located in a cave, and the child was born there. Mary and Joseph raised the child together and instructed him in the ways of Judaism. Jesus grew up and became a rabbi. Mary remained close to her son throughout his public life and was with him when he died on the cross. After his death, Mary went to Ephesus, where she lived out the rest of her years.

Mary's story develops in the cultures of the near East, North Africa, Greece, Turkey, and the mixed cultures of Rome, where the goddess was still very much alive in the minds and hearts of the people. The stories of Mary begin to interact with the goddess culture, and Mary takes on much of the legendary status of the Great Mother.

Womanspeak

Holy Spirit is the third element of the trinity that is composed of God the Father, Jesus the Son, and the Holy Spirit. The Holy Spirit is a concept expressing love and union and is not shown in human form.

Goddess Guide

In the cultures in which Christianity was first introduced, it would be impossible to have a "Father God" without a "Mother God." In the goddess cultures of the Middle East, the female deity was almost always more powerful than the male, who often appeared as her son and/or consort. The Mother Goddess carried with her the means of creation, her body, which was symbolized as the earth, and her ability to care for creation through the sustaining qualities found in nature's abundance.

Mary's image and story have captured the imagination of artists throughout history, making the Madonna and child a primary theme in religious art for all ages. Mary remains as popular today as ever. Her numerous appearances and miracles continue to happen on a regular basis all over the world. For the most part, she is the most accessible heavenly resident and has shown herself to be ultimately of and for the people.

How Women Feel About Mary

Mary has been both the church's biggest nightmare and a one-woman PR department. Women have a wide variety of experiences, feelings, and opinions about Mary. Some Catholic and Protestant women point to the impossibility of trying to live up to her perfection. Some see Mary as powerless, simply a vehicle for getting Jesus here with no real function of her own in religion or in the church. For these women she is a shadow, a background figure with no clear personality, and her image is confusing.

Other women from various Christian traditions find Mary an important source of spirituality. They are not concerned with the logic behind the image, but instead connect to Mary on an intuitive level. Whether as the young virgin girl, the new mother, the woman who places her son in his grave, or in her victory over earthly suffering as Queen of Heaven, they relate to Mary on a woman-to-woman basis.

Yet other women of all faith traditions connect to Mary as Divine Mother in her goddess state. Many talk about feeling this connection to her before they were consciously aware of a goddess culture. Once they began to explore the stories of the Great Mother, they immediately recognized her in the form of Mary. In the ancient religions, goddess consorted with gods, and virgins gave birth regularly, often signaling the arrival of a great person. Biblical references to the birth of Jesus come from Luke 2:7 and say only that he was placed in a manger. Caves were frequently used to house animals in the countryside around Bethlehem. Imagery depicting Jesus' birth often picture a stable inside a cave, and caves have always represented the womb of the Great Mother. Mary most likely delivered him right on the earth floor. The breath of animals warmed them, and a star in the East announced the birth. The essence of the images comes from the ancient Earth religions.

Mary takes a bigger place in Catholic worship than in Protestant; however, differences in how women relate to Mary don't always follow denominational lines. Regardless of whether she is seen as a powerful spiritual character or a problematic one, Catholic and Protestant women "own" her together.

God: An Equal Opportunity Employer

Although the emerging church was directly under its leader, women were treated as equals. This was in direct opposition to the cultural norm of the time. Soon after Jesus' death, this practice came to a quick stop. As the church shifted from a movement to an organization, leadership roles for women were limited and finally eliminated. As the religion grew further and further away from its beginning, it reflected a more secular attitude than a transcended one. An exception to this was the spiritual tradition of monasticism.

Monasticism and the mystical tradition have played an important role in Christianity, almost from the beginning. Life in a monastery involved prayer, meditation, and good works and was often lived in seclusion from the world. In a parallel structure to monasteries, women developed religious life in convents. Convents were under the direction of a woman known as an abbess. Although life in a convent might not seem like much of a choice for today's women, it represented the first autonomous career or vocation for early Christian women. Prior to the development of this tradition, women either lived at home under their fathers' rule or were married and lived under the rule of their husbands.

Women were not considered for ordination in the church, but their position in the religious communities gave them both autonomy and a voice in the church. In addition to prayer and meditation, their spirituality was often expressed through social action, feeding the poor, and treating the sick. This remained true until the middle ages, when papal authority began to usurp the authority of the abbess, attempting to bring women's religious autonomy under male control—something that was easier said than done.

The Holistic Mystic

Hildegard von Bingen (1098–1179) was one of those remarkable women whose spirit would not stay in the box. She was a "first" in many fields. At a time when the contributions of women largely went unnoticed, von Bingen produced major works of theology, visionary writings, and music. When few women were accorded respect, she was consulted by and advised bishops, popes, and kings.

> ### Sophia's Wisdom
>
> Von Bingen is known for her love of music, which she poetically described as the means of recapturing the original joy and beauty of paradise. According to von Bingen, before the fall from Eden, Adam had a pure voice and joined angels in singing praises to God. Von Bingen wrote hymns in honor of saints and Mary. Her importance is reflected in the fact that she is one of the first musical composers whose biography is known.

Von Bingen was an herbalist and a natural healer. She wrote about natural history and medicinal uses of plants, animals, trees, and stones. Her holistic and earthy scientific views were based on the ancient Greek cosmology of the four elements: fire, water, air, and earth. She knew sickness was brought on by an imbalance and that adding the right plant or animal with the missing quality could restore health.

Perhaps even more surprising are von Bingen's unique and progressive ideas about sex. Speculation has it that her writings may contain the first description of the female orgasm: "When a woman is making love with a man, a sense of heat in her brain, which brings with it sensual delight, communicates the taste of that delight during the act and summons forth the emission of the man's seed. And when the seed has fallen into its place, that vehement heat descending from her brain draws the seed to itself and holds it, and soon the woman's sexual organs contract, and all the parts that are ready to open up during the time of menstruation now close, in the same way as a strong man can hold something enclosed in his fist."

> **Mother Knows Best**
>
> Headaches or heavenly messages? It is now generally agreed upon that von Bingen suffered from migraine headaches and that her visions were a result of this condition. Her descriptions point to classic migraine symptoms, during which a person often experiences a clarity that can be likened to a spiritual insight.

Papal Foot-Kissing and Arm-Twisting

Catherine of Sienna (1347–1380) is known as a mystic, a contemplative who devoted herself to prayer, a humanitarian, and a nurse who sought to alleviate the suffering of the poor and the sick. She was a social activist who didn't hesitate to confront the corruption that characterized the church and society of her time.

Catherine believed that spirituality was based in self-knowledge, and her honesty and straightforwardness earned her a reputation as a person of insight and sound judgment. She didn't learn to write until almost the end of her life, but when she retired to Sienna, she recorded an account of her visions and other spiritual experiences along with advice on cultivating a life of prayer. She wrote hundreds of letters in which she shared her practicality and common sense through sage and frank advice.

Catherine wrote in the beautiful Tuscan vernacular of the fourteenth century, and her works are considered among the classics of the Italian language. In them we can see what will come to be an earmark of women's spirituality, the mixing of politics and religion. Many of her letters were written to popes, sovereigns, rulers of republics, and leaders of armies and are of priceless value to history. Others were written to the "regular" folks in her society and remain as illuminating, wise, and practical in their advice and guidance today as they were for those who sought her counsel while she lived. It is impossible in a few words to give an adequate conception of the manifold character and contents of the *Letters*, which are the most complete expression of Catherine's many-sided personality.

Meet a Zen Master and Christian Mystic

Women in the Middle Ages who had the ability, gumption, resources, and sheer spiritual drive to make it in a man's world—and accomplish what the women did—are in no way ordinary or fit the image of "church ladies" we have come to think of. They had to be resourceful, independent, sure of themselves, clear of vision, good businesswomen, innovative, and strong-willed. These things are not generally listed as spiritual qualities.

Womanspeak

Zen or **Zen Buddhism** is a major school of Buddhism originating in twelfth-century China that emphasizes enlightenment through meditation and insight.

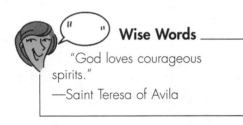

Wise Words

"God loves courageous spirits."

—Saint Teresa of Avila

Teresa of Avila (1515–1577) was all of these things and more. One of her biographers, Tessa Bielecki, describes Teresa as "a maddeningly beautiful young girl with an irrepressible zest for life" (*Teresa of Avila*, Crossroad, 1994). Bielecki goes on to say that Teresa operated with equal grace in the kitchen and in the boardroom. She embraced Christ and was likewise a *Zen* master. She played music, sang, danced, and wrote humorous and insightful poetic notes to friends.

Teresa was born into a wealthy family in Avila, Spain. In the Spain of her time and place, worldliness, militarism, and religion collided dramatically. Teresa reflected this cultural conflict. Her strong spirit was infused with adventure, courage, and religious fervor—a dynamic combination of forces that was confusing and difficult for her to manage.

Teresa took her vows at 22 years old, a difficult decision for her to make and one that caused her great emotional turmoil, resulting in physical illness. Her illness caused her to be sent home, where she once again encountered the sharp contrast to her religious calling that her family wealth and position afforded her. Teresa was caught up in the exciting social life in which she met visitors from all over the world entertaining them with her wit and charm, captivating them, and being captivated by their worldliness. During this time she had a spiritual awakening and a radical conversion that led her back to the mystical life. However, her entire life was characterized by conflict, disruptions, and confusion.

Teresa's legacy lives on through her writing, which is filled with sensuous poetic understandings of God's loving and nurturing nature. She wrote about God desiring our companionship and needing our friendship. Teresa was made a saint in 1622 and later further honored by being elevated to the title Doctor of the Church in 1970 by Pope Paul VI, a high position reserved for those whose contributions are considered to be of benefit to the whole church. Saint Teresa was the first woman to be so honored.

A Witches' "Brew Ha-Ha"

To the modern woman it is incomprehensible that anyone would believe that women flew through the air on broomsticks, mated with animals as well as the devil himself, and caused sickness and death to livestock, crops, and people. Yet the religious and political leaders of Europe preached this message, killing thousands of women they accused of being "witches." Historians now favor the theory that the *Inquisition* of Europe was mainly levied against Christian heretics; however, throughout this 400-year scourge, and particularly in the later stages, Church and political leaders turned their efforts against Jews, Muslims, and women.

Womanspeak

Inquisition describes the relentless process in the Middle Ages by which people were questioned—and even tortured—by church officials to determine whether or not they were heretics.

The Hammer of the Witches

The practices of the Inquisition began as early as the twelfth century and became official in 1484, when the pope issued an order that allowed anyone suspected of *heresy* to be put on trial. Two years later, the *Malleus Maleficarum* (*Hammer of the Witches*) written by two Dominican Monks, Heinrich Kramer and James Sprenger, was published. It became the working handbook for describing the supposed activities of witches and how to convict them—which was essentially through unspeakable torture. The book is rampant with paranoia, blatant misogyny, and the sexual fixation of its authors. It describes women's insatiable lust, infidelity, ambition, and intellectual and moral inferiority. It placed all women in danger; however, midwives, herbalists, and healers who were the specialists in women's health were the favored targets of the celibate, all-male clergy.

The figure of nine million people executed by the Inquisition, most of whom were believed to be women, was widely quoted by many and became an urban legend in the women's movement. Later scholarship, however, does not support this figure. For a long time the Inquisition was directed primarily toward Christians in an attempt to quell various heresies that were arising.

Womanspeak

Heresy describes an opinion or belief that contradicts established religious teaching, especially one that is officially condemned by a religious authority.

Womanspeak

Infidel describes someone who has no belief in the religion of the speaker or writer. It is used most often by Christianity or Islam to describe disbelievers.

It was also directed at Jews and Muslims as "heretics and *infidels*." Pagans were not the primary targets until the later years of the Inquisition, when church and political leaders turned their attention toward witches. The number of people executed is more likely to be between 20,000 and 100,000. Even the adjusted figure is hardly an insignificant number of people to be put to death in the name of religion.

Ashore in the New World

The Inquisition of Europe washed ashore in the New World and gasped one dying breath at Salem, Massachusetts, in 1692 when 141 people were indicted on charges of witchcraft. Of the indicted, 20 went to the gallows, refusing to disgrace their names by giving credence to the outrageous accusations. Of the 20, 14 were women and 6 were men. Middle-aged and older women who had managed to escape the poverty that was the common plight of this population were favorite targets and comprised the majority of those who were accused.

After the execution of the 20 victims in Salem, most of the clergy in the Bay Colony expressed doubt about the practice, and soon authorities admitted they had made grievous mistakes. In 1696, Samuel Parris, who had presided over the Machiavellian nightmare, formally resigned as village minister, bringing an end to the practice in America—for the time being. It continued in Europe, however, and was imported to the New World again through the brutality of the Conquistadors against the native people. Just as African American women talk about racial memory of slavery, many women of European descent carry the emotional imprint of this time of terror.

Sophia's Wisdom

Joan of Arc was one of the most famous women to fall to the Inquisition. Joan was 17 when she heard a voice tell her to go help the king of France recapture the kingdom that he had lost to the English. This young woman, known as the Maid of Orleans, raised an army and rode to the king's defense. The English captured her in battle, and the French failed to come to her aid. She was imprisoned and found guilty of heresy, sorcery, and adultery. Joan was burned at the stake on May 30, 1431, at age 19. Thirty years later she was exonerated by Church officials of all charges and found innocent. She was made a saint in 1920 and has become a symbol of female leadership and power for many women today.

In 1517 Martin Luther took a hammer, a nail, and 95 complaints against the Catholic Church and began a religious revolution that sent Protestants and Catholics on different paths. In the next chapter you'll read about how Christian women—both Catholic and Protestant—who remain in their traditional religion are continuing the heritage of spiritual work and creating a better and more humane world for today.

The Least You Need to Know

◆ Women played important roles in the ministry of Jesus.

◆ Catholics and Protestants share 1,500 years of history. Much of modern-day American Christian religion is rooted in the European culture that was their common ground.

◆ There is a rich tradition of women's spirituality found in the writings of the mystics and of life in the convents, where women lived autonomously and practiced their spirituality according to their own rules.

◆ The Inquisition resulted in the deaths of thousands of Jews, Muslims, and women identified by church and political leaders as heretics.

15

The Spirit of Ecumenism: Working on the Inside

In This Chapter

- ◆ A "guilt-free" Catholic tells all
- ◆ Finding the true power of Eucharist
- ◆ The spirit of St. Joan of Arc—alive and well
- ◆ Working for justice despite injustice
- ◆ Ministering to the dying

Garrison Keillor brings insight into many of our cultural quirks on his popular radio show, *A Prairie Home Companion*. He tells his audience that the difference between Lutherans and Catholics is most pronounced at Christmas. Lutherans put their Christmas trees up on Thanksgiving day and take them down the night after Christmas. Catholics put their trees up on Christmas Eve and leave them up until the second week of January. What Keillor is saying is humorous and, as always, has more than a grain of truth to it. Catholics and Protestants may have more in common than they often think they do, and this is particularly true with women. Today's woman who makes the choice to stay within her religion does so because she is more interested in expressing her spirituality in the world than in theological differences.

Trading Places

The lines between Catholic and Protestant, as well as denominational differences within Protestantism, are soft lines for many women. Many move back and forth between religious "camps" easily, exploring differences and finding what they need to create their full spiritual expression.

Many of today's Protestant women seek a connection to the Catholic sense of mystery and ritual. This is not to say they are seeking Catholicism for its theological statement, but are still attracted to many of its practices—just as many Catholic women find that Protestant denominations offer them a better access to power through the democracy of their structures.

In Search of Mystery

Olivia Martin describes herself by saying, "I'm a guilt-free Catholic, and there aren't very many of us! I was raised in Protestant New England, but in the very predominantly Catholic culture of Boston. In the 1950s you were either Catholic or *non-Catholic*. I was a member of the Congregationalists, but referred to myself as non-Catholic."

I had a conversion experience while attending the rehearsal dinner for a Catholic friend. The dinner was a big family affair. The priest, a lifelong friend of the groom's family, was there, along with the bride's pastor. As we sat around a large table filled with food, I had a tremendous feeling of being included in this ritualistic community from which I had been excluded as a child. There was an interweaving of religion and culture, and I fell in love with it. My daughters were confused when I joined such a patriarchal religion. I assured them it was for the "magic." I am careful not to get sucked into institutional arguments, and I pray for the ordination of women.

"I hadn't been active in any church for more than 30 years and had come to the realization that I would never completely agree with any one formal religion," Martin continued. "I had been raised in a liberal Protestant home, and I have no disagreement with the concepts of my childhood religion. However, it didn't touch me at the personal level. It seemed distant.

Womanspeak

Ecumenical is the promotion of friendly relations among different religions or promoting the unity of Christian churches around the world. **Non-Catholic** was a term once used by Catholics to identify "others." **Hocus pocus** is slang that comes from the sound of the Latin words of the consecration during Catholic Mass, *"Hoc est enim meum"* ("This is my body").

I realized I was looking for the mystical side of religion, which I had not been exposed to in Protestantism. I wanted religion of the heart rather than the head. What I found among Catholics that I didn't find anywhere else was a wide streak of compassion. The mystery and ritual drew me in. What can I say—I loved the '*hocus pocus*.' It gets places you can't reach any other way. I was able to get past 'thinking about God' and tap into the experience of the sacred."

On the Other Hand ...

Eileen O'Leary Norman was born into an Irish Catholic family in New Orleans's French Quarter and attended Catholic school for 12 years. Alcoholism made her home a tumultuous place, and Norman sought the structure the church gave her. "Church was family," she said. During college she took a leave of absence from church. "I hadn't separated God from religion yet, so when I dropped out of church, I became an agnostic. When I married and began having babies, I knew the children would need a church home. This eventually brought me back to Catholicism."

Over the years, Norman has moved in and out of the church, each time wrestling with its use of power. Meanwhile, she read the Bible from cover to cover, and that is where she found her faith. She finally made her peace by leaving the Catholic Church. "I was tired of being angry." Norman joined the Presbyterian Church two years ago. She belongs to a small congregation, which she describes as friendly and involved in the community. What she likes about her new religious home first and foremost is that women have equal power! Elders run the church, and women can become elders! Norman says, "I'm finally not angry anymore!"

Norman has always found her spirituality in nature, where she experiences mystical oneness, and in relationships. "Communion or *Eucharist* is in reaching out to another," she says. It is a spiritual truth she discovered quite by accident one Holy Thursday. A group of women she met with regularly for prayer and meditation was enjoying an early spring day by the creek on her farm. In what seemed at the time to be a quantum leap in consciousness, they decided to have a Eucharist service. They prayed and meditated and broke bread. As they passed the loaf around the circle, each woman took a piece, turned to the woman beside her, and gave it to her. "It seems like that was the paradigm shift for me. I realized that the spiritual power of communion exists in the *giving* of the bread to another."

Womanspeak

Eucharist, also called Holy Communion, is a ceremony in many Christian churches during which bread and wine are blessed and consumed to commemorate the last supper of Jesus Christ and his disciples before his death.

Bits and Pieces of Faith

Ronnie Angelus was born Rosalie Moore in New York City's Polyclinic Hospital at 52nd and Broadway, on the spot where the Schubert Theater now stands. Her mother was a dancer, and her father was a politician. Angelus has combined the personable skills she inherited from her parents into her personality, and the result is a vibrant, composed, outgoing woman of action who loves people. Angelus was raised in an ecumenical family of German Lutherans, Episcopalians, Greek Episcopalians, Methodists, and Tibetan Buddhists. She chose Catholicism at the age of 11 and was baptized into the Catholic Church.

Mother Knows Best

Action, action, action! Satisfaction with parish life depends on how active you are. Those who just show up are dissatisfied. Those who become active find spiritual fulfillment.

When asked to describe spirituality, Angelus begins by saying, "It's not religion. It's not legalistic or bound to rules and codes. It is the totality of who you are. It's how you have internalized the rituals and experiences, how they have become the fabric of your life. Spirituality permeates everything you do, it is how you think, act, and live in the world. It is completely inclusive. It's found in nature, down in the gutter, in temples, churches, and mosques alike. It's what illuminates you. It's all the bits and pieces of faith that get you up when life has knocked you down."

Despite the problems she runs into in the Catholic Church that cause her to take periodic "breaks" from it, ultimately Angelus comes back. This is partially due to the character of her parish, St. Joan of Arc, and also Angelus's ability to set personality aside and work from principles—in this case her desire to be of greater service.

Putting a Face on AIDS

A few years ago Angelus had a dream about working with AIDS patients. The dream said that their stories must be told. Angelus began her career as a writer at age 70, and just a few years later her dream became a reality. She started a writing workshop at Grace House, an assisted-living facility for people with AIDS, originally sponsored by Joan of Arc Catholic Church in Minneapolis. She collects stories and profiles of the residents called "Stories of Grace" for publication on the St. Joan website (www.stjoan.com).

Angelus describes the AIDS patients and the writing process as triumphal and joyous. "They are facing the greatest mystery of all—death—and are having the time of their lives. The stories are heroic and painful—a rich mixture of the best and the worst life has to offer. There are also the stories of all the people who come to care for them. I am both filled with gratitude and humbled by this experience." Angelus is reminding the world that "AIDS has faces."

A John XXIII Catholic

Angelus has been a member of St. Joan of Arc "on and off" for 30 years. Although this parish embraces the inclusive worldview that she shares, "big" church, or the organizational church, often falls short of her ideals. When this happens, she takes a break. "If it wasn't for St. Joan of Arc, there wouldn't be a spiritual home for me." This is a sentiment shared by many who worship there.

Angelus came to St. Joan of Arc after having a spiritual awakening in a church in Columbus, Ohio. She had entered one of those "dark nights of the soul" and felt she had lost everything she held dear. She recalls entering the church and being overtaken by "the smell of molded concrete walls imbedded with the molecules from decades of incense." She felt totally stripped. "I knelt before the altar, my arms stretched wide, and I completely surrendered. Speaking out loud, I said, 'It's over!' Then, suddenly, strength flowed into me; I was filled with grace. In that moment, I realized the sacred exists in the communion of people. The true Eucharist is the trust and respect we give one another."

Angelus considers herself a *John XXIII Catholic* and wonders what ever happened to the changes that were promised at *Vatican II*. "It's like we got all caught up in form rather than substance. For instance, I can get profoundly offended listening to a long discussion on whether to hold the communion wafer in the right hand and put it in your mouth with the left hand or the other way around, while a nation [Africa] is dying of AIDS." She asks, "'What is real communion?' In those moments, I just shrug my shoulders and say to myself, 'You [the institutional church] just don't get it,' and somehow I am able to hold it all a bit lighter. Life has taught me how little can be transformed beyond myself."

Three things that Angelus holds sacred and that nourish her spirit are "(1) Talking with my daughter who opens vistas for me and makes me laugh. She is a mentor, teacher, and guru, and without her I would still be wearing high heels and an apron. (2) Being in the circle of Divas, my writing group, who shout, 'Go Girl' and give me standing ovations with their smiles and tears. We have fallen in love with one another! (3) And sitting next to Mary and Claude Paradis during Sunday Mass at St. Joan of Arc, which is as close to pure goodness as I will know in this lifetime."

> **Wise Words**
>
> "… love is the only thing that we can carry with us when we go, and it makes the end so easy."
>
> —Louisa May Alcott

> **Wise Words**
>
> "I carry deep in me something someone said about the stories. 'I used to think of HIV/AIDS as a separate thing, a terrible disease out there somewhere. But now it has faces—it is William, and Theodore, and Charli, and Clifford.' That's a huge thing to think about. It makes my gratitude to them and love for them even deeper. It was their courage that gave the face to AIDS."
>
> —Ronnie Angelus, writing coach at Grace House in Minneapolis, Minnesota

A Cutting-Edge Church Community: St. Joan of Arc Parish

St. Joan of Arc is an unusual parish. It combines many ministries and many individuals who often fall between the cracks of more traditional churches. Reading the mission statement, it might appear that St. Joan of Arc's mission isn't different from any other Christian mission. The difference might be found in the fact that St. Joan of Arc puts these words into practice in a way that has earned it a national reputation as a cutting-edge church community.

"Have I Told You Lately That I Love You?"

I arrived at St. Joan of Arc Catholic Church not knowing exactly what to expect. Over the years the parish has been characterized as a countercultural statement of radical Christianity, an anachronistic throwback to the "Dawning of the Age of Aquarius," a warm and loving congregation, and everything in between. I arrived with my friend, Kobbe, entering the school auditorium, which was filled to capacity for the 9 A.M. Father's Day service.

Sophia's Wisdom

The following is St. Joan of Arc's mission statement:

St. Joan of Arc is a joyful Christian community, which celebrates the loving Word of God in worship and in action. We transcend traditional boundaries and draw those who seek spiritual growth and social justice. We welcome diverse ideas and encourage reflection on the message of the Gospel. We are committed to the equality of all our members and strive to ensure their full participation through liturgy, education, and service. By these means we seek to empower all who come to grow in wisdom and bring to reality the promise of Christ.

Colorful silk flags waved in the breeze overhead, large screens were suspended from the ceiling, and what looked like the "Lake Wobegon" town band was on the altar preparing to play. Soon we all stood and sang the opening song, "Have I Told You Lately That I Love You?" I was unprepared for the effect that the bridging of the sacred and secular worlds with music would have on me.

I had written about the merging of religion into "real life," yet, I hadn't had the experience of connecting them through music. Somehow, as we sang these old American classics, the accumulated family gatherings of my childhood, childhood experiences with my three kids, now grown with their own families, and thousands of evenings spent watching sparks from a campfire rose into the night sky. While we sang these familiar songs, everything converged in the here and now and became part of the Mass.

A Father's Firsthand Account

It was Father's Day. A young man who told us about what it was like to be a father delivered the homily. He remembered going out into the barn when he was a child to talk with his own dad, who was a dairy farmer, and how the lessons he learned there carried him a long way into his life. He talked about learning how to change diapers and getting the inevitable sprinkling that is the particular rite of initiation by boy babies.

He told us how the sudden illness of his first son took him past his known limit and made it clear that he would have to go to a greater source than his earthly father for strength to deal with the situation. In his greatest need, he drew on Jesus and his divine father—and the people at St. Joan of Arc, who saw him through it. There is no sermon that can come close to the authenticity of a firsthand witness.

Near the end of the service we stood again, and I took the hand of my friend on one side of me and the hand of a stranger in a wheelchair on the other side (I suspect he is a resident of Grace House). Together we sang "Come sit here a while 'ere you leave me, do not hasten to bid me adieu …" So many things get built up in your mind before you have the actual encounter and fail to meet your expectations. This didn't happen that day. (For more about St. Joan of Arc, Grace House, and other ministries, see Appendix C, "Resources.")

Tending the Store

Often a woman's religious vocation and her love for her work keep her inside an organized religion. One such woman is Reverend Janet Wolf, a Methodist minister who knows about the shortcomings of the institutional church yet also knows about the power of community. For the time being at least, Wolf has mastered the art of conciliation, saying, "There is no place where you don't have to compromise." She chooses to work within the structures to remove as much of the injustice both there and in the larger world as she can.

Another woman working within an organized religion is a Dominican nun, Honora Werner, O.P. (Order of Preachers), who will share with you her formula for staying focused on what she feels is the heart of the matter despite the limits placed on her by her church.

Sophia's Wisdom

Order of Preachers (O.P.) is a religious community begun by Saint Dominic in 1216 C.E. Priests, brothers, and nuns who belong to this order are also referred to as Dominicans. Members are dedicated to a life of prayer, study, teaching, and preaching the word of God. Dominicans preach the good news of Jesus' saving grace through published books and periodicals, schools of theology, parish churches, hospitals, and universities all over the world.

Strike Three!

After successfully completing her seminary studies, Wolf was denied ordination three times by a member of the board because of what he described as her "too confrontational" stand on homosexuality and community organizing in the seminary. When Wolf was finally approved, this board member said he would pass on her ordination, but he would "place her in a church where she could not succeed." She was sent to a blatantly misogynistic rural county where one pastor declared he would burn down the church before he would let a woman preach. She was boycotted, harassed, and one of her children was beaten up.

At the same time, Wolf encountered people of unbelievable bravery who put themselves in jeopardy to stand by her and her family. There was the bus driver who made special trips to pick up her son to assure his safety and the cafeteria worker who sat with him during lunch when he was being shunned. "Those people came forward to help, and they would be paying the price long after I left," Wolf said. "Thanks to them, my children remember the closeness of the community, not the ugliness they encountered." As to why she continues to serve the institutional church in the face of its faults and shortcomings, Wolf says it is because of the deeper community that resides within the church. She also knows she has been educated and ordained as a minister, and the most effective place for her to confront injustice is from within the organization.

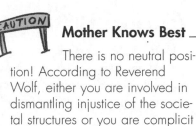

Mother Knows Best

There is no neutral position! According to Reverend Wolf, either you are involved in dismantling injustice of the societal structures or you are complicit with them.

Letting Justice Roll Down

For 12 years, Wolf was the pastor of a congregation characterized as a mixed, lower-income population. She took a year off to travel, studying issues of race, class, and sexual identity. Her present ministry is directed toward issues of incarceration and drug addiction.

Sophia's Wisdom
Barbara Ruckle Heck is considered to be the "mother of American Methodism," having established the first permanent Methodist society in America in 1768. However, women were not given full equality with men until 1956, when the United Methodist Church granted women full rights to ordination. The African Methodist Episcopal Church granted permission in 1948 (eight years before the United Method Church), and the Colored Methodist Episcopal Church followed suit in 1950. Ordination is denied to Catholic women, and all official discussion or consideration has been suspended under the current pope.

Despite the problems, Wolf remains hopeful. She remembers being in South Africa in the 1970s and witnessing the horror and destruction of apartheid. Last year she returned to the same city in South Africa, where blacks and whites, once separated under law, now live, work, and worship together. She believes society can change and that we stand a better chance of being effective in the process by working together.

Preacher Teacher Offers Sage Advice

Honora Werner, O.P., is a Dominican nun who teaches preaching at St. Mary's Seminary and University in Baltimore, Maryland, yet is not allowed by her Catholic religion to preach from the pulpit. Werner is both a progressive and a pragmatist, and when I asked how she manages this unfortunate limitation, she offered some very sage advice:

◆ Acknowledge the injustice of it and deal with the emotions it evokes—anger, frustration, pain—whatever.

◆ Get over it! There are lots of things that need doing that I can do. Make sure the "limits" are theirs, not mine.

Werner further explains, "I'm doing everything I can do, mainly through my teaching, to subvert the mentality that supports the injustice." She defines preaching in the broader context of "bringing the good news of God's all-embracing love." She points out, "There are many places besides the pulpit where this message can be delivered, such as through our individual presence, writing, art, prison ministries, even the Internet." Werner believes that "every creature has a different perception, and all voices are important."

To Die a Good Death

Mary Lou O'Gorman is a chaplain at a large Catholic hospital. Her job is to minister to patients, family, and staff, assisting them in the face of chronic or life-threatening illness or death. She helps them live the life they have left more fully, regardless of the outcome of their treatment. She talks about making peace—when everyone involved with the patient comes to terms with or befriends the limits of the illness. She helps patients, family, and sometimes the attending staff find the hope in the situation. O'Gorman talks about this process as spiritual integration, a time when one examines his or her life and asks the deep questions about meaning and purpose.

Ministering to the Whole Person

O'Gorman approaches her work from an ecumenical position. "It is my job to appreciate the faith tradition of those I serve—to find out what role faith plays in their lives, and to explore with them the things that give them hope and strength," she says. "If that means bringing in someone of their own religion, that is what I do. I talk with the patient and find out what needs to happen for them as they approach their death. I assist them in finding out what is important to them and connect them with it. Recently one woman wanted to leave behind her memoirs; she died just after completing the last page. Others have wanted to make a video or plan their funeral arrangements. We look at it all."

> **Wise Words** _____
>
> "There is nothing easy about becoming conscious. My own life was much easier before I knew about the deeper meaning of choice, the power of choice that accompanies taking responsibility. Abdicating responsibility to an outside source can seem, at least for the moment, so much easier. Once you know better, however, you can't get away with kidding yourself for long."
>
> —Caroline Myss, Ph.D., internationally known medical intuitive and author in *Anatomy of the Spirit* (Harmony Books, 1996)

O'Gorman also teaches medical students and residents about caring for the whole person—the complex network of relationships that go with the patient. And sometimes it can mean teamwork, where staff supports other members of the staff, helping them gain insight into what the patient or the family needs to hear from them. She talked about a situation where a family was agonizing over whether to continue the life-support system on a family member. "They desperately needed the doctor to tell them it was alright to let go. A staff member was able to convey this to the doctor, who then told them what they needed to know. I was able to later tell the doctor how he had helped the patient 'die a good death.' I could see the appreciation in his eyes. I have come to a deeper respect for the doctors—the buck really does stop with them."

> **Wise Words** _____
>
> Speaking at a September 15, 2001, memorial service following the terrorist attacks in New York, Washington, D.C., and Pennsylvania, the Reverend Dr. James A. Forbes Jr., Senior Minister of the Riverside Church in New York City, told Americans to take a deep breath and get into their bodies. He reminded people that "the body knows how to get you through this; the heart knows how to grieve."

Spiritual Bouquet

O'Gorman says her Catholic religion "is not a set of beliefs" for her but instead is "who I am down to the core. It's the lens through which I view life; it's how I frame God's activity in the world." She also sees spirituality as bigger than religion. "It includes all that gives our life purpose, meaning, and hope. It includes our relationships both here and now and with God. It is the totality of our life experiences and expression—it is dynamic and evolves over time." Her own spirituality was formed by her family and by the 15 years she spent in the care of the Visitation nuns, a contemplative order that educated her. The nuns taught O'Gorman about a loving God and about being still and experiencing God's love.

Wise Words

"Religion is the structure of your being and believing. Ritual gives order to your beliefs. Spirit, or spirituality, is the heart of a person—the 'stuff' of a life."

—Mary Lou O'Gorman

Womanspeak

Centering prayer is a centuries-old form of contemplative prayer in which the practitioner quiets her mind, emptying it of all thoughts to be in silence, allowing God to make any changes God thinks best.

O'Gorman supplements religion by nourishing her spirit in a variety of places, such as "getting lost in her garden," where she gets her hands in the dirt and lets the beauty and bounty of nature take over. On a summer day, tomatoes and red peppers line the windowsills of O'Gorman's kitchen. Outside, a small pond is full of water lilies in full bloom, and tall purple flowers tower over everything, climbing the fence and spilling down into the neighbor's yard. A heady and hearty bouquet of smells scream of summer's seemingly inexhaustible supply. The life in O'Gorman's garden brings balance to her work, in which death is often the focus. "I am always amazed at the earth's abundance and the deeper meaning of nature's cycles," she says.

O'Gorman also belongs to a small group of friends who have met every other week over several years for prayer, scripture reading, and reflection. The group has become an important part of her spiritual life-support system. In addition, she reads spiritual material from many sources, including the Buddhist tradition and most recently, *centering prayer*, a Christian form of meditation.

The Least You Need to Know

- Women are less bound by denominational differences and more focused on where they can find the support they need to accomplish what they feel is important.

- Women who find satisfaction working within traditional religions do so by staying active in ministries where they can find expression for their spirituality.

- Women who stay in the traditional church despite its shortcomings do it with eyes wide open—meaning they are aware of the injustice and find they can work for change from the inside and still be effective in their service to the world.

- It is in the nature of systems and structures to become conservative and lose their cutting edge. To avoid this, systems must be challenged by their membership.

Part 4

People of the Earth

The word *religion* comes from the Latin *religare*, meaning "to bind back." We're going to take that definition to heart as we go back to the beginnings of time and take the fascinating journey from ancient Paganism to Celtic Christianity, seeing how religious images have endured throughout this very long period of our history. We'll also take a look at another old religious tradition you've probably heard about and maybe clear up some of the misunderstandings that have shrouded it since the Middle Ages.

Many women who practice women's spirituality feel that most sources of authority in Western society are hopelessly patriarchal, especially those based on religion, and often hold women back. If women's spirituality is not scripture-based, then to what do women turn in developing their ethical and moral codes? In the next chapters you'll read all about this, and learn some fascinating ways you can experience your intuition.

Chapter 16

Native Woman

In This Chapter

- Why native ceremonies went underground
- Discovering our matriarchal heritage
- Women's autonomy among indigenous people
- The first female chief of the Cherokee Nation
- A spiritual teacher who has roots in the ancient world

The spirituality of Native American people is complex and diverse, and one cannot talk about native spirituality or religion as a unified set of beliefs. However, there is a common worldview and shared characteristics that can be recognized in the beliefs of most native people. We'll look at Plains Indians to see how the women of some native societies lived before their culture was disrupted by European occupation. We'll also hear about the woman who became the first Principal Chief of the Cherokee Nation and perhaps clear up some misconceptions of what it's like to be a Native American woman today.

Indian Affairs

The European occupation of the North American continent brought an incomprehensible level of oppression to its native people. One aspect of that oppression that perhaps did more to destroy the culture than any other was the suppression of religion. In 1891 the American government made it illegal for Native Americans to practice their own religion. For the next 87 years religious ceremonies and possession of sacred objects were forbidden by law. Although the ceremonies were taken underground and preserved, without direct access to them, the very structure of Native American society was greatly compromised. Additional destruction to native people happened through practices imposed by both church and government such as the forced removal of children from their parents' homes, the forbidding of speaking native languages, and the imposing of religious conversion. It was only in 1978 that the American Indian Religious Freedom Act was passed and Native Americans were again free to worship through ceremonies and traditional rites.

Each Indian nation is unique and has a particular way to fulfill its spiritual duty; however, there are also certain things held in common. Each native nation has ceremonies that relate to the cycles of planting and harvest and the cycles of the moon, ceremonies of purification and renewal, and ways to maintain traditions and cultivate spiritual awareness. Smudging with cedar or sage is almost universal, as is the understanding of the living spirit that is present in all things. There is a similar understanding of the interdependence of all the earth's creatures and on the elements of air, fire, water, and earth. This sacred relationship is expressed by the Lakota people in the prayer often used as a greeting and said many times each day, Mitakuye Oyasin. It translates to "all our relations," acknowledging the sacred web of life.

Wise Words

"I have noticed that as soon as you have soldiers, the story is called history. Before their arrival it is called myth, folktale, legend, fairy tale, oral poetry, or ethnography. After the soldiers arrive it is called history."

—Paula Gunn Allen, Ph.D. (1939–), professor of English at the University of California in Los Angeles, poet, author, and expert in Native American studies

The Iroquois are known for their superior political organization, and their political system dominated the first 200 years of colonial history in both Canada and the United States. Proper credit is seldom given, but the Europeans learned about democracy from the Iroquois. They had an elaborate system of checks, balances, and supreme law, which directly influenced the American Articles of Confederation and Constitution. On September 16, 1987, the U.S. Senate passed a resolution stating that the U.S. Constitution was explicitly modeled upon the Iroquois Confederation.

According to an essay by Sally Roesch Wagner in *The Untold Story of the Iroquois Influence on Early Feminism* (Sky Carrier Press, 1996), women's rights in Native American tribes included …

- Children belonged to the mother's tribe.

- If a marriage proved to be a bad one, the woman could leave and take the children with her. She was free to marry again.

- When a man brought home the results of a hunt, it was the woman's to use or dispose of as she saw fit. Her decisions were not disputed.

- A woman kept ownership of her belongings even within the marriage.

- Women ruled the home front, and all goods were commonly owned.

- Women voted on tribal affairs.

- Treaties had to be ratified by three quarters of all voters and three quarters of all mothers.

- Women could impeach a chief.

- Women addressed council meetings.

- Women could forbid braves from going to war.

The First Women of the Plains

Most accounts of Native American life have come through the observations of European men. Often the women's lives were not recorded or were interpreted through the cultural lens of the observers. Native women's lives did not seem to be as glamorous as the men's lives and, therefore, not as important. European men often painted a picture of Native American women as downtrodden, mistreated, and subservient, which was not the rule. For the most part, the subtleties of tribal politics were completely lost on early European observers. Later studies have shown that Indian culture among the Plain Indians of North America, for example, was matriarchal. UCLA professor of English and author Paula Gunn Allen is a Native American of mixed heritage who laments the price women pay because they don't know about the prevalence of female-based cultures on this continent prior to European occupation. In looking for models of female leadership, American women need to look no further than the first people of their own land.

Tribal Mothers and Grandmothers

Women were indispensable to tribal life and participated in many activities. Their primary responsibilities, however, were in maintaining the home and family. Women were greatly respected as the life-givers of the tribe. Songs and stories have been passed down through the ages that sing of Mother Earth and the love and honor the people hold for all females as mothers of the tribe. Likewise, parents had great affection for children, and child-rearing rules were permissive. When discipline was needed, grandparents generally administered it. The mother-daughter bond was particularly strong even though (or perhaps because) grandmothers did most of the training—teaching girls to cook, sew, tan hides, and design and make clothing, an art form in itself. Bravery was a highly valued virtue in both boys and girls, and in some tribes girls developed riding and fighting skills. Ordinarily hunting and warring were left to men, but there were some exceptional cases in which women of particular strength of will became warriors.

Wives were not subject to their husbands. Abuse was rare, and the woman's family had the right to intervene and separate her from her husband if there was mistreatment. An Indian woman maintained her own property separate from her husband's. She was free to buy and sell as she desired. After skinning the animals following a hunt, the pelts were given to the woman to be used in any way she wanted—to keep, sell, or trade and keep the money or goods. Most native tribes found the treatment of white women disrespectful, and there was just concern about what might happen to Indian women when they became citizens and lost their rights.

Goddess Guide

White Buffalo Calf Woman was a mystical woman who symbolizes purity and renewal for the Sioux people, who lived on the plains. She brought them the sacred medicine pipe and seven teachings that form the pattern for all Sioux ceremonies. The pipe is a central teaching of the Sioux and is used in all ceremonies. Following White Buffalo Calf Woman's instructions, pipes are made from red pipestone hand-quarried by tribal members from the quarries in Minnesota. The pipe is an altar, and smoking is a prayer. Tobacco is a sacred herb in native culture, and as the smoke rises, it carries prayers to the Great Spirit, Wakan Tonka. Like all sacred teaching, the pipe is not restricted to any one race or people, but is a teaching for all.

Marriage was a tribal affair. It was usually arranged—and not always for love. Women could refuse their chosen mate, but it was not a right often exercised. A suitor might bring gifts of horses or other items to the woman's family and then wait patiently for an answer. If rejected, he got his gifts back. If accepted, the family took possession of them. Both of the couple's families were involved in the wedding arrangements, which included feasting and dancing. The newlyweds generally lived with the bride's parents, because Plains Indians traced descent in the maternal line and children belonged to the clan of the mother.

Wise Words

"They are coming to see this!
I am making this place sacred.
They are coming to see this!
White Buffalo Calf Woman will come.
They are coming to see this!
She will sit in a sacred manner.
They are coming to see this!
They are all coming to see this!"

—Lakota song for womanhood ritual from Patricia Monaghan's *The Goddess Companion*

Women as Shamans and Healers

The Plains Indians knew plants and plant medicine. They gathered and used wild berries and herbs for seasoning food, in ceremonies, and for medicine. Both men and women shared plant knowledge and medicine-making, although it is believed that women excelled at it. In some tribes women studied with the medicine man, and others learned healing from their mothers and grandmothers. Commonly, the road to becoming a medicine woman was a long one. Her powers had to be validated by a visitation of a spirit dream, in which she would receive personal instruction and knowledge. This was followed by many years of study and apprenticeship, learning all there was to know about gathering herbs and preparing them. She generally did not qualify to practice on her own until mid-life or later.

A medicine women was considered to have a personal connection to the spirit world, which gave her the ability to heal. She approached healing with the belief that emotions influenced health, and supernatural powers were required to rescue the soul and restore a person to health. Because disease was understood as an imbalance between the physical and emotional world and the world of the spirit, healers worked with an ally from the spirit world, who guided them. The healer worked to restore balance through the use of herbs and prayer.

Sophia's Wisdom

The end of the childbearing years was an important passage for women of the Plains. Respect and distinction accompanied the older women into her later years. An older woman's opinion was valued for its wisdom, and she kept the tribal history. Because the tasks that fell to the younger women took most of their time, grandmothers spent time with the children, teaching them the ancient traditions, skills, and crafts of the tribe.

The priests of the Plains Indians, called shamans, influenced the spirit world. If a woman wanted to enter this highly respected profession, she did so by seeking training from an established shaman. If she was chosen as the shaman's successor, she inherited the shaman's position and used her predecessor's songs and formulas as well as those of her own making. Shamans cured illness, predicted the future, and were the spiritual guardians of the tribe. The realm of both medicine woman and shaman were the most powerful roles in the Plains Indian's society, and they were open to women.

Chief Wilma Mankiller: Absolute Faith in Her People

Wilma Mankiller, former Principal Chief of the Cherokee Nation of Oklahoma, represented the second-largest tribe in the United States, making her task equal to that of a chief executive officer of a major corporation. Some opposed Mankiller's 1987 candidacy—her tires were slashed and she received death threats. But she eventually won the respect of the Cherokee Nation and made an impact on the culture as she has focused on her mission to bring self-sufficiency to her people. Mankiller, the first female principal leader of the Cherokees, approached her job with "absolute faith and confidence" in her people and their ability to solve their own problems.

> ## Wise Words
>
> "Prior to my election, young Cherokee girls would never have thought that they might grow up and become chief."
>
> —Wilma Mankiller, former Principal Chief of the Cherokee Nation of Oklahoma

The Call to Serve

Mankiller's concern for Native American issues was awakened in the late 1960s, when university students drew attention to concerns of native people by occupying Alcatraz Island, the site of a former prison in San Francisco Bay. According to treaty, federal lands revert back to native hands when they are no longer being used by the government. In 1979 when returning home from classes at the University of Arkansas, Mankiller was almost killed in a head-on collision. During her recovery she began reevaluating her life, and it proved to be a time of deep spiritual awakening. A year after the accident, she was diagnosed with myasthenia gravis, a chronic neuromuscular disease that causes varying degrees of weakness in the voluntary muscles of the body. In a further spiritual awakening, she recalls her realization of how precious life is, which spurred her desire to help her people.

Her success in the projects she took on earned Mankiller national recognition as an expert in community development. Her election to deputy chief did not come until two years later. Meanwhile, yet another life-threatening illness struck. Her love of family and community became a source of strength when kidney problems forced her to have a transplant. During her convalescence, she had many long talks with her family, and it was decided that she would run again for chief to complete the many community projects she had begun.

Sophia's Wisdom

Mankiller recalls that the only thing people wanted to talk about with her when she was running for election as tribal chief was the fact that she was a woman, not the innovative programs she was presenting. In her frustration at the sexism she was encountering, Mankiller called a friend on the staff of *Ms* magazine for advice. They had a good laugh, but Mankiller says she can't repeat the exact conversation. She decided to come to grips with the situation and transcend it. And she did, with the help of some words of wisdom she found printed on the back of a tea box: "Don't ever argue with a fool, because someone walking by and observing you can't tell which one is the fool." She took it as good advice and went on to win the election.

Rebuilding the Cherokee Nation

It is plain to see where Mankiller's unshakable faith in her people is rooted. In a talk given at Sweet Briar College on April 2, 1993, she talked about the removal of her people to Indian Territory and their remarkable recovery as a nation. In 1838 President Jackson, following a plan conceived by former President Jefferson, ordered U.S. Army troops to the Cherokee homes, where their property and land was confiscated and they were forcibly taken to stockades throughout the Southeast. Thus, in 1838 the forced march of the Cherokees to Indian Territory began. By the time the last contingent arrived in Indian Territory in April 1839, one fourth of them were dead, having marched on foot in the winter with inadequate clothing or blankets.

Mankiller credits the recovery of her people as a nation to the loss of all their material possessions. Their survival as a nation was in jeopardy, and they had to rebuild the tribe. Through their brutal experiences and great loss of life, they bonded as a people. In less than 10 years, they made remarkable strides toward reestablishing the Cherokee Nation. They formed a new political system with a new constitution, published a newspaper in English and Cherokee, formed a judicial system, and constructed buildings that still stand today. Most important, according to Mankiller, is that they rebuilt their educational system.

> ## Wise Words
>
> "We built an educational system not only for men, but we built an educational system for women, which was a very radical idea for that particular period of time in that part of the world. Our tribal council had no idea how to run a school for girls, and so they sent a group of emissaries to Mount Holyoke and asked the head of Mount Holyoke to send some teachers back to show us how to put together a school for girls. So we built an educational system and began this process of healing and rebuilding ourselves as a people."
>
> —Wilma Mankiller

Mankiller's leadership earned her an honorary doctorate of humane letters from Dartmouth University in 1991. She has worked tirelessly for the Indian Nation and for advancement of females in general. Known for her community leadership, she has also become a spiritual presence for her people and her nation. Awards Mankiller has received include Oklahoma Women's Hall of Fame, 1986; Woman of the Year, *Ms* magazine, 1987; John W. Gardner Leadership Award, Independent Sector, 1988; and National Women's Hall of Fame, 1993. Mankiller makes her home in Oklahoma with her husband Charlie Soap and his son Winterhawk.

In the Voice of Her Ancestors

Today, as always, Native American women continue to be a powerful presence in their communities. They are active in tribal government and participate in society as doctors, lawyers, teachers, entertainers, artists, and in every other profession.

Venerable Dhyani Ywahoo is a Cherokee leader and elder and the twenty-seventh generation of spiritual teachers who have held the ceremonies and rituals of her clan. She is also a recognized teacher in the Tibetan Buddhism tradition, thus her title, Venerable. She is the author of *Voices of Our Ancestors: Cherokee Teachings from the Wisdom Fire* (Shambhala Publications, 1987) and the founder of Sunray Meditation Society.

Receiving the Teachings

In 1969 the elders of the Cherokee nation made the decision that certain Cherokee teachings previously kept within the clan could now be given to the society at large. Ywahoo was chosen to teach this information. Ywahoo subsequently founded the Sunray Meditation Society in Bristol, Vermont, where she offers instruction in both Native American and Tibetan Buddhist practices.

The Ywahoo lineage reaches back 2,860 years, when it was established by the "Keeper of the Mysteries," the Pale One, a mystical teacher. The Pale One was born in a miraculous manner, appearing in many places all over North America at the same time. Every creature could understand his teachings. He brought instruction to the indigenous people about ceremonies, building temples, training for being a priest, and culti-

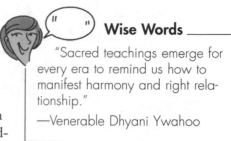

Wise Words

"Sacred teachings emerge for every era to remind us how to manifest harmony and right relationship."

—Venerable Dhyani Ywahoo

vating and maintaining peace within each family, clan, nation, and the planet. This body of knowledge was passed down through oral teachings. Ywahoo received her instructions from her grandfather, Eonah Fisher (Bear Fishing), who received his from Eli Ywahoo, her great grandfather, and from her grandmother, Nellie Ywahoo.

Sunray Meditation Society

The Peacekeeper Mission is the entry level of study offered by the Sunray Meditation Society. The Peacekeeper Mission is a training in personal and communal transformation. It is directed toward instilling peace in the hearts of those who are faithful to the practice. Peacekeeper teachings are rooted in Native American spiritual wisdom of right relationship in the circle of life. The practices include sitting and moving meditations, chanting, work with sacred sound and shape, and community dream practice. The knowledge and skills have an immediate and practical application to one's everyday life. Techniques develop mindfulness and meditation, bringing clarity to the practitioner, which helps in finding life purpose and the skillful means to accomplish one's work in the world. Check Appendix C, "Resources," for information on how to reach Venerable Dhyani Ywahoo and the Sunray Meditation Society.

Many nonnative people are drawn to native spirituality for many reasons. It is the spirituality of this land, and it holds the key to creating the transcended relationship to the earth that many people seek today. Women from many races and religions are hungry for a spirituality that expresses partnership and celebrates the living universe and the presence of the sacred here and now. Paula Gunn Allen reminds women that they do not need to go anywhere else to find a connection to a matriarchy; it is right here on our own continent.

The Least You Need to Know

◆ Most interpretations of native culture come through the eyes of European males and may not give an accurate account, particularly regarding information on women's lives.

◆ The society of many native people is based on matriarchal principles, and women enjoyed a high degree of autonomy in the native cultures before the Europeans arrived.

◆ Native people were denied their religious freedom for almost a century, during which time the survival as a culture was threatened.

◆ Native Americans share a common worldview that includes respect for the earth. Many of these teachings are being shared with nonnative cultures today.

Chapter 17

The Celtic Connection

In This Chapter

- Religious themes of caves and rebirth
- Pagans, Druids, and Neopagans
- What Pagans and Christians share
- All about original grace
- Christianity's wild goose

There's a common thread weaving through the indigenous people of the Bronze Age of Old Europe, the Celtic people of the pre-Christian world, the early Christians, and modern-day Christians. Elemental religious themes have existed through this 25,000-year history, bonding the people to the land and to one another. Despite the fact that to be a Celt means to be of a mixed heritage, the commonalties among these people speak louder than the differences. They have deep connections with one another that have endured throughout time. These connections have provided the "earth" link between Paganism and Christianity, preserving its character as an organic religion connected to the soil of the Near East.

Who Are Pagans?

The term *Pagan* originally comes from the Latin *paganus*, which translates to "country bumpkin" or "hick" and was used as a minor insult by Roman city

Womanspeak

Pagan describes people who practice monotheistic or polytheistic religions based on the deities of the pre-Christian world, exclusive of Judaism. **Neopagan** describes people who reconstruct the religions of the pre-Christian world and follow an ethical and moral system derived from those religions. **Hedonism** is a philosophical belief that holds pleasure as the highest good.

Womanspeak

Original sin refers to the Christian belief that humans were created and then "fell" from God's grace by their sin of disobedience. **Original grace,** although not an officially defined religious term, refers here to humans being born naturally graced by their creator, free from sin.

Goddess Guide

In the 1960s the term *Neopagan* evolved as a description of those people involved in the reconstruction of the old polytheistic pre-Christian religions, or the practice of them adapted to modern time.

folks. Christians began referring to people who worshipped pre-Christian gods and goddesses as Pagans because they often lived in the hinterlands. Over time, *Pagan* became an insulting term tossed around by various religious groups to define anyone who didn't believe the same things they did. Christians called the followers of Islam Pagans, Protestants called Catholics Pagans, and Catholics returned the favor. *Pagan* gradually gained the connotation of those who don't believe in the monotheistic Judeo/Christian God, lumping together atheists and agnostics and with *hedonists* sometimes thrown in for good measure.

Today many people practice the polytheistic religions of the ancient world. New versions of Pagans have reappropriated the term, calling themselves Pagans or more specifically, *Neopagans*.

Original Grace

It could be said that Neopagans believe in *original grace* rather than *original sin*. They believe that life is good and to be alive is rich with spiritual potential. They accept that we are all born ethically and morally neutral and that the community plays a big part in developing spiritual values. Those who believe in reincarnation might say that certain behaviors are carried over from other lifetimes or incarnations, but the belief in karma is not the same as original sin, and not all Neopagans believe in reincarnation.

Neopagans believe that men and women are spiritually equal. They honor both a female and male deity referred to as the goddess and god. Sometimes this godhead is expressed singularly, but more often it occurs as a *pantheon*. Values generally associated as masculine and feminine are respected equally in these communities. However, they are often committed to emphasizing feminine values as a means of balancing today's patriarchal culture. An observer would notice a prominence of goddesses in Neopagan myths and rites, and quite a few Neopagans worship only female deities.

Practice, Don't Preach

Neopaganism, like any other religion, is a way of life. However, people fall short of ideals and make mistakes. In that case, the emphasis is on restitution and reaffirming one's commitment to the ideals s/he stands for, rather than emphasizing punishment. Although there is a wide variety of beliefs within the community of Neopagans regarding the afterlife, it's not a main focus. Pagans put more energy into the spirituality of living in this world rather than the next. It's commonly accepted that wrongdoing carries its own punishment. There is no concept of eternal punishment or damnation. Neopaganism operates from an ethical base rather than from laws and rules.

Neopagans strike a balance between the need for personal autonomy and an awareness that all actions impact the whole of society. For them, society includes other living beings, including the earth. They understand this relationship between individual and community as a dynamic one that is constantly needing renegotiation.

Like other "living" relationships, Neopaganism calls for introspection and self-honesty. Thus, many Neopagans become vegetarians, animal-rights activists, pacifists, and environmental activists. However, individual choice prevails, and depending upon their individual beliefs, you may find Neopagans eating Big Macs at McDonald's, grabbing organic salads at health food stores, or steaming their own veggies at home. Neopagans leave caffeine, tobacco, sugar, alcohol, and other substances up to personal choice.

The Neopagan community considers sex to be one of the good things of life to be enjoyed without guilt and without abuse. Neopagans are tolerant of sexual preferences and alternative relationship lifestyles. In the Neopagan community you will find heterosexuals, homosexuals, bisexuals, transgenders, and some who are undecided. Neopagans may be in a monogamous relationship, be in one or more polyamorous relationships, or

Womanspeak

Pantheon means all the deities of a particular religion considered collectively.

Mother Knows Best

Please don't confuse the worship of Satan with Paganism. One cannot be a Satanist and a Neopagan at the same time. The devil is a character in the Christian worldview. It is not present in Pagan philosophy or religion.

Goddess Guide

Neopagans respect and love nature and believe people are part of it and not the "rulers over it." In fact, what has come to be known as "the Gaia hypothesis" is commonly attributed to a Neopagan by the name of Tim Zell. The Gaia hypothesis states that our planet is a living being. A scientist, James Lovelock, popularized it.

have no romantic relationships at all. A Neopagan may live in a nuclear family, a traditional extended family, or an untraditional extended one.

Many Christian religions struggle with issues of sexuality—gender bias, sexual preference, traditional marriages, and so on. Because Paganism is not of patriarchal derivation, it is almost free of such bias. Judaism's relationship with sex is far more tolerant than Christianity. At the same time, Jewish, Catholic, and Protestant religions have not openly come out for the ordination of gay and lesbian members, and Conservative Jews and Catholics don't ordain women. Catholics still refuse a woman control over her body regarding abortion and artificial birth control, both of which are forbidden. Traditional Judeo-Christian churches tussle with definitions of family. Sexual tolerance is present among certain people and certain congregations, but not really structured into the religions themselves.

Ritual and Ceremony

Neopagans hold a common vision of a peaceful world in which justice reigns and ecological balance is maintained. This vision is expressed in their rituals and ceremonies, which are continually evolving. Rituals are designed to be intellectually stimulating, aesthetically pleasing, and involving the whole person, body, and soul. Neopagans observe the solstices, equinoxes, and the points in between. They also observe the phases of the moon and various ceremonies marking rites of passage such as birth, puberty, personal dedication to a given deity or group, marriage, ordination, and death. (You will find the earth calendar and holidays discussed in greater detail throughout Part 2, "Meeting Goddess.")

Most Neopagans believe that people are involved in a spiritual process throughout their lifetimes and that actions and decisions have meaning as well as obvious consequences.

> **CAUTION**
>
> **Mother Knows Best**
>
> Check your facts before you speak, and don't participate in religion-bashing. Neopagans don't engage in human or animal sacrifices or satanic rituals. Any individual or group who participates in bizarre or criminal behavior is not acting in accord with traditions or principles of any recognized spiritual belief system.

Most believe that healthy religions should have a minimum amount of rigidity and a maximum amount of flexibility. You will find people in the Neopagan community who practice other religions, and they place a high value on respecting one another's beliefs. There is virtually no concept of heresy. Most Neopagans enjoy participating in ecumenical activities with members of other faiths who share similar values, such as Unitarian Universalists, reform Jews, and liberal Catholics. The Unitarian Universalists are one of the first established religious traditions in the United States to officially recognize the Pagan community, and the Covenant of Unitarian Universalist Pagans (CUUPS) has become one of the largest and most active subgroups of the Unitarian Church.

The Modern-Day Druid

Paganism and Neopaganism are sometimes considered religions, and sometimes the name is used as an umbrella to cover a general philosophy that includes many other spiritual communities. Druidism and Wicca are two Neopagan groups that are growing in popularity.

Druid: Person or Religion?

Druidism is a philosophy that includes polytheism or monotheism—god or goddess. You can be a member of a traditional religion and still be a Druid. Some present-day Druids attempt to reconstruct the beliefs and practices of ancient religions, and others create a new version based on the principles of Paganism. Since ancient Druidism was an oral tradition, they did not have a set of written-down scriptures. Some Druidic teachings have survived in Wales, Ireland, and Scotland; in medieval manuscripts; and in oral tradition through folklore and ritual.

The term *Druid* or *Druidism* can be a bit confusing because it describes the priestly class within the Celtic tradition and also a religion that predates the Celts. Remember, these religions developed over many thousands of years without a written text. They endured numerous cultural adaptations, yet historic references show us that they maintained their essential character and beliefs. So if you can be flexible regarding what the religion is called, or what the practitioners are called, the underlying principles remain intact and are the best way of recognizing it.

Womanspeak

Druid comes from a Greek word meaning "oak" and "knowledge," and is a title given to learned men and women in the Celtic tradition who were said to possess "oak knowledge" or wisdom. The same word (Druid) describes the religion itself and the priests within it. **Druidism** is an ancient philosophy that includes both monotheism and polytheism and believes in the sacredness of the earth.

The Players

Three groups or classes of people existed in the ancient Druid culture: bards, ovates, and druids.

- **Bards** kept the memory of the tribe. In Ireland, they trained for many years to become great storytellers, poets, and philosophers.

Mother Knows Best ___

Modern Druidism connects the ancestors' reverence of nature with the scientific knowledge of today to realize we are in trouble if we don't make some changes fast. The belief in having dominion over creation joined with the idea that we are "just passing through" has resulted in ecological arrogance. Druids, like other Pagans, believe in a living universe, with an ethic of mutual respect.

- ◆ **Ovates** worked with the processes of death and regeneration. They were the native healers of the Celts. They specialized in divination, conversing with the ancestors, and prophesizing the future.

- ◆ **Druids,** both men and women, formed the professional class in Celtic society.

Druids performed the functions of modern-day priests, teachers, ambassadors, astronomers, genealogists, philosophers, musicians, theologians, scientists, poets, and judges. They underwent lengthy training—some sources say 20 years. Druids led all public rituals, which were normally held outdoors in groves of sacred trees. Most leaders mentioned in the surviving records were male; however, Christian monks might have deleted references to women exercising religious power from the record during the Celtic Christian era.

The Belly of the Mother

The first spiritual practices in Europe that we know about date back about 25,000 years. Ceremonies involved spending a period of time in a cave, which represented the belly of the Great Mother, followed by a ritual reemergence into the light of day as initiates were reborn. Caves found at Lascaux in France and Altimira in Spain are decorated with mystical paintings of wild animals.

Twenty thousand years later, in approximately 4000 to 3000 B.C.E., in New Grange, Ireland, evidence of the same ritual of rebirth is found. There, a shaft is positioned in the ground to chart the movement of the sun on the winter solstice, marking its path and focusing its light onto huge ceremonial mounds of earth. Following an ancient pattern, disciples held a vigil inside the earth where they sat in darkness and emerged into the morning sunlight to be ritually reborn.

Mother Knows Best ___

Like the names of all other religions, Pagan and Paganism are capitalized, just like Buddhist, Christian, Protestant, or any other religion.

A time of megalithic building produced the great mounds in New Grange, the more famous Stonehenge, and other stone circles all across the landscape of old Europe. The construction of these gigantic structures testifies to the considerable knowledge of astronomy and engineering skills of the cultures that built them. They used "Pythagorean" mathematics 2,000 years before Pythagoras was born!

Stonehenge is a complex of standing stones located in South Central England. Although many people have attributed its construction to the Celts, it was actually built circa 3500 B.C.E., and its current formation was completed circa 1500 B.C.E., almost 1,000 years before the start of Celtic civilization. Whether or not the Celts built the monuments, they most likely performed rituals there and understood its astronomical meanings and uses. The same is true of many ancient altars, beds, rings, stones, stone circles, and temples found in Ireland and Great Britain.

As the Christian church absorbed much of Celtic religion, many of the stories of many Pagan gods and goddesses became entwined with Christian saints. Sacred springs and wells and other Pagan temple sites became the locations of cathedrals. By the seventh century C.E., Druidism itself was fragmented or driven deeply underground throughout most of the formerly Celtic lands.

Goddess Guide

Some historians suggest ancient Druids performed human sacrifices. The references can be traced back to the writings of one individual, Julius Caesar, who may well have been prejudiced against the Celts because of their continual warfare with the Romans and the fact that in war, the enemy is routinely demonized. Some remains of executions have been found in the archaeological record, but it is not obvious whether the victims were killed during religious rituals or to carry out the sentence of a court. There is one reference to human sacrifice in Celtic literature, but it appears to be a Christian forgery. So the bottom line on the subject is that it is undecided whether the ancient Celts engaged in ritual killing; certainly other contemporary societies did. Modern Druids, of course, do not.

Spiritual Inheritance

The ancient teachings of the Druids add an important dimension to the Western spiritual and mystical tradition. Druids were magicians and poets, counselors and healers, shamans and philosophers. In the early days as pre-Celts, they built stone circles and worshipped the forces of nature. Later the Celts blended earlier esoteric teaching and mathematical and engineering skills of the megalithic people with their own artistry and wisdom traditions to create their religion.

Druids worshipped a pantheon of gods and goddesses. Whether they understood this as manifestations of one deity is not known. No Druidic creation story appears to have survived, although there are numerous accounts of the supernatural creation of islands, mountains, and other natural wonders.

Although partly suppressed with the coming of Christianity, Druidism continued to live through schools, folk traditions, songs, and customs of Ireland, Scotland, Wales, England,

and Brittany. It is not entirely clear whether Christianity absorbed it or whether it assimilated into Christianity. Certainly Druidism has survived, and Celtic Christianity maintains a uniqueness that is Druid at the core. The eighteenth century saw a revival of Druid practice, which continues to this day. Today's Celtic Christianity connects its followers to their roots in the ancient cultures of Europe.

They've Got That Magic Touch

The current revival of Celtic culture through music, dance, art, and spirituality speaks to a need within many people to link to their past, feed their ecological imagination, and ground their spirituality back into the soil from which it sprang. Nothing so captures the imagination as Irish folklore and Celtic stories, sometimes making it difficult to separate fact from fiction regarding these tribal, magical, and mysterious people. Perhaps that is precisely the appeal this tradition holds today for those who are searching for the magic missing in our overly technological world. For whatever reasons, many people are exploring the Celtic world through Celtic Christianity and Celtic spirituality.

Grandmother Belle: Root Woman

The Celtic people were intimately involved with the sacred through the constant interplay of ritual and life, acknowledging the divine presence in the natural world. Like other indigenous people, they transmitted their teaching by oral tradition rather than by written word. The Celts used poetry, song, and mythological stories both as poetic expression and to facilitate memory. The Celtic people were tribal, and they bonded through their connection to local gods and goddesses who inhabited the forest, lakes, and streams, making religion and landscape one. Always, the divine spoke to them through nature. This story shows how one woman found her roots through her Celtic heritage.

Emmy lives in Helena, Montana, but grew up in the hills of Kentucky. She is in her mid-30s, with a 7-year-old son and a 5-year-old daughter. Emmy works for the state, and her husband teaches junior high school. "I was raised Christian, and we went to church every time the door opened. I belong to a large 'clan' of family and close friends who got together every Sunday—it is like a family reunion, only it's a regular occasion. I miss them, but I also like being way out here on our own, too. I guess sometimes you have to leave home to find it. I discovered my Celtic culture here, through friends. When I began to trace my spiritual roots back to the soil, my life began to make sense for the first time." Emmy talks about her Celtic connection as a "homecoming."

> **Wise Words**
>
> "Thou King of deeds and power above, Thy fishing blessing pour down on us. I will cast down my hook, the first fish which I bring up, in the name of Christ, King of the elements, the poor shall have it at his wish."
>
> —A Celtic fisherman's prayer

"My grandmother Belle was a root lady. People used to come to her for all kinds of remedies. She had things in jars all over the house, herbs hanging from the ceiling, stuff soaking in barrels, and concoctions simmering on her wood stove. She taught me how to gather, and when I was with her, I felt completely at peace. It was both being with her and gathering the herbs that gave me a sense of my spirituality. I didn't have the words for it until much later, looking back.

"Christianity just didn't make sense to me. I won't say Jesus didn't make sense—I understood him as a healer. But the religion never took hold in me. It has always felt like hearing someone else's stories—stories about people who lived far away on a different kind of land. I always came away from church with a sense of longing, wondering when it would come alive for me. I figured something was wrong with me.

Goddess Guide

The wild goose represents the Holy Spirit for the Celtic people. They found the dove, the traditional Christian symbol for the Holy Spirit, too tame. As they set out from the beach in their small boats, Celts prayed that the wind of the Holy Spirit would take them in the right direction.

Mother Knows Best

It is interesting to note that the overwhelming majority of all human beings who have ever lived were or currently are Pagans.

"I am still a Christian, but now it's not just ideas, it's in my bones. I can see it, taste it, touch it, hear it, walk on it, and lay on it. The Celts are my people. They see God in the plants and trees. Christianity connects for me, when it goes back into the ground. The images of sacred wells and lakes and the spirits that live in them fill me with awe. Christ is the mystery of the forest, the freedom and grace of a field in spring.

"The Holy Spirit is the wind as it comes screaming down the mountain pass out there [Emmy points out her window to the mountains on the horizon], driving a snowstorm into the valley. The spirit of Great Mother is everywhere present. She holds us in her apron, her bounty is endless, and her love is beyond measure. When the natural world becomes the spiritual world, I no longer feel that separation and loneliness. I am back gathering herbs with Grandmother Belle."

Celtic Women: From the Battlefield to the Bedroom

Because women's position in the culture is often ignored or misinterpreted, no one seems to know or agree on the precise status of women in Celtic society. Some sources say that Celtic women occupied an equal place with men in the culture—owning property, choosing their marriage partners, and retaining their independent status and property in marriage. Other sources say that their place was almost equal to men. Still another source reports that it varied from region to region, and over time, and believes women seem to have had some rights and liberties. Regardless, the relationships between men and women was generally good.

In *Sacred Texts by and About Women*, editor Serenity Young (Crossroad, 1994) points out that women seemed to have more status in practice than by law. For example, some codes show limits on women's ownership and sale of property, yet deeds, wills, and the oral literary traditions indicate they frequently inherited, bought, and sold property. In Moyra Caldecott's book, *Women in Celtic Mythology* (Destiny Books, 1988), she tells us that women enjoyed a high place in Celtic society and that it is revealed through their mythology. Oliver Davies and Fiona Bowie, in *Celtic Christian Spirituality* (Continuum, 1995), caution the reader not to think Celtic women enjoyed too great a privilege in the culture—despite powerful stories such as those told about Bridget, the ancient goddess who became a Christian saint, the culture was only marginally less patriarchal than other societies of its time.

> **Wise Words**
>
> "May the road rise up and welcome thee, / May the wind always be upon thy back, / May the sun always warm thy face, / And may the rain fall softly on thy fields."
> —A Celtic prayer of blessing

Heroism certainly was not the exclusive realm of males. Women were known to be fierce fighters, battling side-by-side with their men. Celtic heroes were even named for their mothers. Women took part in politics, but to a lesser degree than men. A woman's primary role was wife and mother. However, a Celtic woman could get a separation from her husband and remarry, thus her status was not as property.

All sources agree that the status of some Celtic women was high and that women in northern Celtic lands enjoyed a higher place in society than they did under Christianity. Celtic women were respected in their culture, even becoming priests, a practice that at this time was not common in the neighboring cultures. Celtic women were known to be "seers" and soothsayers and were consulted as intermediaries between the natural and supernatural worlds. According to some stories, St. Bridget became the bishop of Kildare. As the Celts met the Catholics, it was over the status of women that they had their greatest disagreements. Women were ordained in the Celtic church but not in the Catholic church.

Goddess Guide

Bridget, a favorite goddess of the Celtic people, was later adapted into Christian stories, where her legend continued as Saint Bridget. Her feast is celebrated on February 2. Bridget's praises have been sung, and prayers such as the following one have been offered to her for thousands of years.

"Every day, every night that I pray to the goddess, I know I shall be safe: I shall not be chased, I shall not be caught, I shall not be harmed. Fire, sun, and moon cannot burn me. Not lake nor stream nor sea can drown me. Fairy arrow cannot pierce me. I am safe, safe, safe, singing her praises."

—The Shield of Brigid, Irish Prayer from *The Goddess Companion* by Patricia Monaghan

Celtic Christianity

Celtic Christianity maintained its original character due, in part, to the good sense of St. Patrick. He arrived in Ireland in 432 C.E. and spent his life converting the natives to Christianity. He didn't attempt to abolish existing customs, though. He proposed alterations only where they were in direct conflict with Christian doctrine. Patrick established monasteries across the country where language and theology could be studied, and he introduced the Latin alphabet. Irish monks began to record the great wealth of oral traditions and history.

The character of Irish monasteries and the monks themselves departed from tradition. It is said that Celtic monks carried on a continuous song of praise throughout the day and night in their monasteries, and they often chose their places of prayer in the most remote places in nature. They even stood in the middle of a storm and prayed. They wanted to pray and, at the same time, hear the roaring of the waves. They believed that the storm helped lift their prayers up to the throne. They believed that through their prayers out in the open air they were ministering as priests, uniting heaven and earth.

Sophia's Wisdom

During the Dark Ages in Europe, Irish monasteries served as sanctuary to many of the great scholars and theologians of the day. Many important documents belonging to Western civilization were preserved for all time in Irish monasteries. The great manuscripts of Ireland, most notably *The Book of Kells*, were produced at this time. It is a beautifully illustrated manuscript completed in 800 C.E. The vellum (calfskin) manuscript contains transcriptions of the four Gospels and is lavishly illustrated and ornamented. The scribes and artists who created *The Book of Kells* were monks who lived in a monastery on the remote island of Iona, off the west coast of Scotland. An Irish monk, St. Colm Cille, founded the monastery in the late sixth century.

Celtic Christianity remains close to the ground, keeping its link with the natural world and its poetic understanding of God's mystical presence. Where once gods and goddesses spoke to the Celtic people, it is now the voice of the risen Christ who dwells in nature who speaks. The presence of the Holy Spirit as a creative force in the Celtic imagination is as apparent today as it was in the past. The Celts continue this living relationship through poetry, music, dance, the arts, and most profoundly in their continued connection to nature. Celtic Christianity is calling Christians back to their roots in Celtic soil.

Regardless of whether the women achieved the positions of power in the Celtic religion and social structure that some people believe they did—and there is evidence that points both ways—the structure itself was more affirming of feminine values than what many women experience in today's institutions. The characteristics of Celtic spirituality that have been passed down through history to Christians today are the same qualities that many women strongly identify with and are seeking today:

◆ Intuitive

◆ Imaginative

◆ Lyrical and poetic

◆ Interconnected

◆ Earthy

◆ Sense of world as community

The Least You Need to Know

◆ There is a common thread running throughout history that connects the religions of the ancient world to modern time.

◆ *Neopagan* is a term being reappropriated by today's spiritual seekers who seek connection to the values of an earlier time.

◆ The primary focuses of today's Neopagans are respect for the earth, love of community, freedom to express their religion, and freedom for others to express their religion.

◆ The Celtic culture of old Europe provides a vital link to today's practice of Christianity. It grounds people to an earth-centered spirituality and connects them to their historic roots.

◆ The women who look to Neopaganism, Druidism, and Celtic spirituality do so because their values are affirmed there.

Chapter 18

Wicca: They're Back!

In This Chapter

- ◆ Is Wicca a religion for today's world?
- ◆ Witches: Would you want your sister to marry one?
- ◆ Putting the "magic" back into imagination
- ◆ Hexing—Budapest style
- ◆ Challenges for tomorrow's witch

The practice of Wicca is becoming more mainstream in today's subculture and is rearing its head in traditional places as well. It has gained notoriety and popularity among feminists and also among New Age communities. Wicca falls under the general heading of Pagan religion or spirituality, leaning more toward spirituality. It's practiced in small groups called covens, and it professes no doctrine but instead works from an ethical base. The craft has no written codes and is taught according to oral tradition. However, there is an increasing amount of material written on the subject, and workshops and seminars abound.

If your head is filled with images of black hats, black cats, and broomsticks, you might be in for a surprise—the woman standing next to you in line at the supermarket might be a witch!

Today's Craft

There are many different ways of practicing the ancient art of witchcraft. There is no witchcraft central office or board of directors. Each group is autonomous. The rules of the craft are simple—in fact, you can make that "rule" rather than "rules." The rule is simple: Do what you will and harm no one. In only the most rare cases do witches engage in the practice of "hexing," although they do work "magic" regularly. There are essentially two basic expressions of the craft today: Gardnerian and Dianic.

Which Witch Are You?

Wicca, sometimes called witchcraft, is a revitalizing of an old folk religion that is constantly changing form. It officially reentered the culture about 40 years ago, and since then it has continued gaining popularity in Western society. A person who practices Wicca is called a *witch*, although many witches don't identify themselves with that title due to the huge amount of trouble it has caused in the past, and opt for the title *Wiccans*.

Womanspeak

Wicca stems from the Saxon word *witega*, meaning "a seer or diviner." A **witch** in tribal societies is one who practices healing, divining, or other magical powers.

In 1951 the last of the English laws against witchcraft listing it as a capital crime were repealed. It quickly became clear that the craft had not gone away but had existed just below the surface of society. A retired British civil servant of Scottish descent named Gerald B. Gardner is attributed by many to be the "grandfather" of the neo-Wiccan movement. The story goes that Gardner was initiated into a coven of witches in the New Forest region of England in 1939 by a high priestess named "Old Dorothy" Clutterbuck.

In 1949 Gardner wrote a novel about medieval witchcraft in which he described some of the practices used by the New Forest coven. He published under a pen name because the craft was still against the law. Shortly after the laws were repealed, Gardner released his first nonfiction book, *Witchcraft Today*, in 1954. It supported the theory that modern witchcraft is the surviving remnant of organized Pagan religion that existed during the European witchhunts. As a result of his writing, new groups began forming in the United States in the early 1960s.

Feminist witchcraft, sometimes called *Dianic*, most often honors the goddess exclusively and consists of women-only covens. These groups tend to be freely structured and non-hierarchical, using consensus in decision-making. They have a feminist and ecological focus and are intimate and personally and emotionally supportive. Most covens are open to women of all sexual, cultural, and religious orientations.

Both men and women practice in *Gardnerian* groups, which honor both god and goddess. Sometimes the groups can be somewhat authoritarian and organized hierarchically. Many women's groups have spun off from Gardnerian for just these reasons. They resist the authority and hierarchy and prefer more spontaneity in their rituals. Spin-off groups often continue to have both men and women practicing. They evoke the deity as both goddess and god, although there is more emphasis on goddess. This is done in acknowledgement that there needs to be more female energy to bring balance to the predominantly male culture. These groups usually have both an ecological and feminist agenda. As is common among all Pagan groups, there is an acceptance of different sexual expressions and religious backgrounds.

Womanspeak

Dianic comes from Diana, the Roman version of Artemis, the virgin Goddess of the Moon. The term is used here to describe a particular branch of modern witchcraft that is exclusively female. **Gardnerian** describes a branch of witchcraft that is practiced in mixed groups of men and women and honors both god and goddess.

The Devil Does Not Make Them Do It!

Flip Wilson, an American comedian popular in the 1980s, used to issue the disclaimer, "The devil made me do it!" And indeed, many people blame the devil for a lot of things, giving him credit for a lot more than he actually deserves. Nowhere is that more true than in the practice of witchcraft. Many confuse witchcraft with the alleged devil worship of late medieval and early modern Europe. For many years, mainstay Western religions of Judaism, Christianity, and Islam have held witchcraft in fear and contempt, perhaps falling victim to some of their own press in the process. In so doing, they have lumped together many practices such as tarot cards, *runes*, magic, sorcery, New Age philosophy, crystals, yoga, and sometimes meditation all under the description of the occult, attributing them to devil worship.

Witchcraft has no association with the devil. People who practice the craft point out that the devil is actually a character belonging to Christianity. When Christianity separated the world into spirit and matter, it gave heaven to God and the world to the devil. Since Pagans associate their spirituality with the earth, Christianity named the practice "devil worship."

Womanspeak

Runes are characters from a number of ancient Germanic alphabets usually inscribed on small stones and used like tarot cards to bring insight.

Goddess Guide _____

Wicca belongs to the Pagan revival of this century and has its roots in Europe. Some people claim family lineage that connects them to pre-Christian time. Many of today's Wiccans practice a version of the craft, often combining many philosophies with bits and pieces gleaned from Siberian shamanism, Native American beliefs, Greek Paganism, Egyptian magic, or Celtic spirituality.

In all its forms, Wicca is a religion based on the worship of the Mother Goddess in any of her manifestations. Practitioners answer critics regarding the mixing of different beliefs—when the fact is that all religions have always done the same thing, and it is the nature of the craft to indigenize in each time and place. It blooms where it is planted.

Mother Knows Best _____

Whether you call it privacy or secrecy, Wicca has always preserved its confidentiality. The rule used by many today is an old one: Anyone seeking membership in a coven must wait a year and a day after formally presenting her or his request. This gives the group an opportunity to find out if they want the new member, and the year also is used as a time of study and preparation for entrance.

Imagination, Magic, and Manifesting

Magic is extremely important to the practice of Wicca. It's how thought materializes in the world. Magic follows the same law as any other creative act; it begins in the imagination. For example, someone imagined the Statue of Liberty, the Golden Gate Bridge, and even democracy. They energized the image, and it became manifest. The practice of magic works the same way. Magic begins by imagining a situation or a condition the way you would like it to be. For example, a powerful way to work for world peace is to imagine the world already living in peace and harmony rather than thinking about war.

Goddess Guide _____

The most powerful prayer is a prayer of gratitude, in which you thank the goddess or God in advance because your faith tells you that you have been heard and you believe help is on the way.

The logic behind magic is that we create what we are imaging. Here's how it works. Every thought or mental picture has an emotion tied to it. Most people agree that war is the product of fear. When you are thinking about war and the destruction it brings, you will be generating the emotion fear. Without magic, you have added more fear to the fear already present. There has been no transformation.

Rather than focusing on the destruction of war, magic, a word that describes transformation, uses the power of the imagination to create the opposite image—in this case an image of peace. As the practitioner focuses on the peaceful image and wills it out into the world, feelings of peace are generated and released into the world. In the craft, this is called raising a cone of power. When enough people imagine something, it is said that the idea has caught the public imagination, and it is created.

Imaging world peace does not rule out the need for working for peace in a more active form, too. In fact, personal integrity often requires that kind of direct action. As you go out into the world, do it with a sense of peace about you. The underlying principle is that transformation or change in culture happens as each person takes the responsibility to create the transformed quality in her or his life.

The four traditional essential characteristics of a witch are as follows:

- Faith
- Will
- Imagination
- Freedom

Bewitched and Bothered, but Definitely Not Bewildered

Starhawk is the hands-down living goddess of the Wiccan arm of the women's spirituality movement. She leads rituals, teaches earth spirituality, and counsels women. She was born Miriam Simos in 1951 in St. Paul, Minnesota, raised Jewish, and given a Hebrew education. She went on to the University of California and later received a Master's degree in feminist therapy at Antioch University.

Starhawk taught at the Institute for Creation Centered Spirituality under the direction of Matthew Fox, theologian and former Dominican priest. His institute was housed at Holy Names College in Oakland for many years. It was Starhawk's presence on the faculty that caused the pope to censure Fox, silencing him for one year. Silencing is just what it says—the recipient must not speak publicly or publish during the allotted time. Such a papal order is seldom invoked in modern time.

Spiral Dancing with Starhawk

Starhawk is a popular leader in the Pagan and Wiccan movements. She is the founder of Reclaiming: A Center for Feminist Spirituality and Counseling. The Reclaiming community offers classes, workshops, and public rituals. Star, as she is sometimes called, is a feminist who includes men in her ceremonies and as members of the community. Her "theology" is based on the sacredness of the earth and integrates social and ecological activism into her spirituality and rituals. The Reclaiming community was one of the first pagan groups to directly engage the political structures and has participated in demonstrations against nuclear plants and military bases.

Starhawk has written extensively on the connection between politics and spirituality, and her book, *Spiral Dance: A Rebirth of the Ancient Religion of the Great Goddess*, mentioned in Chapter 13, "How Jewish Women Do It," is a classic among witches and pagans. She teaches and lectures at seminars around the country and at colleges and universities, including Union Theological Seminary in New York, the University of California at San Francisco, and California State University at San Jose and Chico.

The Charge of the Goddess

The Charge of the Goddess appears in many places, but no one knows its exact origins. Starhawk's version, in which she has updated the language, appears in her book *The Spiral Dance*. Here is a part of the piece; the rest can be found in her book (see Appendix C, "Resources"):

"I, who am the beauty of the green earth and the white moon among the stars and the mysteries of the waters, I call upon your soul to arise and come unto me. For I am the soul of nature that gives life to the universe. From me all things proceed and unto me they must return. Let my worship be in the heart that rejoices, for behold—all acts of love and pleasure are my rituals. Let there be beauty and strength, power and compassion, honor and humility, mirth and reverence within you. And you who seek to know me, know that your seeking and yearning will avail you not, unless you know the Mystery; for if that which you seek, you find not within yourself, you will never find it without. For behold, I have been with you from the beginning, and I am that which is attained at the end of desire."

Margot Draws Down the Moon

Margot Adler is the New York Bureau Chief for National Public Radio and author of *Drawing Down the Moon*, a comprehensive study of Neopaganism written in 1979 that is still considered one of the definitive books on the subject. Margot is a witch who travels (by plane, not broomstick) throughout the United States, leading rituals and workshops and speaking about Wicca and other Neopagan traditions.

Ritual Born of Desire

Adler's longing for ritual ignited when she saw her Catholic friend's first Communion dress and veil. Adler was raised in a Jewish/Marxist/Atheist home; her father told her she belonged to "the brotherhood of man," a neighborhood she found spiritually boring. Now Adler talks about ritual as a way human beings can connect to each other, ending the feeling of alienation by feeling connection to the earth community. She says, "Ritual returns us to our sense of attunement with the universe, to reconnect us with who we really are."

Adler knows that in our busy lives it is difficult to squeeze in one more thing. That is why she talks about calling on the elements as you take a shower or in blessing your food. Sometimes a ritual is accomplished by a quick glance at her altar on top of the filing cabinet at the office. Adler demystifies ritual by reminding people that they don't have to have all the bells and whistles.

She likes Paganism because it isn't about beliefs or creed; it's about practice and ceremony, and she likes its sense of tribe. Adler was introduced to the craft through the Gardnerian tradition but has adapted her own version of it. She finds the craft today much less sexist and much more focused on the environment than when she first encountered it. She feels that both she and Starhawk had an influence in shaping its present feminist and political character. Starhawk's *The Spiral Dance* came out the same year Adler's book was published, and both are classics in the movement.

Encounters with Artemis and Athena

Adler knows the importance of having young girls grow up with powerful images of women. She remembers encounters she had with Artemis and Athena during a year she spent studying in Greece when she was only 12. The basic philosophy of women's spirituality is that *we* are sacred. Both the women's movement and earth spirituality give women permission to celebrate their body and mind—making everything we do sacred. Adler sees women's spirituality as supporting and enriching feminism by empowering women, removing any limits to what they can accomplish in their own lives and in their communities, giving them the power to remake the world.

> **Wise Words**
>
> "I believe the women's spirituality movement has gained such tremendous momentum so quickly because it helps women see themselves as part of divine reality. Traditional religions don't have a place for women—we were disinherited from the ministry centuries ago. Let's face it—women were left out of the deity game."
>
> —Margot Adler

A challenge Adler sees as the movement grows is how to avoid the temptation to institutionalize as it shifts from a private spirituality to a more public one. She wonders if the movement will sacrifice autonomy and diversity and how it will handle issues of power and dogma if it goes mainstream. Adler believes it does well as a minority religion because it provides a critique of the larger society. Regardless of the challenges, she is in it for the long haul. She agrees with the philosophy of women's spirituality and finds the practice satisfying.

Straight up with Zsuzsanna Budapest

Uncontrollable, outspoken, charismatic, troublemaker, and visionary are words used to describe the legendary Zsuzsanna Budapest, founder of the feminist religion Dianic witchcraft. Budapest, or "Z" as she is known, was born in Hungary in the middle of a Siberian blizzard in 1940 and calls herself a genetic witch. Her early goddess consciousness was formed at her mother's knee, watching her sculpt statues of the female divinity. She learned herbal remedies from her grandmother and was raised with the stories of the gods and goddesses. Budapest traces her family tree back to 1270. She is an author, ritual leader, and teacher.

Like other forms of Wicca, Dianic witchcraft is a nature-based religion that pays respect to both the god and goddess; however, only the goddess is worshipped. In tipping her hat to the male principle of the universe, she assures students that he is a "good boy," but "we just don't pray to male gods." In her teaching she also points out that women are daughters of the moon; the female's reproductive cycles and psyche are ruled by the moon. Dianic witchcraft allows only women.

Progression of Witchcraft in Modern Time	
1951	Witchcraft is removed from the capital crimes list in England.
1954	Gerald Gardner publishes *Witchcraft Today*.
1960s	The craft reenters the counterculture as part of an underground movement.
1970s	Zsuzsanna Budapest publishes *Feminist Book of Lights and Shadows*. Feminist spirituality is born.
1979	*The Spiral Dance* is published, in which Starhawk sets out the principles and structure of witchcraft. *Drawing Down the Moon*, a comprehensive survey of the movement, is published by reporter Margot Adler.
1987	*The Goddesses and Gods of Old Europe* by Marija Gimbutas presents a comprehensive look at the images of the pre-Christian world.
1990s	Appropriation of witchcraft by numerous communities.
2001	Still growing …

Living-Room Witches Need Apply

In the early 1970s the feminist movement made little mention of religion or spirituality. Many feminists dismissed spirituality as navel-gazing, which took time and energy away from activism. Budapest saw it differently. She believed the movement needed spiritual underpinnings, and she offered what she describes as "a new kind of trust ... we are learning to trust our souls." She brought the spiritual and political camps together and created a new religion that affirmed feminist values—Dianic wicca. Budapest takes credit for originating the term "feminist spirituality."

> **Wise Words**
>
> "A witch bows to no man. Feminist witchcraft is natural female power, fueled by emotional necessity, and delivered by those brave women who consider slavery of the soul and emptiness of the heart more of a threat than not being safe."
>
> —Zsuzsanna Budapest

Budapest has nothing but ill-disguised disdain for "living-room" witches—a term to describe women she feels don't make the full commitment to the tradition. She believes true witchcraft is spontaneous, passionate, and comes from the heart. She finds some modern versions of it boring. In her version, papers with written instructions are not allowed! Her practice and her teaching community are nonhierarchical, and the rituals have only the most minimal structure. Here she lays out the bare bones of a ritual: Four people call in the four corners of the universe, everyone holds the intention of the ritual that is decided by group consensus, power is raised and released, and the four corners are thanked. Those who are participating improvise the middle part of the ritual.

Pushing the Hexing Envelope

Of all the concerns raised from both those practicing the craft and outsiders, the one guaranteed to make the hair on the collective necks of all involved stand straight up is hexing! Hexing smacks of lawlessness, black-pointed hats, and dolls with pins in their backs. Isn't hexing the very thing most witches are accused of and staunchly deny? It is no wonder that when Budapest advocates for it she pushes the hexing envelope off the edge of the desk. Yet when you hear her out, a different understanding emerges.

Budapest is talking about women taking back their power specifically and only in cases of rape. She encourages them to plead their case to the goddess, to seek retribution through her, but make no requests as to how that retribution should happen. Rather than collapsing into a victim mentality, the hex or spell becomes a proactive demand for justice. How that is affected is left up to the goddess; the woman performing the hex simply asks that justice be done. According to Budapest, the fear people have about hexing translates as fear of women gaining power.

Goddess Guide

Florence Anderson of California tells of being accused in court of law of casting a spell on her son-in-law, who died quite suddenly and unexpectedly of rectal cancer after molesting her three-year-old granddaughter. The man's mother protested Anderson gaining custody of the child, accusing her of being a witch. In fact, a healing circle had preceded the unexpected news of her son-in-law's illness, in which many women prayed for justice to be served. What really happened? Florence shrugs her shoulders, and with eyes wide open and the corners of her mouth turning upward ever so slightly says, "Thy will be done!"

For Budapest, the goddess has a cheekier aspect than some want to acknowledge. However, the goddess has always dealt in death and destruction as well as birth and nurturing—protection of women was one of Artemis's primary roles. Budapest has no problem calling on this power when it is appropriate. Giving women a sense of a powerful figure in their corner backing them up is a necessary part of healing. Budapest reminds us what we're really talking about here is balancing the patriarchal scales and the absolute imperative of the craft that whatever one wishes upon another will be returned to sender times three!

The Least You Need to Know

◆ Wicca is part of the Pagan movement that is currently resurfacing in the United States as well as in many other parts of the world.

◆ Wicca is a religion that has roots in pre-Christian Europe but is not to be confused with false accusations that were made about it during the late Middle Ages and early modern time in European history.

◆ The practice of Wicca in no way invokes the devil or engages in negative behavior such as wishing bad things on people.

◆ Wicca promotes positive images for women, equality between men and women, and ecologically sound living.

Chapter 19

Spiritual Instinct

In This Chapter

- ◆ Is morality in your body?
- ◆ How intuition really works
- ◆ Getting in touch with yourself
- ◆ You can dowse for water; can you dowse for a new job?

A substantial number of women believe that much of what they were taught about religion, particularly as it pertains to women and their place in the world, has not been true, and they don't draw on traditional sources of authority. Does it leave them flying the ethical skies with no moral compass? Not necessarily. They believe there's a source within each of us that offers guidance based on common sense, a source that can be trusted. You can call this moral system *spiritual instinct*.

Morality Is in Your Titty!

I once had the privilege of studying with Luisha Teisch, and I have never forgotten her instructions on intuition and spiritual instinct. The institute where she was teaching attracted people willing to step outside their world and look at new perspectives. Teisch certainly offered that.

I can see her now as she paced back and forth in front of the class in an exaggerated strut, declaring, "Morality is in your titty! It is in your big toe, your gut, your neck, and in your titty!" The declaration was accompanied by appropriate gestures. What she was saying is that if you are thinking about doing something that isn't good for you emotionally, physically, or morally, some part of your body will give you an indication that you are on the wrong track. She's describing spiritual instinct. *Instinct* are those innate aspects of intelligence or behavior that are not learned—they are innate. Instinct and *intuition* are installed by the creator; they're Goddess- or God-given. Another way of describing innate knowing is that it refers to the indwelling of Holy Spirit. It is our spiritual instinct.

Sniffing the Wind

Many of the practices you've been reading about, such as building your home altar, creating a ritual to honor what you need honored, meditating, going on guided journeys, and just taking a day to yourself when you need to, are about reconnecting to your instincts. Living instinctively means following your inner guidance, and that sometimes puts you at odds with the culture. The culture tells you if you follow a certain pattern (theirs), you will be successful and happy. The truth is, this very seldom happens. If following the "norm" does not harmonize with your personal tune, you will be flying into the fan, swimming upstream, fighting an uphill battle—take your pick of these or mix your own metaphor!

Following your instincts often means doing things that don't have the immediate sense of logic that we have grown accustomed to. The intuitive mind is logical; however, it doesn't use a linear process. It works from what might seem to be a random pattern, but then when you least expect it, a very "logical" decision has been made—something emerges that is of greater proportion and depth than you would have imagined possible.

Joseph Campbell, world-renowned scholar and authority on mythology, talked about following your bliss during interviews with journalist Bill Moyers for the popular book, *The Power of Myth* (Doubleday, 1988). Most people talk about following their heart or what brings them joy. We're going to talk about following your spirit. That seems easy enough. Then why do so few people actually do it? There are two reasons that immediately come to mind. The first is that we are conditioned to not trust our inner guidance, to disbelieve it, to "get that idea right out of your head." Second, our connection to inner guidance has become dulled, and some people don't even hear it. Neither of these reasons is good enough to keep you locked into dull and uncreative situations. We'll look at a couple ways you can practice sharpening your intuitive skills and get the lines of communication flowing between you and your instinct.

Your Bi-Cameral Mind

You might remember the word *bi-cameral* from grade school. It describes the House of Representatives and the Senate, which have slightly different functions and work to balance one another. In order to have a law passed, both bodies have to agree. Your brain works a bit like that. One hemisphere is the intuitive side, and the other is the structural side. The right hemisphere connects you to your inner world. It monitors your physical body, your emotions, your dream world, and your imagination. It's your source of inspiration and where your new ideas come from. The left hemisphere sorts through your inspirations, makes practical decisions, and carries out plans. It connects you with the world outside yourself and is involved with form and structure. Think of the two hemispheres as a unified effort.

The following table lists the brain functions belonging to each side of the brain. As you can see, one quality is not better than the other; we need access to corresponding skills to be fully functioning and balanced. Holistic thinking engages both hemispheres of the brain, using the dual nature of each quality in a complementary way.

Right Hemisphere	Left Hemisphere
Primary (cause)	Secondary (effect)
Internal/subjective	External/objective
Sensate	Verbal
Feeling	Thinking
Concrete	Abstract
Free	Directed
Metaphoric/symbolic	Material
Imaginative	Structural/form
Emotional	Mental
Relational (sees connections)	Differentiates
Intuitive logic	Rational logic
Gestalt/concurrent	Linear/sequential

continues

continued

Right Hemisphere	Left Hemisphere
Receives revelation	Discernment
Spirituality	Religion
Faith	Law/rule/set of beliefs

Setting Your Body Clock

Most of us operate from the left hemisphere of the brain as we go about the day. Every 90 minutes or so the dominance switches, and we swing over to the other hemisphere, where we'll spend about 20 to 30 minutes, relaxing and regenerating. I probably don't need to tell you that most of us override our body's natural process of relaxing every hour and a half. This is when you find you're feeling tired, concentration becomes difficult or even impossible, and you keep spacing out no matter how hard you try to remain alert. This is when you often take a trip to the water cooler, the coffee pot, the smoking room, or the candy machine!

However, if you allow yourself to go through your whole cycle of resting and relaxing, you will disconnect from the external world and become internally focused for a while. You will not be aware of what your body is doing in those internal moments; you will just be resting. Your brain waves will slow down; your thinking mind will become quiet; and your brain will be busy attending to internal affairs. Stress is released; blood pressure is regulated; the immune system is strengthened—every single physical system is checked and adjusted. And your instinct talks to you, giving you information that will help you make healthy decisions.

When this is finished, your focus shifts back to the external world, and you return to what you were doing, refreshed and relaxed. This looping back and forth is called your *ultradian* rhythm. It corresponds to the dream cycle you experience at night.

Womanspeak

Ultradian describes the cycle of right- and left-brain dominance that goes on throughout the day, corresponding to the REM dream cycle of sleep.

So what has all this got to do with instinct? Well, for one thing, it's a good way to understand that our instinct is functioning all the time, even if we don't realize it.

Your instinct knows a lot about you. It knows what you need, when you need it, and how much of it you need. The left hemisphere, which is subject to social conditioning, can override this information and keep on keeping on, even when your health is in danger.

When this happens routinely, your body will get a cold or some other physical condition that will shut things down for a while and let you rest.

Following Your Spirit

In religious or spiritual terms, the right brain's instinctive process equates to innate wisdom or divine instructions, and the left brain, or rational mind, equates to free will. Your instinctive mind will let you know whether something is having a positive or a negative effect on you. You have the choice of how you respond. You've probably been taught to practice moral behavior toward others. Most religious instruction covers that area. We're going to turn the tables a bit and focus morality within—meaning it has to do with how *you* treat *you!* Of course, in the long run both are important.

Goddess Guide

There are times when it serves a greater good to override the body's signals and stay on task. For example, a parent tending to a sick child might realize he or she is tired but choose to stay with the vigil. This is a matter of individual choice, and making healthy choices requires that we first become aware of the signals we are getting, assess the situation, and make our choice with spiritual awareness.

As you will learn in the next chapter, scientists and psychologists are now discovering how our moral choices affect our health. Good decisions are reflected in strengthening your spirit, or life force, and making your body strong. Poor decisions have the opposite effect—they weaken your life force. It doesn't matter whether the decision is about selecting the right food, getting enough rest, or telling a lie. It all registers as a negative in your body.

Does this mean that sickness is a sign that we aren't being moral? No, not necessarily. There are many reasons for illness. However, we are willing to say that health is often the result of your making good choices about what you eat, how you rest and exercise, where and with whom you spend time, etc. These decisions form the basis of your relationship with you, which is the first step to moral development. You can learn how to use your intuition to determine if your choices are physically healthful—and morally right.

A Meeting of Your Minds

To make contact with your intuitive mind, you must first learn how to go into an alpha state, or learn how to relax. Here is an exercise that will lower your brain waves and let you relax enough to be able to feel what is going on in your body. The slower you go with it and the more you focus, the better it works.

Take six deep breaths all the way down into your belly. Make them slow and very intentional. As you pay close attention to the breath, feel it as it enters your nostrils, goes down your windpipe, and fills your belly with air. Hold it in your belly for a few seconds. As you release the breath, stay aware of it as it leaves your body. Notice how your body feels as you release the air. Repeat the process again, slowly. Each time you release the air, feel how your body softens. Feel how you relax. After you have taken six belly breaths, relax and allow your breathing to continue at its own pace. Notice how it feels inside your body.

Let your imagination take you to a place in nature you really like to visit. It can be a real place, or it can be a place you completely invent in your mind. Maybe you will see it on your inner screen, or maybe you will connect to it another way by sensing you're there. When you find yourself at your place in nature, take a deep breath and draw the feelings of the place into your body. Answer these questions silently: What does the air smell like? What sounds are there? Do you hear water, birds, the movement of the wind in the trees? What are the colors? What shapes? What textures? Are you up high or down low? What is the temperature? Is the air moving? What kind of light is there? Is it daytime or night? Take a deep breath and notice how your body feels in this image.

From this relaxed place, learn how your body feels when it is telling you "no." Repeat the word over and over in your mind, and then pause and see what sensations you are receiving from your body.

Now do the same thing with "yes."

Go back and forth, focusing on no, then on yes. Allow time to let the feelings surface. Before long you will begin to feel a definite difference between yes and no.

Things that have a negative result on your body weaken your spirit or life force. Your body loses energy even when you are *thinking* about something that isn't good for you, whether it's something to eat or drink, a relationship, or an action you are considering taking. Likewise, your life force strengthens when you approach something that is good for you. Both responses have a physical feeling that you will eventually be able to get in touch with. That's your innate moral instinct.

Here's another way you can access your innate wisdom. Begin with your belly-breathing exercise. Wait until you feel you are connected with your inner world, then stand up, close your eyes, and imagine whatever it is you are seeking information about. If it's a product, you can hold it in your hand, but that isn't mandatory. As you are imagining your question, does your body swing forward or backward? Swinging forward generally means positive, and swinging backward means negative, but you may want to check your own set of responses.

Goddess Guide

Working with a partner, extend your arm out in front of you straight from your shoulder. Your partner will stand alongside your arm but not in front of you. Say, "Partner: Give me a yes response," and your partner will place her hand on your wrist and gently push down on your extended arm. Resist and attempt to hold your arm at the same level. Let your arm rest before going on. Next, using the same arm, repeat the exercise saying "no." Your body loses energy when the answer is no, and you cannot hold your strength. After you establish your yes and no responses, it doesn't matter what you're asking; your instinct knows whether it is good for you or not.

Dowsing: Intuition in Motion

Did you ever wonder how people found out about the natural world before there were science laboratories? How did they discover which herbs worked for what condition and which ones you should step over with caution? They didn't give them to the cat to eat while they watched to see if it passed out on the kitchen floor; they used their intuition. Your body will tell you what is good for it and what isn't. You just have to learn how to listen and how to trust it. Another name for this is *sixth sense*. Sixth sense is way of perceiving in addition to the five senses—touch, taste, smell, sight, and sound. As scientific principles developed, we began to rely on them rather than on instinct. Yet it's good to remember that every scientific principle has evolved from an intuitive process. Someone got a hunch about how something worked and began to experiment.

Tuning In to Cosmic Resonance

Dowsing is one way your instinct can communicate with you. Dowsing uses a forked stick or metal object to sense underground water or other minerals. It's not the stick that senses the water, it's you. The stick only measures your reaction. Dowsing is thousands of years old yet still used today by engineers and farmers alike. It is based on the principle of a living universe. Everything is energy in motion—all substances vibrate. Each individual "thing" has its own frequency. Your body contains countless atoms and molecules that are made from the same elements that exist in the earth. (This may sound familiar to you: Scripture says that we were formed from the clay of the earth.) Each cell in your body is resonating at a particular frequency, which becomes your personal cosmic tune, or harmonic resonance.

We are also part of the cosmic symphony. We are continually receiving and reacting to the symphonic resonance coming from many sources. The dynamics of this energetic exchange alter the chemical balance in your brain, forming your moods and emotions. Sometimes these exchanges are very obvious, such as a sudden clap of thunder or a crack of lightning. We're very aware of the physical and emotional surges this causes. More often these changes are quite subtle, and we may be totally unaware of what has caused them.

Sophia's Wisdom

The theory of resonance says that when a note is struck in one instrument, such as a piano on one side of the room, the same note begins to vibrate in another instrument on the other side of the room. Your body works on the same principle. You resonate with the vibrations of many different frequencies all around you, usually at a very subtle level that is barely discernable. You can sharpen your instincts to the point you can actually sense the different signals and know what you are sensing. Many indigenous people have a highly developed relationship with their environment that allows them to perceive even the slightest variations.

You are constantly receiving vibrations, through both the technological world and the natural one. Every first-grade teacher will tell you that kids can predict the weather. Just before the barometer drops and a rain blows in, they are registering it in their bodies and are getting restless. Cows are still used to predict earthquakes and can do it better than scientific equipment. Then there are Grandma's arthritic knees and the emergency room at the hospital, which fills up on nights of the full moon. You're in constant communication with your environment on a physical level. You can't pay attention to it all the time, or you wouldn't get anything done. Because you have many layers of perceptions, most of the sorting goes on at the subconscious level, unless it is something you need to know, in which case your subconscious mind brings it to conscious level. Dowsing is a tool that amplifies these subtle or subconscious reactions. It shows you what your body is reacting to.

Old-Time Dowsing

Our ancestors practiced dowsing, although they probably didn't need an object to amplify it, because they would have felt it through one of their physical senses. Technically, you can feel it without an object, too, although few people want to spend that much time developing the skill. Using an object lends an extra bit of proof that something is going on and it makes it more believable. As you practice dowsing, you can't help but make the association between the dowsing tool and your internal sensor. Eventually, your ability to read your signals will improve. Living in the technological world makes it necessary to filter many of your perceptions. That's one reason why getting out in the country makes you feel good. As your senses awaken, you literally "come alive!"

Mother Knows Best

Knowing things intuitively is easy. Allowing yourself to know what you know is the challenge!

The survival of our early ancestors depended on their ability to sense the smallest and most subtle changes in their environment. To be able to "feel" danger well before it became a physical threat meant that they were able to survive. You don't have to sharpen your skills to that degree, but you could if you wanted to. Dowsing registers responses coming from your physical, emotional, and intuitive aspects.

◆ **Physical.** Dowsing can amplify reactions you are having to your natural or artificial environment. You can find out if particular places, plants, foods, or just about anything is good for you. You can even find those missing keys, glasses, or even your cell phone. But you can't find your missing dowsing rods!

◆ **Emotional.** Dowsing can bring insight to emotional patterns that may be complicating a situation and tell you what will work and what won't in changing it.

◆ **Intuitive.** Dowsing can give you psychic or intuitive information that falls outside of your normal perception of linear time, space, physical consciousness, or reality.

Sophia's Wisdom

Everyone has the ability to dowse. When you are willing to explore something with a beginner's mind and suspend critical judgment, you open up enough space for new information to reach you. You can always analyze it later.

As the Pendulum Swings

The pendulum is probably the easiest dowsing tool to make. It's simple to carry (you can wear it!) and can be made of almost any type of material. To make a pendulum, you need a string or chain—any length from a few inches to 10 or 12 inches—and an object of sufficient weight so that it will swing freely. Hold the string with your first and second fingers and thumb, suspending the object so that it swings freely. Here's how to begin making friends with your pendulum.

Getting to Know You

When you work with a pendulum, you are really working with your own energy. The pendulum is only a tool to measure impulses or very slight movements. Often people attempt to discount the information gained through a pendulum by saying "Oh, you're making it move." Well, they're right—but they are missing the point. You are making the pendulum move from your subconscious mind. It is true that you can influence it from the conscious level if you want to; however, what would be the point? Working with a pendulum can put you in touch with information that is generally not available in normal awareness. It is a valuable tool for gaining insight.

Here is a short exercise showing how to begin working with a pendulum. Take time to meditate for a few minutes before you begin. It's necessary to be in a relaxed or alpha state so that your subconscious mind can be engaged.

- Relax, breathe, and enter an alpha state.
- Speak to the pendulum as if it were a separate thing from you (even though it isn't).
- Ask it to show you its neutral position.
- Ask the pendulum to show you what a "yes" answer is.
- Return to neutral.
- Ask the pendulum to show you what a "no" answer is.
- Return to neutral.
- Repeat the exercise one more time to make certain you have connected with your pendulum.
- Relax.

Mother Knows Best

Don't try to boss your pendulum around. If you "think" you know how it is supposed to work, you'll stop the process. Your conscious mind has just taken over. Always ask for it to tell you its signal system while you go into a passive or receptive mode.

Now you're ready to use your pendulum. Here's how:

- Breathe, relax, and enter an alpha state.
- Let your pendulum operate in neutral position for 30 seconds while you and "it" get into sync with each other.
- Focus on your question and ask the pendulum if this is an appropriate subject.
- You can only ask yes or no questions.
- If the answer is no, either go to another subject or leave it until another time.

Some Do's and Don'ts on Dowsing

Here are some suggestions that will help you become a successful dowser. Remember, everything that uses your instinct or intuition works best when you suspend judgment, and just see what happens. You can always judge it later.

- Do take a couple of deep breaths and relax before dowsing. Go into an alpha state.

- Do pay attention or focus on the object or situation you are dowsing about.

- Do practice. The more you do it, the better you get.

- Don't continue if your pendulum says no when you ask for permission. Reframe your question, or come back to it later.

- Do suspend judgment and approach it with a sense of exploration. Use a kindergarten mind.

- Don't do tricks for others. Dowsing is personal, and doesn't respond well to being shown off.

- Do be humble and respectful of the process.

Remember that the pendulum, like other dowsing tools, is an extension of your deeper knowing. Sometimes asking questions that have a lot of emotional charge to them interferes with the accuracy. In this case, you can have someone else dowse for you. The surrogate dowser can ask the question directly, or you can ask it through them. Oh, just in case you're wondering, it isn't ethical to ask for information about another person without permission. You wouldn't be able to trust the answer anyway.

The Least You Need to Know

- You have an inborn sense of right and wrong called spiritual instinct.

- The functions of the two hemispheres of the brain complement one another and together create the whole.

- With practice and concentration, you can learn how to directly read your innate system and know what is good for you and what is not.

- Dowsing is an ancient way of interacting with your intuitive mind to help bring insight to a situation.

- There is really no limit on what you can dowse for, although it isn't considered ethical to dowse for information about someone else unless they have asked you to do so.

Chapter 20

The Soulbody

In This Chapter

- How right living is your best insurance plan
- Mystical teachings encoded in the body
- Locating the body's natural wisdom centers
- How your body leads you to enlightenment

There are seven major energy centers in the body. Each governs the functions of particular organs and emotions, and also contains the process for spiritual development. These energy centers are called chakras. *Chakra* is a *Sanskrit* word meaning "whirling light." Each chakra relates to a Hindu god or goddess, showing the embodied spirituality of the system. Your body's chemistry not only takes you through physical developmental stages of growth but also has the chemicals for your transcendence, as well.

Body and Soul

Soulbody describes the unified physical, emotional, mental, and spiritual aspects of a person. *Holistic healing* describes the healing techniques that engage the soulbody. Many holistic healing techniques have been in constant use for more than 4,000 years and are used all over the world, yet have not been adopted by the medical system in the United States. For example, the medicinal use of herbs is standard in Europe, India, Asia, Africa, and the Americas, and acupuncture is widely practiced all over Asia as well as in many other countries around the world, yet both are just beginning to be accepted into Western medicine.

Womanspeak

Sanskrit is the old Indo-European language of ancient India. **Chakra** is a Sanskrit word meaning "whirling light." It describes energy centers in the body that generate physical, emotional, and spiritual well-being. **Soulbody** is a term that describes our simultaneous and unified experience of self as physical, emotional, mental, and spiritual beings. **Holistic healing** describes healing practices that integrate the whole person in the healing process addressing the physical, emotional, mental, and spiritual levels, thus the whole self.

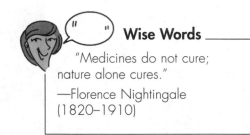

Wise Words

"Medicines do not cure; nature alone cures."

—Florence Nightingale (1820–1910)

This atmosphere is changing, however, as a growing number of medical doctors are realizing that some of their patients are healing faster and more effectively when they are treated with both Western and holistic medicine. Many people are now educating themselves in the variety of healing methods available to them and are combining the best of both worlds.

What Is Holistic Healing?

Holistic healing is both a philosophy and a method of health care that integrates the whole person—body, mind, emotion, and spirit—in the healing process. It believes that

Sophia's Wisdom

Holism is based on a philosophical understanding of the interconnection of our physical, emotional, mental, and spiritual parts (soulbody) and how they all interact in creating health and well being. There are many healing modalities based on holistic philosophy. All work from a common understanding of the life force and have an integrated understanding of how health is maintained.

when those four systems are balanced and supported, the soulbody generates healing energy. Holistic healing utilizes natural healing techniques and remedies to help find that balance and to create the necessary support and requires the patient to become active in his or her healing process through personal desire, intent, and lifestyle choices that support health. It is fair to say that holistic healing is as much dependent on self-healing as it is on direct treatment by a practitioner. Patients are encouraged to lead balanced lives including eating a healthful diet, getting regular exercise and enough rest, experiencing some form of creative expression, working toward a positive self-image, and participating in a spiritual practice. Like many things in nature, this philosophy has a high degree of common sense behind it.

In addition to anatomy and physiology, holistic healing is based on the energetic system that flows through the body, the life force or *chi*. When the energy is open and flowing, the body enjoys its naturally healthy state. When the energy is weakened as can happen for a variety of reasons—such as poor diet, toxins, worry, or any other sources of stress you might encounter—the flow of chi is blocked and health is compromised.

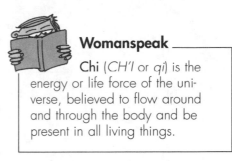

Womanspeak

Chi (*CH'I* or *qi*) is the energy or life force of the universe, believed to flow around and through the body and be present in all living things.

Holistic healing supports the soulbody to keep the energy flowing, which strengthens the life force. When the life force is strong, the body's natural defense systems protect it from disease.

Common Holistic Practices

The following are descriptions of several common holistic practices currently being used in traditional Western medical settings as well as holistic clinics throughout the country. They are based on a 4,000-year-old "new" paradigm and have been proven to be effective in assisting the body heal disease and alleviate stress by supporting the soulbody. They are often used in combination with traditional treatments.

- **Acupuncture** originated in China and is used to treat a variety of disorders by inserting needles into the skin at points where the flow of energy is blocked.
- **Acupressure** is based on the same principles as acupuncture but uses finger pressure rather than needles on specific points along the body.
- **Reflexology** applies direct pressure to points on the feet or hands that correspond to organs and systems in the body, relieving tension and resulting in positive changes in the soulbody.
- **Herbology** applies knowledge of the healing property of plants both internally and externally to prevent illness and to rejuvenate the soulbody's systems.
- **Imagery** is an ancient technique that heals through the imagination, directly engaging a person in his or her healing process.
- **Reiki** is a healing technique in which practitioner senses the client's energy field and, through a series of movements, assists the flow of energy.

Meet a Medically Intuitive Theologian

Caroline Myss earned her Bachelor's degree in journalism in 1974, her Master's degree in theology in 1979, and her Ph.D. in energy medicine in 1996. She is a *medical intuitive* who draws on theology as well as biology and is able to accurately diagnose illness through her

Womanspeak

A **medical intuitive** is someone who can diagnose illness through perceptional insight rather than through the five senses.

Goddess Guide

There is a Buddhist saying that tells us that the way to the "higher self" is through the "lower self." This means that if we aren't feeling safe and secure, it is difficult to address life at the aesthetic or philosophical level.

intuition. She also has the medical training to understand what her intuition is telling her. She has discovered that the great spiritual teachings of four world religions—Hinduism, Buddhism, Judaism, and Christianity—are all saying the same thing—spirituality is encoded in the body.

Myss's observations and study of the spiritual teachings of those four world religions have shown her how the ideas of the separate religions can combine to bring people a deeper understanding of life as a soul journey. Her observations show how the chakra system of Hinduism and Buddhism, the mystical teaching of the Jewish Kabbalah, and the Christian sacraments form an integrated spiritual instruction book for health and well-being. Myss describes her discovery as "The universal jewel within the four major religious is that the Divine is locked into our biological system in seven stages of power that lead us to become more refined and transcendent in our personal power."

Chakras: The Soulbody's Energy Centers

The body has vortexes or centers that energize our physical, emotional, and spiritual systems. These vortexes are called chakras, and they correspond to the major nerve or endocrine centers in the human body. Knowledge of chakras comes to us from the *Vedas*, the oldest written tradition in India (2000 B.C.E.–600 C.E.) and the foundational scriptures of the Hindus.

Like all sacred material, the teachings of the Veda belong to the whole world. They are particularly important to our discussion for several reasons. One is because of their holistic basis. They work on the body and soul as one integrated whole. Another is because they create a link between today's religious and scientific understanding and that of the ancient world, when an integrated understanding was common. Again, many other cultures base their medical knowledge on this holistic paradigm.

Womanspeak

Veda comes from the root *Vid*, meaning "to know." Vedas are sacred revelations of the Hindu religion.

Using Myss's discoveries along with information from a variety of sources, let's look at the seven major chakras, or biological energy centers, and the spiritual power each one contains.

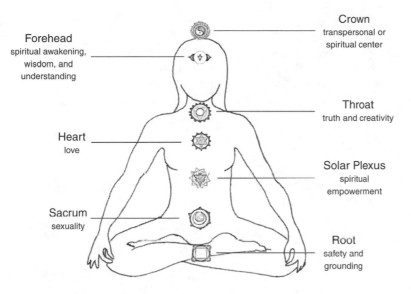

Forehead
spiritual awakening,
wisdom, and
understanding

Crown
transpersonal or
spiritual center

Throat
truth and creativity

Heart
love

Solar Plexus
spiritual
empowerment

Sacrum
sexuality

Root
safety and
grounding

The major chakras, or energy centers, from bottom to top.

Root Chakra: Oneness

The first chakra is called the root chakra. It is foundational to your health and well-being. In women the root chakra is located at the opening of the vagina; in men it relates to the gonads. The root chakra governs reproduction and contains our instincts for security needs, such as food and shelter. Because these needs are associated with belonging to our tribe, it is also the tribal chakra.

- The first chakra corresponds to the Kabbalah's teaching called Shekhinah, God's feminine name, honoring nurturing and the unity of all people. It also relates to the Christian sacrament of baptism, an initiation into the "tribe." It instructs us on our relationship with the human tribe.

- Parts of the body: legs, feet, bones, large intestine, spine, nervous system, red blood cells, womb, menstrual cycle, and fertility.

- Emotions: positive: enthusiasm, belonging, and joy; negative: fear of survival, insecurity, disconnectedness, longing, and distrust.

- The first chakra contains our inborn instructions on how to establish trust, safety, health, home, and family or tribe.

- Moral instruction: right relationship flows from our feelings of safety, belonging, trust, and bonding with tribe.

Wise Words

"If a person is able to sense intuitively that he or she is losing energy because of a stressful situation—and then acts to correct that loss of energy—then the likelihood of that stress developing into a physical crisis is reduced, if not eliminated completely."
—Caroline Myss

Sacral: Union

The second chakra, or sacral chakra, is located halfway between the pubis and the navel. It relates to the ovaries in women and the spleen in men. Its functions overlap somewhat with the root chakra in women, because it governs some aspects of fertility and menstruation. Issues of sexuality are located in the sacral chakra—not just sexuality pertaining to reproduction but matters of sexuality and gender in a broader sense. It also contains intuition and emotional memory.

- The second chakra connects with the Kabbalah's teaching regarding the procreative force of God. It relates to the Christian sacrament of holy communion, honoring union.

- Parts of the body: skin, reproduction organs, kidneys, bladder, circulatory system, and lymphatic system adrenals; orgasm; the flow of fluids in the body. Imbalance: asthma, allergies, epilepsy, coughs, kidney disease, arthritis.

- Emotions: positive: receptivity, ease or comfort with self and others, ability to give and receive pleasure, desire, and passion; negative: fear, anxiety, lust, and hanging onto painful emotions.

- Our instinctual instructions for partnership are contained in the second chakra. Relationship begins with our ability to accept sensual pleasure, which creates capacity for emotional intimacy. Creativity originates here.

- Moral instruction: Good relations begin with family. If this does not happen, relationships must be healed, or dishonor in personal or professional relationships will result and bad health will follow.

Solar Plexus: Personal Power

The third chakra is in the solar plexus, located just above the navel. It is the center of personal power by which we are able to be effective in the world.

- The third chakra connects to the Kabbalah's teachings of endurance and strength. It relates to the Christian sacrament of confirmation, which also imparts endurance and strength in the practice of one's faith.

- Parts of the body: intake and absorption of food, digestion and absorption glands, diaphragm, stomach, duodenum gall bladder and liver, and endocrine part of pancreas. Imbalance: diabetes hypoglycemia, eating disorders, digestive upsets, ulcers, urinary infections, and skin problems.

The sacraments are a physical acknowledgement of God's grace being bestowed on us as assistance through particular passages throughout our lifetime. They have a particular form, which includes the application or use of elements such as water, oil, holy candles, bread, and saying certain words. The seven sacraments of the Catholic Church are as follows:

- Baptism
- Eucharist or communion
- Confirmation
- Marriage
- Reconciliation or confession
- Holy orders or ordination into the priesthood
- Extreme unction or sacrament of the dying

- Emotions: positive: willpower, self-empowerment, ability to get needs met, ability to be effective in the world, self-confidence, and taking things to completion; negative: mood swings, depression, powerlessness, feelings of victimization, excessive introversion, and loss of the will to live.

- The third chakra contains the instinct for personal power and right use of will, development of a code of ethics, and the strength of character to be true to our ideals.

- Moral instruction: compromise of one's integrity affects physical strength, and corresponding organs will be negatively affected.

Heart: All Is Love

The fourth chakra is the heart chakra and is located under the breastbone between the breasts.

- The heart chakra connects to the Kabbalah's teaching on compassion, harmony, and beauty. It relates to the Christian sacrament of marriage, opening the heart and blessing love.

- Parts of the body: heart, thymus/immune system, strengthening circulation; infections; lungs; respiratory system; arms; and hands. Imbalance: heart disease and weakened immune system, causing infections.

◆ Emotions: positive: giving and receiving love, good self-image, trust, openness, compassion, charity, altruism, beauty, sensitivity, belonging, and joy; negative: loneliness, isolation, longing, self-hate, bitterness, resentment, fear, and guilt.

◆ The fourth chakra contains our instinctual understanding of the power of love; our innate need to love and be loved to survive; instructions to cultivate forgiveness; and energy for imagination, the magical child within, and playfulness.

◆ Moral instruction: Love and forgiveness is necessary for our physical and emotional strength.

 Wise Words

"The mystique of the heart has been a major part of cultural rituals for ages. Every year we celebrate St. Valentine's Day with the ritual giving of symbolic hearts to our loved ones. The heart was once thought to be the 'seat of the soul' and has been incorporated into our emotional language, with phrases such as 'breaking my heart' and 'heartfelt.' Although science and medicine now explain to us that the heart is just one of many organs and systems that make us whole living beings, our reverence for the importance of the heart still lingers."

—Jeanne Achterberg, Barbara Dossy, and Leslie Kolkmeier, *Rituals of Healing* (Bantam Books, 1994)

Throat: Creativity and Truth

The fifth chakra is in the throat, and is the creative center, especially after menopause when the creative energy of a woman's reproductive center in the second chakra is transmitted to the fifth (unless she is on hormone replacement therapy). The fifth, sixth, and seventh chakras are associated not with emotions but rather with abilities.

◆ The fifth chakra relates to the Kabbalah's teachings on how speaking with love and mercy make our communications truly powerful. It relates to the Christian sacrament of confession, in which forgiveness is granted through the spoken word.

◆ Parts of the body: nervous system, female reproductive organs, vocal cords, ears, thyroid, and parathyroid. Imbalance: headaches, migraines, sore throats, creative blocks, anger, asthma, anemia, laryngitis, and skin or respiratory problems.

◆ The fifth chakra strengthens our ability to communicate, to find our voice and speak our truth. It helps us hear the deeper meanings in communication and energizes singing, music, and deep insight.

- The throat chakra contains our instinctual instructions for speech and the need for clear, honest communication. It energizes all creative projects, sending them out into the world.

- Moral instruction: We must speak our truth to be strong and healthy. Living a lie creates negative consequences in the body, mind, and emotions.

Sophia's Wisdom

Paraphrasing Jacquelyn Small, historically, the priests of various religions have attempted to keep universal spiritual truth codified in language not easily understood by the people they serve, teaching a specific dogma that is based on the truth rather than teaching the truth itself. Teaching the real truth about the self means moving into wild and dangerous territories, because it gives us the key to our power—and the responsibility. This makes us no longer subject to being a passive follower of any limited orthodoxy. Meister Eckhart, a thirteenth-century Christian mystic, was excommunicated for teaching the truth to his people in a lay language they would understand. Dominican priest Matthew Fox was silenced by the Vatican for speaking of creative, more feminine, and participatory spirituality.

Forehead: Awakening Wisdom

The sixth chakra is called the "third eye" and is located on the center of the forehead between the two eyebrows. It energizes intuitive perception and governs wisdom: It allows us to see the paradoxical nature of truth.

- The sixth chakra connects with Kabbalah's wisdom teachings. It corresponds to the Christian sacrament of ordination and raises all occupations to the level of a priestly vocation.

- Parts of the body: eyes, nose, ears, brain, pituitary gland (main hormone balancer), women's intuition and knowing, and white blood cells. Imbalance: multiple sclerosis, degenerative disease, headaches and migraines, mental and nervous disorders, colds, flu, pneumonia, sinus, rigid thoughts, irritability, confusion, stress, and neuritis.

- Abilities: psychic development, clairvoyance, and telepathy; wisdom; finding our right work; integration on many levels, including merging of your male and female self; living by your own rules; and spiritual awakening.

- Moral instruction: contains our instinct for spiritual awakening, discernment of truth and the acquisition of wisdom, and instruction for coming into one's own being and living our truth.

Crown: Union with Goddess

The seventh chakra is located outside the body, just above the crown of the head, over the baby's soft spot. It is our energetic connection to the divine source.

◆ The seventh chakra is the source of our spiritual energy system and corresponds with the Kabbalah's teaching on "the supreme crown of God." It also relates to the Christian sacrament of extreme unction, assisting in time of death.

◆ Parts of the body: endocrine or pineal white blood cells. Imbalance causes: vision problems, stress disorders, insomnia, anxiety, mental and nervous issues, tumors, and strokes.

◆ Abilities: The energy from this chakra connects us with the eternal life. It is the fulfillment of spirit become human.

◆ Moral instruction: The seventh chakra contains the instinct for fulfilling our spiritual journey, or enlightenment, and the realization that there is no death. Self and other are no longer experienced as separate. There is unification.

The chakra system shows how the body and spirit are one, and how our spiritual journey is energized by our connection to the source and unfolds from within us.

> **Wise Words**
>
> "Biography becomes biology. All our thoughts … enter our system as energy. Those that carry emotional, mental, psychological, or spiritual energy produce biological responses that are woven into our biological systems. Gradually, slowly, everyday."
>
> —Caroline Myss

> **Wise Words**
>
> "Spirituality is our deepest sense of connection to self, to nature, and to God or Spirit, characterized by feelings of love, harmony, and being in the moment—accompanied by awe and belonging."
>
> —Joan Borysenko, *A Woman's Book of Life: The Biology, Psychology, and Spirituality of the Feminine Life Cycle* (Riverhead Books, 1996)

Biology: Spiritual Wiring

Joan Borysenko holds a Ph.D. in biology and is a licensed psychologist and a leader in mind/body medicine. She brings a further understanding of a spiritual instinct grounded in the body, showing how it is activated through natural biological functions a woman goes through during her lifetime. Borysenko has identified this spiritual map, and in so doing has become a spokesperson for others who believe spirituality is not separate from biology. As we saw earlier in this chapter, present-day religious ceremonies originated to help believers successfully navigate natural life processes. They have their roots in tribal ceremonies used to assist members in understanding and maximizing the spiritual and physical power that was being unlocked as one matured. Today, women are reclaiming both their understanding of spirituality as a natural process and their feminine power.

Straight from the Heart

Remember when you knew that rocks and trees had feelings? Dr. Borysenko describes the intuitive, holistic thinking of little girls from birth to age seven as one of life's greatest gifts. Their moral compass is guided at this young age by their intuitive understanding that the world is alive—it all has spirit. Brain scans on children show more activity in the right hemisphere in girls than in boys. Relational skills, imagination, and mystical experiences take place in the right hemisphere. This natural edge combines with socialization to create a kind of spirituality that is both organic and centered in relationships.

Little girls are treated differently than little boys. Family and friends relate to girls with more emotion, smiling more when speaking to them and holding and cuddling them more than they do boys. This encourages relational skills such as emotional development, intuition, and empathy in girls. From then on, girls draw on these relational qualities in making decisions in all areas of life, including how they understand moral truth. Borysenko calls this "heart" logic and natural wisdom.

Becoming Whole-Brained

Carol Gilligan, psychologist, professor of gender studies at Harvard University, and author of *In a Different Voice: Psychological Theory and Women's Development* (reissue edition, Harvard University Press, 1993), identified essential differences in how males and females approach moral decisions. She found that males come from an understanding that individuals have basic rights that must be protected. For them, morality is a system of limits such as those expressed in the Ten Commandments as "thou shalt not's." Females naturally perceive morality as a responsibility to others. Morality calls them to care for others such as that expressed in the biblical mandate "love one another."

As girls grow, they add left hemisphere skills to their natural intuitive skills and become whole-brained. They have more connective tissue between the right and left hemispheres of the brain than males, giving females a balanced and holistic way of thinking and making decisions. In making choices, including moral choices, girls perceive the complexities of a situation, seeing a big picture that includes the motives and circumstances of everyone involved. They engage the morality in an interactive dynamic that is informed by the "law" and guided by the spirit.

Sophia's Wisdom

There is a story that has been around for a while about a seven-year-old girl who tip-toes into her new sibling's room. Her parents see her and wisely stand back to see what she is up to. As she approaches her little brother's bed, he looks up to greet her. The siblings exchange a knowing look, and the girl makes her request to her brother: "Tell me about God. I'm beginning to forget." Whether this story is true or not doesn't really matter. It captures the process of this transition in a child's life and makes the point for us as adults.

Borysenko points out that as a young girl approaches the onset of her menstrual cycle, the chemicals produced in her brain deepen her emotions, making her especially vulnerable to what others say about her. If she is receiving positive messages about herself, she grows strong and confident and has a clear sense of herself. If not, which is unfortunately often the case, she begins to question herself at the deepest level.

Traditional Religion and the Female Dilemma

Women's psychological process shows that females, being naturally relational, must go through a process of *individuation* to become personally powerful in our society. They must be encouraged to experience themselves as important, independent of their relationships as well as through their relationships. This passage was once addressed with rites of initiation. Today's young woman instead often faces a decline in support as she goes through this very important transition.

Borysenko describes this crucial time as a growing girl's essential spiritual task or challenge. A young woman must resolve what she perceives as an either/or dilemma of choosing either herself or "others." This challenge often requires assistance. Important people in her life can instruct her in establishing the primary bond with herself, which will then enable her to be of assistance to others without sacrificing her own needs in the process. The healthy self-esteem that results from being firmly anchored in her own center allows a woman's natural empathy and relational skills to be used without losing herself in the process.

Womanspeak

Individuation describes a psychological process by which females understand their worth as individuals separate from their worth gained through their interactions with society.

The window of opportunity for a woman to individuate closes by her mid-20s. If the dilemma is unresolved at that time, she will be left with deep feelings of inadequacy that play out in a variety of ways. When the young woman does not successfully negotiate this crucial passage, she will spend many years struggling against issues of self-worth. Poor body image, eating disorders, addictions, caring more about other's opinions than her own, and depression engulf her. Rather than being effective in the world, she will spend much of her life dealing with her damaged ego.

Sophia's Wisdom

Two important challenges young girls face in their spiritual development are self-esteem and connecting with other women who will help them understand themselves. In her book, *The Wild Girls: The Path of the Young Goddess* (Llewellyn Publications, 2001), Patricia Monagham presents many suggestions to assist girls in developing a positive self-image and in learning more about themselves. She encourages girls to make a self-confidence alphabet by writing one word for every letter that describes positive qualities about themselves. She also urges girls to talk to female relatives until they find one who will talk to them about the womanly history of the family.

It's at this juncture that traditional religion, which excludes women's experience and is based on male experience, can seriously hamper young women's spiritual development. Relational skills such as awareness and sensitivity to the needs of others are essential spiritual tasks that must be developed in males, but the opposite is true for females. Females need support in knowing their own hopes and dreams are important, and that it is proper and necessary to attend to their personal needs before giving to others. Religious instruction that continually directs a woman outside herself to focus on the needs of others without spending adequate time developing her sense of self increases pressure and adds guilt. Girls are left with the feeling that no matter how much they give it isn't enough. Women point out that while religion remains predominately in the hands of men, this is the message it gives to women.

Mother Knows Best

Take care of yourself first! Flight attendants always caution passengers to put their own oxygen mask on first before attending to their child or other passenger. Imagine for a moment how different it might be if a woman's spiritual lessons included learning how to take care of herself first.

Women are offered a second chance to individuate at mid-life, when biology creates another powerful mixture of chemicals presenting an opportunity to complete their individuation process as their menstrual cycles begin to decline. Mentoring by a woman who has passed through this gate, or belonging to a women's group focused on self-discovery rather than doing for others, is an important part of successfully making this transition.

Growing Old and Wearing Purple!

Sandra Haldeman-Martz's *When I Am an Old Woman I Shall Wear Purple* goes a long way toward reframing how many people feel about aging. The book gives poetic insight into the freedom of growing older and the innate wisdom that accompanies the process. Dr. Borysenko adds to our understanding of aging by giving us the biological basis of this freedom and wisdom. Chemicals produced by menopause open "conduits of higher wisdom," as she describes them. Now we'll look at the years from 63 to 84 and beyond. It's a time of great perspective and personal power that produces freedom and authenticity. This is when women speak their truth, regardless of the consequences.

Listening to the Soul

The spiritually vibrant woman has broken through her conditioning; she has met her true self and likes it! A real confrontation with death only raises the bar as far as truth and integrity are concerned, and there is a rededication to the principles one holds dearest. Here is a story of a woman who has just entered this phase of her life.

> **Mother Knows Best**
>
> If you have a fear of getting older, consider the option! It might help to know the Cherokee people believe that you don't even become an adult until age 51.

At age 65, Dorothy has spent 40 years as a professional actor, director, producer, and writer. She is now exploring the world of digital movie making. She describes the shift that began for her a couple of years ago as "becoming aware of life's rhythms—natural processes. I have become a 'seer.' I 'see' why things have happened in my life and understand the innate wisdom of the experiences. I can 'see' the evolution of my consciousness, my soul. I also 'see' through the propaganda of the culture!"

"I think most organized religion completely misses the boat. All those rules—as if you can control spirituality—or need to!" Dorothy defines spirituality as "knowing you fit into the universe," a place she describes as both "simple and vast." She nourishes her spirit through sleep and early mornings spent looking out her window at the river. "I am lazy in the morning. I don't want words or thoughts infringing. It's my time for just being."

The Glamour Girls of WWII

Being with people is important throughout our lives, and in the elder years friendships take on new dimensions. By her 70s and beyond, a woman has passed through all the gates—she is a natural teacher, having something of value to say to any stage of life. Here's a story of the friendship of four women and how it felt to be in their company.

They have known one another for more than 80 years, meet weekly for lunch, and spend holidays together. I recently went home to Minneapolis to visit my aunt, one of the women, and was invited to attend a special seventy-fifth birthday lunch.

As we drove across town, I was given the history of every important building along the way. We dined at an old speakeasy dating back to the Roaring Twenties, and I heard their stories about that, too! I have known these women all my life. They were the glamour girls of World War II. I remember their upswept hairdos and fancy snoods. They brought soldiers and sailors home, rolled up the living room rug, played be-bop music, and danced the Lindy Hop as I watched wide-eyed from the stairs.

Spending the day with them brought me a realization of the importance of "old" friend-ships, and since that time I have deepened my appreciation of the people in my life. This is how wisdom is transmitted; not by direct instruction, but through an experience that shifts your perceptions. By spending time with these women, laughing together over their old stories—the Roaring Twenties, Prohibition, the Great Depression of the 1930s, World War II, seeing history through their eyes, and experiencing what it feels like to celebrate three quarters of a century and more together, I came away with a greater value of friends and family, even of place. The city in which we had all grown up took on a transformed and transforming quality as well.

The Least You Need to Know

- Soulbody describes our unified nature—the physical, emotional, and spiritual aspects happening simultaneously.

- Holistic health operates from soulbody philosophy, supporting the whole person and engaging natural healing ability.

- Energy centers in the body called chakras maintain physical and emotional health and contain our spiritual instructions.

- The sacred teaching of four world religions—Hinduism, Buddhism, Judaism, and Christianity—address the same spiritual principles and affirm that our spirituality is encoded in our bodies.

- Grace is within. Throughout our lives, chemicals in our bodies open levels of con-sciousness according to a divine plan. Our job is to be aware of them.

Part 5

Mending the Split in the Patriarch's Pants

Earlier in the book we identified the patriarchal separation of body and soul as the primary problem with Western religion and culture. Now we'll read how this split is being mended.

In this part you are going to see how women's holistic understanding of spirituality is finding its way into everyday life and culture. As you know, society didn't always think of the body and soul as separate. For many thousands of years, most people in the world practiced an integrated and holistic kind of spirituality. Many still do today.

There are countless ways of living the belief in the goddess's presence in the world and honoring the sacred web of life. Now you'll meet women whose life work is directed toward healing the separation between mind and body. They have dedicated themselves to focusing the vision that many of us share. They are professionals who often work outside the traditional areas of employment. They are holistic practitioners, teachers, healers, artists, and other "creatives," who are finding new ways of living and doing business that not only reflect the values of women's spirituality but offer healing to others as well.

Chapter 21

Creativity and Spirituality

In This Chapter

- ◆ Thirty-nine women who came to dinner
- ◆ Meet Minton Sparks, who has a little piece of all of us in her!
- ◆ Memories of music, family, and friends
- ◆ Raising babies and making prayer beads

We are co-creators in a universe that is still unfolding, and something within our soul longs to participate in this process. In the past as well as now, women's creative spirit has contributed to the development of culture through art, music, dance, literature, and philosophy. We're going to look at a megalithic project of the 1970s, Judy Chicago's *The Dinner Party*, and meet several artists, a musician, an entrepreneur, and a poet who are continuing the tradition of women, spirituality, and creativity.

The Dinner Party

Judy Chicago's legendary art project, *The Dinner Party*, celebrates women's contributions to Western civilization in all areas of society. The concept began to develop in the 1960s as a result of her search for women's history and the realization that women's contributions to society were missing. There are several factors to consider. One is that women's contributions are often belittled, their importance diminished. At the same time, the exact opposite is true: Because women's observations are extremely poignant and significant, they have often been written out of the historic records. Not only does the culture suffer from this loss, but as Chicago points out, it also results in the loss of any platform for women to stand on. Rather than building on the discoveries of one another, women are, in effect, having to reinvent the wheel from generation to generation.

Chicago set out to correct some of this by documenting women's specific contributions through her project, creating a "symbolic history" to convey women's long struggle for freedom and justice. In addition, she designed a working model for the project honoring women's communal style.

Generation After Generation

The Dinner Party is a multimedia work consisting of three banquet tables that form a triangle, each elaborately and beautifully decorated with 39 place settings. Each setting includes ceramics, china, painting, and needlework commemorating a goddess or an historic or important woman. To find her unsung heroes Chicago combed myth, literature, history, and popular entertainment. Alongside each "celebrity" at the table are embroidered the names of many other women who were involved in similar endeavors.

The entire art piece resides on "The Heritage Floor," which is made of 2,300 hand-cast white porcelain tiles bearing the names of 999 more women of achievement. According to Chicago, the symbolism operates in many ways. It symbolizes all women and merely suggests a beginning platform for the discovery and honoring of thousands more. It also symbolizes the supportive foundation of those who came before us and upon whose work we build. It challenges the false bootstrap theory that tells women (and other groups of people) that success is merely a matter of pulling oneself up by one's own bootstraps. "History," Chicago reminds us, "isn't made of a series of individual efforts, but builds on itself generation after generation."

Wise Words

"Men develop ideas and systems of explanations by absorbing past knowledge and critiquing and superseding it. Women, ignorant of their own history [do] not know what women before them had thought and taught. So generation after generation, they [struggle] for insights others had already had before them … [resulting in] the constant reinventing of the wheel."

—Gerda Lerner, feminist, author, and historian in the history department of the University of Wisconsin in Madison, in *The Creation of Feminist Consciousness* (Oxford Press reprint, 1994)

Each place setting also represents an historical period of history, which have always been measured by men's accomplishments. For example, rather than referencing fifth-century Greek thought through Plato and Socrates, Aspasia, female scholar and philosopher of the same time, is honored.

Looking for Home

The Dinner Party premiered in San Francisco's Museum of Modern Art on March 14, 1979. Over the next 10 years, the exhibition visited 14 institutions in 6 different countries, creating both awe and controversy, sparking hot debate in Congress, the Christian Television Network, art critics, and columnists. It seems that the focus went to the images on the dinner plates, thought to too closely resemble women's vaginal areas, rather than to the artistic, intellectual, philosophical, and historic content of the work. The project, having been viewed by more than a million people, was again displayed in a commemorative exhibition in Los Angeles in 1996. Since that time it has regretfully been in storage, awaiting permanent housing.

Minnie Pearl Meets Lily Tomlin

Minton Sparks is a woman of slight build and cast iron. She is not a worldly sort, but she is by no means dumb. Christianity is rooted deep in her bones; it's the rock she stands on, the rules she lives by, but she doesn't go to church. Her spirit is the spirit of the working-class rural southern woman and the dark humor that allows her to laugh in the face of life's hardest blows. Minton Sparks is the alter-ego character of Jill Webb-Hill, a performance poet who celebrates the spirit of the women in her family through her writing and through Minton's thought-provoking, hilarious, and infinitely human monologues.

Minton, who might be described as a cross between Minnie Pearl and Lily Tomlin, is based on true-life encounters with real people such as 91-year-old Trella, who was beaten by her husband of 65 years and outlived him to fulfill her lifelong dream of selling vegetables on the side of the road. She is almost blind yet continues to garden, setting her produce on a card table, where she earns the first money she has ever had to call her own. *Pathetic* or *victim* is not in the vocabulary of these women, nor would they be accurate descriptions of them. The women Webb-Hill characterizes are survivors, and they have a lot to say to today's women about the spirituality of endurance and resurrection.

Southern Spirit

Webb-Hill grew up in middle Tennessee thinking she might marry a minister. She later discovered she could be one herself, so she went to divinity school. Since college Webb-Hill has taught school, and in her own words, "been an experiential education freak," had a company called Corporate Adventure, been a therapist, written scripts for radio and television, and produced a body of poetry. *Spirituality* isn't a word Webb-Hill would have thrown around casually growing up; it was in the same camp as *sacred* or *holy*.

During divinity school, Webb-Hill participated in a five-year research project on women's collaborative leadership along with 60 other women from a variety of backgrounds. Issues of women's community living, sexuality, race, age, and economics were examined through personal stories. "We told and retold our stories, in a process of refining and rethinking everything," Webb-Hill recalls. It took her a long time to make the paradigm shift from patriarchy to self-definition and autonomy after growing up Baptist, but she quickly understood how story and spirituality entwine.

I asked Webb-Hill where she receives spiritual support, and she said, "The Sisters of Loretto, in the hills of Kentucky near Louisville. They are the one organized group of Christians I feel I can explore spirituality with to the fullest. I am a co-member of their community. This is a formal affiliation where one can be as involved in the life of Loretto as she wants to be. I went through a year and a half process and joined the order because it is where I feel God's presence unmistakably. I totally support the work of the Sisters of Loretto in the world. They are clearly the most self-defined women's community that I have ever met, totally expressing the spirit of God, the earth, and justice for the poor. They are my place of renewal."

Sophia's Wisdom

Like her character Minton Sparks, Webb-Hill still has Christianity deep in her bones. She envies the unquestioned faith of her mother's and grandmother's generation. "They have a solid unshakable belief that sustains them through broken relationships, poverty, anything that life delivers," she says. "They pick up the Bible and read it and are deeply comforted. I used to be able to do that, too. Now I question the organized church. For instance, I'd like to read the Bible for comfort in times of distress, but for the most part I can't—the images are too violent, too misogynist. I am left with several Psalms, a couple verses in Isaiah, and a bit of John!" Webb-Hill, her husband, and their two children attend the Glendale Church, which she describes as "benign enough—meaning they don't do the devil."

White Shoulders and a Time-Torn Dress

Webb-Hill found her ministry in articulating her stories and calling others to theirs. She describes the innate spirituality of storytelling as "how we know who we are through telling our story to others." A favorite quotation of hers comes from Nell Morton, who describes the sacred act of listening as, "to hear people into speech."

Minton Sparks evolved out of writing Webb-Hill did for her grandmother and mother about some of the "nut cakes" in the family. She feels connected to the spirit of the women she writes about and is often surprised at what comes out of her mouth during a performance. "It feels like they have lent me their spirits," she says. She tells about how she spends the day preparing for a performance. "I'm definitely not the fussy type. I go around in sweat pants and a T-shirt with my hair pinned up most of the time, but when I am getting ready for Minton, I spend the day primping."

Minton has the kind of curls many of us can remember from the old days, and to reproduce them, Webb-Hill spends the day in rollers. "I roll my hair up, pick out one of my grandmother's dresses, and slowly prepare," she says. "I enjoy sitting around in Minton's costume, stewing in the juices until I feel myself turning into her. The final touch comes as I spritz a little White Shoulders on just before I walk out of the house." The following poem by Webb-Hill describes the dress Minton wears, the dress we can all remember someone in our family wearing.

> **Sorrow Knows This Dress**
>
> Sorrow knows this dress,
> cotton-made, time-torn.
> It's not the color or the cut that cries out
> but the slack-shouldered emptiness—a scarecrow
> exposed to a parched dusty yard.
> Reveals more than a housedress should.
> Around the hemline, shame shows.
> Embarrassed, a shy collarbone
> protrudes. Pale daisy-print cloth
> forgetful now of summer days,
> blowing on the line between the Sweet Gums.
>
> Breasts nag at the waistline—
> hungry old mares.
> Belly slack from child bearing and buttered bread.
> The knees poke through,
> cotton worn so thin it shines.
> I wrestle this place.
> This cotton-field-of-a-dress.
>
> —Jill Webb-Hill

There's (at Least) One in Every Family!

"Minton's purse is an essential part of the costume," Webb-Hill says. "It kind of brings it all together for me. My favorite story is about finding my grandmother's purse 20 years after she died. Someone had put it away just as she left it. When I opened it, the smell of old perfume, Juicy Fruit gum, and butterscotch Lifesavers wafted out. I left it exactly the way I found it, and that is the purse I carry onstage.

"There have been times when I have felt intimidated by my audience. Especially when they are business people or folks that present as 'together,' and here I am in old worn-out housedresses talking about being poor and uneducated—and a little crazy. Every time when I'm finished, people come up and say things like 'You must have known my grand-mother' or 'I have an aunt just like that.'" The character of Minton Sparks transcends cul-tural boundaries, education, and sophistication. Everybody has one in their family!

Webb-Hill and Minton Sparks are taking the show on the road in 2001. They will be vis-iting colleges, where Minton will share her wisdom with students, and Webb-Hill will teach a class on writing, storytelling, and spirituality. This reminded me of an important question I almost forgot to ask, "What is Minton's idea of spirituality?" Webb-Hill describes it as being "Like a song out in the woods she can hear; something she is thirsty for, like a drink of water."

You can find out how to reach Jill Webb-Hill and Minton Sparks in Appendix C, "Resources."

Music, Music, Music

Gertrude was born in Minneapolis, Minnesota, on June 16, 1917, the "baby" of an Irish Catholic family. "I was born at home and weighed only three pounds," she says. "Family stories have it that I was kept in the oven with the door open as an incubator! The doctor didn't expect me to live. When I did, he predicted I would never walk." She survived and was entertaining friends by singing and dancing at the age of four. "My father used to take me to a bar near his workplace where he put me up on the piano and I sang, 'We Are Tenting Tonight on the Old Camp Grounds,' and other World War I songs. I sang, and an old dog in the back howled," she remembers, laughing.

"Don't Sit Under the Apple Tree ..."

Music has been central to Gertrude's spirituality and religion. She sang in the choir for more than 60 years, performing the solos at Christmas and Easter, and singing at wed-dings and funerals all over town. "Singing has always been effortless for me," she says. "It was something I could contribute that I really loved doing. It made me happy." She grew up in a house filled with music. "Mother was a wonderful musician, and when John Philip Sousa came to town, she was asked to accompany him on the piano. Other times she played the best ragtime you've ever heard." Although the family wasn't wealthy, their piano was the finest that money could buy, "A Merlin with a full harp—quite rare by today's standards." Besides music, Gertrude's spirituality is deeply rooted in family.

Silver Slippers and Streetcars

As teenagers, Gertrude and her best friend, Ruth, loved to sing the latest hit songs they heard on the radio. Ruth took the words down in shorthand, and Gertrude typed them. Together they sounded out the melody on the piano—songs like "I'll Be Seeing You (in All the Old Familiar Places)" "(Kiss Me Once, Kiss Me Twice, and Kiss Me Once Again) It's Been a Long, Long Time" "Don't Sit Under the Apple Tree (with Anyone Else but Me)." Gertrude confessed that the two of them used to sneak out of their houses wearing their best silver slippers and long dresses and ride a streetcar across town to the Marigold Ballroom to go dancing. "Life was all about lightheartedness, music, fun, friendship, and family."

Gertrude thinks of spirituality as a gift "that brings out the best in a person. I've always had a deep feeling that if I prayed, I would be given what I needed." She rocks back and forth in a big padded recliner with her sleeping cat draped across her neck and shoulders. Her heart aches for the days when everyone was together. "Sometimes I fight depression. When I feel it coming on, I ask God to please not let me go there—and it lifts. I wasn't even supposed to survive, and now I have outlived them all. I guess I do have a strong spirit!"

Friendship Beading Company

Elizabeth is a young woman in her early 40s, married, with two children. She and her husband feel the early years of child-rearing are important, and despite the fact that they cut their income in half, they are willing to make the financial sacrifice for her to be a stay-at-home mom. Elizabeth took three years off from her career to be with their daughter, who is now eight, and is approaching the three-year anniversary of the time she took off to be with their son. Elizabeth has enjoyed her career in nursing; however, as she drew closer to reentry, she felt she wanted to do something different. As she looked at options, it was clear that she wanted to explore her creativity.

A Solution Is Born

"About a year ago, one of my friends at church needed a birthday gift for someone, and I offered to make her a piece of jewelry," Elizabeth recalls. "I got the catalog out and began looking for beads and realized that if I ordered enough for 10 pieces I could save a lot of money. Even though I had no idea what I would do with the extra nine, I ordered the larger amount. I needed 'grown-up' time, so I got the idea of having a bead party. I used to make quilts, and I know how great it is to sit around and work on a quilt together. I wondered if this feeling would translate into beading. It did, and Friendship Beading Company was born.

"I began having parties regularly and also going out to other people's houses who would invite their friends to come over and bead. Kind of a cross between *How to Make an American Quilt* and Tupperware! It was fun, and everyone left really happy and proud of the creation they took with them. I charged them for the beads and a slight fee for instructions, but my goal wasn't necessarily to make a lot of money. I attend Unity Church and believe in tithing, and I did it right from the start. My beading parties increased, and people wanted to buy my finished products, too. I began to take special orders, and a local shop started carrying my stuff and it is selling very well."

Letting Go and Letting Goddess

"As I am approaching going back to work on a full-time basis, my company is about ready to take off," Elizabeth says. "My husband is in the Coast Guard and will retire soon. He is going to help me with the marketing and sales. The business part of this has been almost 100 percent organic and intuitive. All I have done is follow what makes me happy. I have always loved handwork in any form—beading, quilting, knitting, you name it—and I like people.

"I was raised Catholic, and I guess beads get into your genes or something. I have also developed my spirituality through a 12-step program. As I said, I belong to Unity, and I also follow an Earth-based spirituality. Again, by pure synchronicity, all this has converged into one of my best designs—affirmation beads."

The Affirmation Three beads represent mind/body/spirit. The four sections represent the four directions and the four elements. Individual beads set the intention for that decade. There are 10 beads in each section, because 10 represents completion.

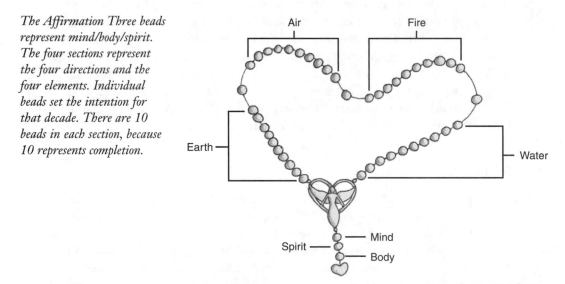

"I don't know where this will take us; I have not placed any expectations on it but am open to responding to what ever happens next. So far it has revealed itself one step at a time, and I assume it will continue. All I can say to others is to stay true to what you 'feel'

like you want to do, and let go of trying to figure it all out. If it's supposed to develop, it will. This is a spiritual principle that I have been attempting to integrate into my life since I first heard it in the 12-step world as 'Let go and let God.' I don't think I was able to really get what that meant. Friendship Beading Company is teaching me."

Following the Impulse

Sculptor Sydney Reichman nestled into a slice of land between two steep Tennessee hills 24 years ago and built a house and studio. She designed the space and created almost everything in it, from the bathroom sink to the 11 hand-crafted doors. Much of who she is grew out of her relationship to the land.

Pushing the Edges

Reichman pushes her art to the boundaries. Her life as an artist began as a result of what she was "not"—in this case, a good student. "When I couldn't make a nice, smooth handle for a clay pot, I made them into tree trunks or other irregular forms," she says. "Later I mastered the techniques, but my personal style had been created out of those earlier shapes. When I couldn't keep my pots perfectly centered on the wheel, my art pushed deeper into the boundaries of that irregularity. My difficulties at school left me searching for the thing that would give me a place on the planet. Art became the vehicle for that search. Clay provided a strong physical connection—I loved its earthy sensuousness and what I discovered evolved naturally out of me." Reichman is an artist of many mediums; she sees them as extensions of the same impulse.

Here Reichman describes her relationship with her land and her art. "I live in a valley of water and light moving the seasons. Between soft round mounds of moss and frosted stars. Long limbs of naked winter hardwood in dance ever-changing from whatever moon, wind, mist, storm breathes a new view. I eat and drink these images, and they have become the seeds of dreams. Chant of the angel toads and vibration of a woodpecker's African drumming on the edge of a spring-lit forest. This texture is the soil of soul and calls me home gut-driven and working across an alchemist playground. Hammering a vision. Welding the puzzle. Pounding the subtext. Carving the rhythm. It's the beat of the earth I work. A journey longing for form from chaos and madness to some kind of peace. Built out of land, the hand, and a large dose of magic."

 **Wise Words**

"We're every age we've been; our history is imprinted in us. Our visual image changes as we grow; the old form breaks open and new forms emerge. My job as an artist is to open the form and give the new one freedom to fly."

—Sydney Reichman

Hornet Spit and Ginger Ale

A large copper sculpture mounted on a wooden platform floated across the pond in front of us, and water trickled over rocks and down a waterfall she built. Reichman points to the sourwood trees growing along the bank and talks of the particularly sweet honey that comes from them. A newly formed hornets' nest hangs on a low branch just outside the screen porch. "Did you know that whole thing is made of fly wings and hornet spit?" she asked. I didn't, but was totally captured by the image.

Reichman doesn't separate spirituality from nature and from her artistic expression. She talks about the balance between masculine and feminine that is the natural order. When that balance is compromised, as it is among humans right now, there are problems. She referred to the out-of-control building going on all over her county as "the male psyche run amok," adding that women participate in this craziness, too. "When nature is balanced, there is an amazing dance of creation." We tossed around our ideas on this topic and came to the conclusion that "nature" will survive, even if our little corner of creation as human beings might not! Just then a small troop of hornets came out of their nest and began repairing the paper-thin layers that make their home—spitting and patting the fly wings. We lifted our ginger ales and toasted them.

Feeding the Body and Nourishing the Soul

Mary Weiland lives on a small lake near Star Prairie, Wisconsin, and it is the gathering place for family and friends from the Twin Cities an hour and a half away. She says she can feel a sense of relief and connection when she crosses the St. Croix River and heads toward home. "It feels like the rules change. I can breathe deeper." After living almost 60 years in the city, it was almost as if she opened the door and walked out of one life and into the next. For her, spirituality is natural, not supernatural. The closer she is to nature, the easier it is to connect spiritually. Weiland describes spirituality as sensuousness. "The senses connect us to life, nature, people—everything."

Wise Words

"I'll tell you right now, the doors to the world of wild women are few but precious. If you have a deep scar, that is a door; if you have an old, old story, that is a door. If you love the sky and the water so much you almost cannot bear it, that is a door. If you yearn for a deeper life, a full life, a sane life, that is a door."

—Clarissa Pinkola Estés, Ph.D., *Women Who Run with the Wolves* (Ballantine Books, 1992)

Mom's Chocolate-Chip Date Cake

Weiland talks about communion as the ritual of cooking "sacred recipes" passed down through her family. She recalls her mother's chocolate-chip date cake, and how there was always enough to share, regardless of who showed up at her table. "When people eat alone, they don't absorb the nutrients as well as when they eat with other people." She uses the word *conviviality* to describe getting together and sharing food. Her spirituality is bound up with the senses, food, and good conversation. "It's the coming alive of the spirit in the body."

As we spoke, Sadie, the neighbor's brown-and-white springer spaniel, appeared in the kitchen window, her nose pushed hard against the glass. There was a look of fierce determination as Sadie locked eyes with Weiland, insisting on help. Just then we heard thunder growling in the distance, across the lake to the north. Sadie intensified her efforts. Weiland opened the door, and the dog made a beeline to the narrow space between the couch and the wall, where she took shelter from the storm. Outside, the rain began to pelt against the front window, wiping out our view of the water below.

> ### Sophia's Wisdom
>
> Mary Weiland sees spirituality as understanding ourselves as an extension of God. She loves setting people free in their minds and bodies. "Here, in our country, we aren't oppressed in the same way [people] in other places in the world [are], for us the struggle goes on inside of ourselves. We are oppressed by greed—sometimes our own and sometimes the greed of others. In the materialism of this culture, people lose touch with reverence and respect for life." Every day Weiland spends at her home by the lake brings her an opportunity to participate in the observance of a holy day.

An earlier bout with depression and an overdose of organized religion left Weiland feeling despair. "Today I have a growing satisfaction with my life," she says. "I journal every morning, spend time in nature, and am nourished by my Artist's Way group—they have become my tribe. Sometimes I visit the Quaker Meeting House and enjoy quiet respectful meditation there. And my music is coming back to me. I have always been able to sing my way out of anything! I want to get back to my guitar and my singing. When I play I feel myself yielding to the creative spirit, and time and space are suspended." Weiland is "pastor shy," as she describes it. "Religious leaders have the definite tendency to take over the show," she believes. "It quickly becomes about them and the church, not about the people and God."

"Over the Rainbow ..."

The storm moved through and the sun glinted off wet branches, dripping on our heads as we walked down the hill to the lake and boarded Weiland's new boat. With her at the wheel and Sadie riding shotgun, I pushed off and jumped onboard. We putted around the lake, slowly savoring each view like turning the pages of an old photograph album. The air smelled as if someone had just opened a fresh bottle of ozone, and the colors were surreal. Long purple stripes stretched across the persimmon sky.

After dinner, Weiland turned down the quilts on an old iron bed on the sleeping porch, and I crawled in between flannel sheets, which felt just right on this midsummer night. Sadie was sleeping on the back porch, and our hostess was down the hall in her room. The storm thundered back through again, and I slept what my mother used to refer to as the sleep of the just and awakened to the morning chatter of a bird outside my window and the smell of coffee.

Creativity is an important part of Weiland's spirituality, and so is community. She is currently developing the Rainbow River Artist's and Writer's Retreat Center at her lake place, claiming her family heritage of hospitality—fixing good food and providing a comfortable bed and quiet time for others to regenerate. She envisions her retreats with boat trips up the St. Croix River, music, campfires, and good coffee—to which I'll attest. Not to forget a special serving of her mother's chocolate-chip date cake, guaranteed to renew the spirit.

See Appendix C for Rainbow River Retreats contact information.

The Least You Need to Know

- Spirituality celebrates our ongoing contributions to the unfolding of creation.
- Women's contributions create an important platform for us to stand on and from which we continue to grow.
- Through our creative expressions, we learn more about ourselves, the human story, and God's action in the world.
- Creativity is both the making of something—an object—or a new way of solving a problem.
- Nature feeds the soul and fosters the creative process. It is also a brilliant spiritual teacher.

Chapter 22

Mother's Medicine Chest

In This Chapter

- ◆ Making medicine
- ◆ All about real flower power
- ◆ Moon Time herbal remedies
- ◆ Harry Potter and the School for Witchlets
- ◆ Back to the sea

Throughout this book we've talked about the belief that the earth is a living organism with consciousness and that it interacts with us to heal, nurture, and support us. Nowhere is that more clearly shown than in the use of medicinal herbs and plants. We have talked about intuition and how our bodies resonate with the plants and minerals of the earth to tell us what is good for us and what to avoid—and how God directs us through our inner knowing.

Singing Their Praises

Catherine Abby Rich has been an herbalist for more than 30 years and has studied the wild medicinal herbs of Europe, India, and the United States. She lives in Marin County, California, and earns her living gathering herbs, making medicine, and teaching others how to listen to the secrets of the wild plants. Her earliest encounter with the plant spirits came at age nine, when she read the biography of George Washington Carver and his spiritual understanding of the plants. "In the book he said that he learned everything by watching and loving them," Rich says. "The plants gave him direct transmissions on how to use them. His book filled me with inspiration."

Rich refers to herself as a "culinary Jew" rather than a religious one. I asked her to clarify that for me, and she said it means that she knows how to make matzo ball soup but she doesn't attend services in the temple. She was raised in a Jewish home without traditional religious training but very much in accord with Jewish ethics. Her parents were liberals who walked in picket lines. They believed in education, kindness, nonsectarianism, service, and peace. Rich says that the infusion of these things is her "truth." Her spirituality is expressed through her love of nature and the healing herbs, and she says "The creation brought me to the creator."

Plants + Prayer = Power

It was more than three decades ago that Rich left Queens, New York, where she was an elementary school teacher, "to have an adventure of a totally new kind." Her adventure took her to Bavaria, where the local midwife introduced her to the world of plants and plant medicine. "They opened up my intelligence—ignited my spirit. My passion to learn about herbs and making medicine was voracious." For the next five years she worked with local teachers, beginning with plants that were used to support pregnancy, childbirth, and child-rearing. She later expanded her interests to a wider variety of conditions. She learned German and Dutch so she could read as many local herb books as she could and collaborated with friends to write her own book, which became a best-seller in Germany.

Rich left Bavaria for India, where she met and worked with an *ayurvedic* doctor in Poona, Dr. Lad, assisting him in making medicine. They shared their love of plants and exchanged information—Rich taught him what she knew of western herbs, and he instructed her in the making of eastern medicine. "He taught by singing the plants. As we ground the roots, he honored the plant by singing its story. He sang of the plant's history on Earth and how it was used for more than 6,000 years to heal people. He would sing the specific qualities of the plant, praising it and thanking it. He chanted and I ommmm-mmmmed! From him I learned the formula of making medicine: Plants + prayer = healing power."

Today, Rich makes her medicine as Dr. Lad taught her, and every batch contains praise and gratitude for the plants and prayers for the health of those who will receive it. In India she was given another important instruction by way of three yarrow sticks brought to her by an elderly woman herbalist. "She told me I would go on to make powerful medicine but reminded me that God put the power in the plants, I did not," Rich recalls. "To remind me of this she gave me three yarrow stalks, the symbol of balance, to use as stirring sticks. She cautioned me to never call myself a healer. I can pick the herbs and prepare them, I can know how to extract the properties, and I can add my prayers, but it is not by my power that the healing happens. That is done by the creator."

Liquid Prayer

Rich also makes flower essences, a relatively new form of herbal medicine developed by Dr. Edward Bach in the 1930s.

"Dr. Bach was a physician in England who understood the healing properties of the flowers and devised a method of transmitting their vibrations into medicine. I make my own essences and teach others, adding what I learned in India. We sing the flower's story, and each bottle is filled with prayers and meditation. It becomes a liquid prayer."

Sophia's Wisdom

Dr. Edward Bach, an English bacteriologist, pathologist, and surgeon, felt dissatisfied with the way doctors were expected to concentrate on diseases and ignore the whole person. In 1930 he gave up his lucrative Harley Street practice and left London, determined to devote the rest of his life to the new system of medicine that he was sure could be found in nature. He found the remedies he wanted in the flowers, discovering that different flowers treated particular mental or emotional state and thus worked on the causes of physical illness. He abandoned formal medicine, relying on his natural gifts as a healer and intuition to guide him. Dr. Bach died in 1936, leaving his system of natural medicine that is now used all over the world.

Unlike aromatherapy, flower essences don't impart an aroma but instead heal by energy vibration. Here are a few common flowers and their therapeutic properties:

◆ **Blackberry** for healing depression, grief, and loss and for accepting change.

◆ **Petunia** for focus.

◆ **St. John's wort** for easing fears both known and hidden.

◆ **Iris** for creativity.

◆ **Snapdragon** for communication—both speaking up and knowing when to hold your tongue.

◆ **Rose** for passion and intention in love and life.

◆ **Zinnia** for laughter as a healing medicine.

Kids Are Naturals

Rich moved to California in 1984, and for the last 15 years she has had a stand at the Farmers' Market in San Raphael, where she has introduced thousands of people to flowers, herbs, and medicine-making. That's where I first met her. I wove my way through a crowd of children and adults to her table, which was strewn with wild flowers, herbs in various stages of drying, and baskets full of bottles and jars of all shapes and sizes.

Rich sells her herbal products at the market, and she also enrolls students for her various herb walks and medicine-making classes. She has a degree in elementary education and prefers teaching in nature to the classroom. She finds children are especially drawn to the herbs and love knowing the uses of the plants. In addition to being some of her best students, the kids have given her some great business ideas. The recent Harry Potter craze has definitely improved business, and she has opened a School for Witchlets.

Becoming a Woman: Moon Parties

"Children are naturals," Rich says. "They haven't been taught that the spirits of the plants don't exist, so all I have to do is introduce them to the plants and they begin talking with each other. One young girl who had just begun her period came to me one day and asked if I would have a 'moon' party for her and her girlfriends. I asked her what she had in mind. She told me she would like a ritual and maybe a flower essence bar. I was intrigued and asked her to tell me more about her idea. She and her mother had been customers of mine for many years, and she was familiar with how the flower essences work. She said that we could set up a bar with essences that relate to girls her age as they go through this change and let them mix their own medicine and label it. Naming the medicine is one of the important things I have people do. This sets the direction of their healing."

"I asked her what she saw were the concerns she and her friends were facing and what flower essences she thought we should use. She began without hesitation, 'Well, we could have some Jasmine for self-esteem, Naked Lady for loving your body through all its changes, and Wild Pink Rose for dissolving barriers and opening to life's direction.' She went on, naming some of my best remedies. Needless to say, we had the ritual and the party, and it was a huge success. A

Mother Knows Best

Plants have feelings, too! Experiments in Russia show the presence of electrical impulses in plants similar to the nerve impulses in humans. Plants talk, according to Russian scientists, and can communicate their feelings.

Goddess Guide

You know, we actually are making headway. We used to call our menstruation the "curse." Now the girls call it their "moon time."

favorite concoction was a tea we made called 'Becoming a Woman.' It's a time-honored formula I learned in Bavaria and contains common herbs that balance the hormonal changes and harmonize the menstrual cycle. I tell the girls that they can be in charge of their menstrual life."

Boo-Boo Balm

Rich goes on to tell about how the moon parties led to herbal birthday parties. "We gather herbs and take them to my house, where they are prepared while we recant the story of the plant's healing history, continuing the tradition I learned in India. When the medicine is finished steeping, we form a circle, holding the Crock-Pot, and we make our prayers. Then we prepare ointments, salves, or balms. The favorites are a lip balm that the kids can pick the color and flavor for and Boo-Boo Balm, which is guaranteed to fix any cut or scraped knee. Then we serve the ice cream and cake and open the gifts. When the kids go home, they have a product they are very proud of—and a whole bunch of new friends in the plants."

Mother Knows Best

Don't panic if you are so unfortunate as to encounter poison ivy or poison oak; you will find the antidote growing nearby. Plantain is a common herb that will neutralize the toxin. It will also stop bleeding, sooth insect bites and bee and wasp stings, carries natural antiseptic, and coagulates blood. Crush the fresh leaf between your fingers until it juices and apply to the injury. Plantain grows almost everywhere—even in the cracks in the sidewalks of New York City.

School for Witchlets

Harry Potter brought potion-making out of obscurity, and his interest therein has resulted in a new approach to herbal education: the School for Witchlets. "Now kids are seeking me out," Rich says. "They want to know if I can show them how to make a spell—in the first class! I tell them we call it prayer, and yes we can do that." Even though Rich has never had children of her own, she feels she was born to be a mother. Working with the kids has helped her express that side of herself, and she has numerous "fairy god-children."

In the School for Witchlets kids have an opportunity to develop their natural sensitivity to the environment through intuition training. They are taught to be careful with plants and to respect nature. Rich says, "Even children with short attention spans become enthralled when looking for plants. Because they're closer to the ground, they see things that adults miss. They find caterpillars, ants, and every little thing completely interesting. They learn to identify many plants and to give thanks to the creator for this glorious creation."

" " Wise Words _____

George Washington Carver worked with more than just peanuts. He knew the benefits of flowers and spirituality: "When I touch that flower, I am touching infinity. It existed long before there were human beings on this earth and will continue to exist for millions of years to come. Through the flower, I talk to the Infinite, which is only a silent force. This is not a physical contact. It is not in the earthquake, wind, or fire. It is in the invisible world. It is that still small voice that calls up the fairies."

—Peter Tompkins and Christopher Bird, _The Secret Life of Plants_

Rich believes that our experiences as an immigrant nation left us disconnected from our roots, from our home soil, and from nature. When her students reconnect to nature, their inborn connection to it is reawakened. She watches their power of observation increase. "Soon, what was simply a flat field of green suddenly takes on shape and form—and meaning." She feels she demystifies medicine-making, empowers her students with knowledge and skills of the natural world, and helps them become friends with the plants.

Back to the Sea

After more than a quarter of a century of working with the land plants of three continents, Rich was recently reintroduced to the sea and seaweed medicine. She met a professional seaweed gatherer who invited her to meet the ocean. They arose before dawn to get to the shoreline for the lowest tide of the year. There they walked out onto the ocean floor and saw plants that, for the rest of the year when the tide is higher, are hidden beneath the water.

Seaweed Medicine

Rich described the experience of gathering seaweed with her friend: "She walked out into the surf and wrapped herself in the long ropes of kelp, extending her arms high over her head. She held it in her hands and began to sing a beautiful song of the seaweed. 'Since the beginning of time, whenever the people were hungry, in times of drought or times of war, when the crops failed or when for any reason they were without nourishment, they came to the sea. And the sea fed them.'"

Rich talks about the seaweed's ability to heal. "Seaweed matches the salt content of the blood and cell makeup, and it works in harmony with the body's natural healing ability, pulling toxins out, converting them to harmless salts that can then go through the body's elimination system. Seaweed is a natural detoxifier of the ocean itself as well as our own bodies." Although there are limits to when and where individuals can harvest seaweed—and it is a task of considerable effort—many good products can be found in Asian markets and in health food stores. For the beginner, Rich recommends just sprinkling a bit of the dried flakes into your soup or stew.

Beyond Chicken Soup

Here is a recipe for a delicious and nutritious soup that will boost your immune system and warm your tummy! (Many of the ingredients can be found in Asian markets or health food stores.)

Mother Knows Best

You don't have to go deep-sea diving to enjoy seaweed. Seaweed sprinkles can be made by tearing a sheet of nori (a dried, pressed seaweed used to wrap sushi) into small pieces and running it through a clean coffee grinder. Mix the sprinkles with your favorite seasoning such as garlic powder, chili flakes, roasted sesame seeds, or other herbs, and sprinkle on toast, popcorn, or baked potatoes for additional—tasty—nutrition.

Mother's Medicine Soup

1 handful dried nettles (or fresh if you know where to find them)

About 2 inches of seaweed (Kombu or nori)

1 burdock root, sliced

4 to 5 garlic cloves, crushed

Several shiitake mushrooms, chopped

2 red onions, chopped

1 carrot, sliced

2 celery stalks, chopped

2 handfuls spinach or kale leaves

Chili flakes to taste

1 handful cilantro, chopped

1 handful fresh parsley, chopped

$\frac{1}{4}$ cup Bragg's All Natural Liquid Aminos

3 quarts water

Optional seasonings: basil, Italian parsley, dill

Boil ingredients in large pot for 15 minutes or so. Freeze leftovers!

Goddess Guide _____

Food is potential medicine. If possible, eat locally grown organic produce and seasonal food—the fresher the better. Shopping at farmers' markets can give you the opportunity to look into the eyes of the person who grew your food! You can find the nutritional or medical information you need in a book and then eat the things that you need. For example, blueberries are good for gout, nettles are good for arthritis, and corn silk is good for the kidneys. There are common foods and seasonings that are powerful medicine when prepared properly. Garlic, parsley, cilantro, shiitake mushrooms, ginger, all the seasonal vegetables, oregano, basil, thyme, chili flakes, and cayenne all have medicinal qualities. You can boost your mood and your immune system at the same time by adding the right seasonings to your soup.

The Least You Need to Know

- Plants have a long history of healing and maintaining health for human beings. Many other cultures have always understood this and relied on plants as a primary source for their food and medicine.

- You can reconnect to the natural healing properties of plants. Simply find a beginner's book and identify a few plants that live close to your house. From then on, your intuition will guide you.

- Children have a natural connection to their environment and learn plant identification and medicine-making quickly.

- Intuition and your inner voice will often let you know what's next in your life, and you can learn to hear it and follow it.

- For thousands of years the ocean has been used as a major resource for vitamins, minerals, and healing plants. As a culture, we are just beginning to understand the importance of natural healing.

Chapter 23

Embodying Prayer

In This Chapter

- ◆ Rewiring the brain and balancing the body
- ◆ Making room for the spirit
- ◆ Finding God in 12-step recovery
- ◆ Circling the wagons

The custom regarding prayer and meditation within women's spirituality is strictly one of personal choice. Many women rely on very traditional forms, and many women use nontraditional practices you may not have thought of as spiritual disciplines. Rather than specific prayers, I've chosen to explore some time-honored practices that are somewhat unconventional for the Western mind and also some newer approaches to renewing the spirit.

Ancient Mind/Body Meditation

Labyrinths are circular geometric forms that define sacred space. They have been found in almost every culture and date back as far as 4,500 years. They've been found carved or scratched on stones and graves, etched on pottery, and printed on coins in Greece, Egypt, India, France, England, Ireland, Algeria, Scandinavia, and Iceland as well as in Native American and Mayan cultures. The most famous remaining labyrinth is in Chartres Cathedral, built about 1200 C.E. near Paris, France. Like cathedrals, Stonehenge, and the pyramids, labyrinths show how physical (external) space interacts with spiritual (inner) space, bringing insight by connecting us to a natural and very physical sense of spirituality.

Seven Circuits: Seven Chakras

Labyrinths exist in three basic designs: 7-circuit, 11-circuit, and 12-circuit. The most common design found today is the seven-circuit design pictured here.

The seven paths of a seven-circuit labyrinth design resemble the brain.

The seven-circuit design is also called the Cretan Labyrinth, because it was found on coins there. The seven paths take you to the center and correspond to the seven chakras. You might remember from Chapter 20, "The Soulbody," that the chakras are energy centers felt in the body and located along the spine and skull. As the brain is stimulated, the spinal fluid is affected and the chakras are energized. The brain experiences an unwinding, centering, and rewinding during the process of walking a labyrinth.

As you follow the labyrinth's path, you wander along a series of circuits, each one composed of 180-degree switchbacks. As you look at a labyrinth's pattern, you might notice how it looks like a diagram of the brain. The turns actually do "wake up" the brain by stimulating the right and left hemispheres, bringing balance, and quieting the mind. As you move deeper into the circular design, you move deeper into your inner world.

Christians adapted the labyrinth as the threefold path of Purgation, Illumination, and Union to represent three stages in a labyrinth walk.

1. **Releasing (Purgation).** The entrance to the center is the path of letting go. There is a release and an emptying of worries and concerns.

2. **Receiving (Illumination).** At the center, illumination, insight, clarity, and focus occur. This is a receptive, prayerful, meditative state.

3. **Integrating (Union).** The path out is one of integration. The insight is being woven into your thoughts, energized and ready to be manifested in the world.

Walking the Labyrinth

Although each person who walks the labyrinth's path has a different experience, the design symbolizes the womb. Walking it represents the soul's journey into the center of creation and its return again to the external world through rebirth. The Hopi people consider the labyrinth a symbol for "mother earth," and its function is similar to a ceremonial Kiva.

Walking a labyrinth is about the journey, not the destination. Before beginning your labyrinth journey, pause at the entrance for a few moments to collect yourself. Take a couple deep breaths, and let your mind clear. You might begin your meditation by calling on the higher power you honor. Walk slowly until you reach the center. Spend as long as you like in the center in quiet awareness. When it feels right, begin your journey out again, walking slowly and with mindfulness. It is recommended that you spend some time in further reflection on your experience after you exit the labyrinth. Like other meditative experiences, the labyrinth will continue to bring you new insights long after you finish your walk through it.

A labyrinth meditation is said to clear your mind, and as you meander toward the labyrinth's center, your journey can help you find your own center. Many people use it as a way of resolving difficulties, entering the labyrinth with a concern or question and emerging feeling much different about the situation, even finding helpful insight. Walking a labyrinth can be used as a time for prayer, meditation, reflection, personal healing, creativity enhancement, relaxation, and sometimes just an enjoyable experience.

> **Goddess Guide**
>
> The power of the circular configuration is both ancient and mysterious. Many who are familiar with this form of sacred space talk about its interactive quality. It seems that a labyrinth both gives and receives from those who participate in its unique prayer form. Using the labyrinth adds energy to it and increases its capacity to transform, as well as energizing those who travel it.

Shekhinah's Labyrinth

My first experience walking a labyrinth was at the Shekhinah Center's Kathy Norris Breast Cancer Help Program for Women, where a group of people had built a large 11-circuit labyrinth on a hill overlooking a sprawling valley below. The site was on a farm belonging to the director of the program, Patty Silver. The labyrinth was built as a group process, working with dowsing rods to determine the exact placement of the each rock—a total of 13 tons of rocks was used. The entire effort took almost six months and involved many people, including students from Silver's son's elementary school, who came to study the configuration and to participate in building it.

Goddess Guide

Children love making laby-rinths, and one can be made very easily by raking a spiral path through your fall leaves, in the sand at the beach, or by using other elements of nature's bounty. You don't have to attempt the most difficult configuration first. Begin with a simple spiral version, and experiment from there.

As I walked the circuits of the labyrinth, I felt a deep-ening and quieting come over me. I experienced a slight disorientation—as if I was unwiring my brain. Silver told me to stop anywhere along the way and spend as much time in meditation as I felt like doing. The labyrinth was designed to balance the chakras, and so sometimes you might need to spend more time with one circuit than another if you need to balance certain chakras. By the time I reached the center, I didn't really know what to expect. As I stood there, I felt my body swaying in a circular motion, and I felt "inside of myself." On the way out of the labyrinth, I was aware of a feeling of mental clarity—my mind felt quiet and open.

The labyrinth at the Shekhinah Center's Kathy Norris Breast Cancer Help Program for Women, in Knoxville, Tennessee.

Goddess Guide

You can draw a labyrinth and trace its path with your finger. Even this very slight connection will give you an idea how it works. If it catches your imagination, you can always experiment further. Like many of the ancient practices you have been reading about in this book, it wouldn't have been in so many cultures for so long if it didn't transmit spiritual wisdom.

Yoga: Five Thousand Years of Holistic Health

Like the labyrinth, *yoga* is a spiritual practice that works with the physical body. The main purpose of yoga is to open space in your body for more breath—your life force. Yoga is often associated with Hinduism, but it is actually a much older spiritual practice—perhaps the oldest physical discipline in existence. Its exact origins are not known, but the earliest evidence of yoga can be traced back to about 3000 B.C.E., making it at least 5,000 years old. The original purpose of the postures and breathing exercises was to bring stability and relaxation to the body to prepare the practitioner to enter the stillness of meditation. That intention remains true today.

Womanspeak

Yoga is a Sanskrit word that means "to merge, join, or unite" and describes a group of related disciplines that promote the unity of the individual and a supreme being through a system of breathing exercises, postures, and rituals.

Union with God

The word *yoga* comes from the Sanskrit language and means "to merge, join, or unite." It refers to the practitioner's desire to find union with God. By controlling the breath and holding the body in a steady posture, yoga balances and harmonizes the body, mind, and emotions. Using movement, breath, posture, relaxation, and meditation, yoga assists in creating a quiet space within, which translates to a balanced life and harmony with one's environment and in relationships with others. The essence of yoga is to take command of your life through control of the body. It's a lifelong pursuit and is accomplished through practice.

In the practice of yoga, you are never in competition with anyone but yourself. Postures range from basic to complex. As you progress in your practice, you are rewarded by your own improvement and feelings of well-being. Many stress-management programs and hospitals now recognize the health-promoting aspects of yoga and include gentle yoga postures and breathing techniques to aid the recovery of patients with heart disease, because of both its physical strengthening and its calming and meditative qualities.

Wise Words

"The supreme godhead resides in the heart of every being."
—Yoga saying

Hatha Yoga Is Better Than No Yoga at All

There are many different systems within the practice of yoga; the one most familiar to Westerners is called Hatha yoga. The word *Hatha* is a combination of *ha*, which means "sun," and *tha*, which means "moon." Yoga is the union of the two, suggesting that the healthy joining of opposites—yin and yang, mind and body, engagement and relaxation—leads to health, vitality, and peace of mind.

Yoga complements any spiritual path or religion. Although yoga is not a religion, it is centered in a set of ethics. Its ethical principles promote the following:

- Nonviolence
- Truthfulness
- Honesty

- Chastity
- Generosity
- Purity
- Contentment
- Self-discipline
- Self-study
- Centering on the divine

Womanspeak

Hatha is a Sanskrit word combining *ha*, which means "sun," and *tha*, which means "moon," thus showing its emphasis on bringing balance.

Wise Words

The benefits of yoga are becoming widely acknowledged as more hospitals and medical centers sponsor classes and integrate yoga or tai chi moves in patient care. Christy Wagner, my copy and production editor (and yoga and tai chi practicer of several years), says: "My yoga classes are offered through the wellness department of the largest hospital here in Indianapolis. Even my 80-year-old grandmother, who is in physical therapy recovering from a broken bone, has been given some basic yoga and tai chi postures to help her strengthen not only her leg, but her whole body."

Yoga continues to gain popularity as an estimated six million Americans practice it today. In addition to gaining recognition among the medical profession, an increasing number of churches offer classes, particularly those that promote mind/body spirituality. Part of its attractiveness lies in the fact that it can be practiced by young and old alike. Specially trained instructors are able to assist even the physically challenged individual to create a specifically tailored yoga workout that will maximize health and promote well-being.

> ### Goddess Guide _____
>
> In yoga, the body is gently worked in all directions, and every muscle gets stretched and toned. A yoga workout massages the internal organs, helping improve their functions. The spine is flexed, extended, rotated, and twisted. This creates greater joint mobility and is encouraged to maintain a healthy, upright, and pain-free condition. The circulation is improved. The breathing capacity and elasticity of the lungs is enhanced.

Keeping It Simple

Since its humble beginnings in 1939, Alcoholics Anonymous (AA) has helped millions of people recover from the disease of alcohol addiction. Over the years it has spawned many other programs, each focusing on different areas of addiction recovery and based on the 12 steps and 12 traditions found in the *Big Book of Alcoholics Anonymous*. The program is entirely self-supporting, refuses to own property, and each group functions autonomously, following the guidelines laid out in the traditions. The 12-step programs are based on the understanding of unity with one another through a relationship with the higher power, regardless of how you name that being. Leadership is based on service work. Here are the stories of two women who have found their spirituality within the 12-step communities.

> ### Sophia's Wisdom
>
> We're taking a closer look at Alcoholics Anonymous for a couple reasons. One is because of its importance to contemporary society—many have found it to be a valuable spiritual path. And second, because it provides a proven example of how a spiritual program can function according to what might be described as "feminine principles," in that AA is a spiritual program with no stated theology. It is built on the idea of a higher power, which is defined through each individual's understanding. There are no commandments (only suggestions), no hierarchy, and no authority outside of self as expressed through the group's consciousness. Wisdom is shared through stories in which personal experiences are shared.

Divorcing God

Deborah P. joined Alcoholics Anonymous in 1983, and she says "I believe in recovery." For her, recovery is all about living life more fully. "Living life more fully often requires us getting bigger, and I am willing to grow. You do that by taking a good look at yourself and being willing to make changes." Deborah began to make those changes the day she walked into her first meeting. She is an African American woman who grew up in a segregated world. She carries many scars from those experiences as well as the pain of childhood abuse in her own home. She had to change how she felt about white people, and she also had to change Gods. "I had my mother's God, not mine. Her God was mean, judgmental, and punishing. He was out to get me if I wasn't perfect. I knew I wasn't, so that meant only one thing!" The people Deborah met (at the all-white meeting) were kind, patient, and loving. They just kept saying, "Keep coming back." And she did. "If I missed a meeting, someone called me right away to find out if I was all right or if I needed a ride. I wasn't prepared for that!"

Deborah says, "I divorced my mother's God and got one of my own! My God is loving, patient, caring, just, and never, never, judgmental. He has no color, and I don't mind saying he is a male—he is the father I never had." Alcoholism is a family disease, and Deborah, like many others in recovery, has survived a difficult childhood. "There were times when I just wanted to die. I remember lying out in a field in a rainstorm with thunder and lightning all around me, just wishing I would die. I was nine years old." Today, she knows she never has to feel that way again, and she never has to be alone.

Deborah has been a sponsor to many people in her almost 20 years of recovery. It's a familiar sight to find her and one or two other women in close conversation over dinner in a local restaurant. "Fourteen of the women I worked with now have more than 10 years in recovery!" she says proudly.

Deborah is an alcohol and drug counselor in a treatment facility, a mother, and a grandmother. Her spirituality is one of service. She follows the suggestions of the 12-step program and relies on prayer, meditation, and working with others to support her spirituality. She also likes the poetry of Maya Angelou, whom she finds to be a model of self-esteem and self-love. She especially likes the poem "Still I Rise" for its hope and because she has lived it!

> **Wise Words**
>
> "I see God in everything—especially in the faces of recovering people."
>
> —Deborah P., recovering alcoholic

> **Wise Words**
>
> "Just like moons and like suns,
> With the certainty of tides,
> Just like hopes springing high,
> Still I rise."
>
> —From Maya Angelou's, "Still I Rise"

Finding *Your* Higher Power

Laurie S. is a member of Narcotics Anonymous (NA) and also practices women's spirituality. In fact, it was through NA that she discovered her higher power was the goddess. Here is her story:

"The 12-step recovery programs all refer to the 'higher power' (H.P.) or the God of your understanding," she says. "There is no definition or spin put on it. You are free to imagine God in any way that works for you. At any given meeting, everyone in the room is praying to a "different" H.P.! There is never an argument over God, because it is all about the one of your understanding. About six weeks into my recovery I began to get an image of a 'Big Mama.' I didn't know about the goddess, but later when I saw statues of her, she and Big Mama looked a lot alike."

Laurie describes her prayer life: "Every morning I get down on my knees and ask my higher power to take charge of my day, to keep me clean and sober, and to help me remember to be of service in every interaction. Before going to sleep at night, I again get down on my knees and say thanks to H.P. for another day. I'm a 10-, 11-, and 12-stepper. When I get in bed, I take out my tenth-step notebook and I reflect on my day." I asked her to explain the tenth-step process.

Into Action

"'The Spiritual Life is not a theory. *We have to live it.*' This is from the *Big Book of Alcoholics Anonymous.* There are 12 steps and 12 traditions that are like the backbone of the program. It is all about action! The tenth step says: 'Continued to take personal inventory and when we were wrong promptly admitted it.' The program is about taking responsibility for your actions. The way I do my tenth step is to go over my day and see if I might be getting sloppy in my interactions with others. It lets you see right away if there is a pattern developing. It also lets you feel good about yourself as you see that you are being a 'good neighbor' to the world.

"The eleventh step tells me to continue prayer and mediation to improve my conscious contact with God. In the morning, I read a page out of a daily meditation book and then sit still for about 10 to 20 minutes. I have also found that when I stop throughout the day for just a few minutes, it slows me down enough that I feel connected."

Wise Words

"If there is something I need to set straight, I do it right away. I don't make a big deal about it, but I clean up the little spills as I go. It is amazing how good it makes me feel."

—Laurie S., recovering narcotic addict

Sophia's Wisdom

Laurie describes how, "slowly over the years, the 12 steps have built a container in my head for my mind. It used to like to run wild, fiercely resisting everyone and everything. Today I have a sense of order. Today I can sit and listen to someone with whom I have a disagreement and not feel threatened or feel the need to argue. I guess that is called tolerance. Today I know that I am better off to be of service than to seek recognition. I guess that is about developing humility. This is a 'we' program. It says that together we are doing what none of us could do alone. Today I know how to ask for help. I don't know what you call that, but it sure works for me."

Going in Circles

The film *How to Make an American Quilt* showed how a group of women used an old tradition of a quilting circle as their centering point. At one level, they met to make quilts. At a deeper level, their circle was where they shared their lives, solved problems, and found deeper meaning to life. It also became the way they passed important information on to the next generation. If you are interested in exploring your spiritual process through women's spirituality, you might want to draw a group of friends together and work from the traditional place: a circle. Working with a group of women in a circle is a powerful way of connecting with your wisdom and also with the accumulated wisdom we all share.

Circles of Time

A circle is probably the most intrinsically female geometric form. It represents the roundness of the female body, hips, breasts, and womb. Our very first experience of the world is in our mother's round belly. The roundness of the earth itself reminds us of safety, nurturing, and home. As the earth rotates and moves in a circular path around the sun, it forms our understanding of life in roundness and rotation. The moon, the turning of the seasons, birth, death, and rebirth are ancient circular patterns and feminine images.

Early tribal villages were built with round shapes—round hearths, round houses, and round ceremonial circles that echoed the primal circular pattern. In a circle, all members face each other; all are equal. In the circle, as backs are turned to the "outside" world, the energy is pulled into the center. It represents sacred or consecrated space. A circle offers protection against the world.

Tribal dancing follows circular patterns, as do later folk dances. Prehistoric sites such as Stonehenge were built in a circular shape, and King Arthur designed his famous Round Table based on the classic symbol of equality. It showed that all who sat at the table were equal; there was no hierarchical ranking there.

Sophia's Wisdom

The snake, also a mystical symbol, is often pictured forming a circle with its tail in its mouth, symbolizing the unending aspect of eternal life, the divine, which has no beginning and no end (see the figure in Chapter 3). In addition to the circular shape of the snake, the shedding of its skin is a symbol of resurrection and the ongoing evolution of life. The snake also symbolizes our spirit as it is at home in the underworld (the unconscious or spirit world) as well as the upper world in which we live.

Throughout the ancient world, it was commonly believed that the female form gave birth to the universe. This is a likely conclusion, because all of nature was observed to function this way. A variation of the circle, the egg is also an archetypal feminine form that is associated with birthing and with divine origins and represents the Great Mother, who gave birth to all of creation.

As architecture developed, circles gave birth to domes. Pagan temples such as the Pantheon in Rome have survived from ancient time. Domes represented the sky and were often painted blue with stars in the form of constellations. Romans further developed the art of constructing domes, and they become one of the primary architectural forms associated with temples, churches, and mosques.

Wise Words

"'God is a circle whose circumference is nowhere and whose center is everywhere,' is a Hindu saying, and God as the unbroken circle was an image for the Gnostic communities."

—Barbara G. Walker, *Symbols and Sacred Objects* (Harper, 1988)

Talking in Circles

If you have decided you want to create a circle, we suggest you work with one or two other women who are also interested. Decide what kind of group you want, and let the others come together around it.

Some things to decide are …

- ◆ Will this circle be based on a religious faith or move outside traditional religion?
- ◆ Will the goddess be the focus of your circle?
- ◆ Are you going to explore Earth spirituality?
- ◆ What sources will you draw on?

Your core group will guide the rest of the group. Once it has been assembled, other issues on how the circle will function can be group decisions, but for now, you or your core members can determine what its essential nature will be. Next, you will begin to invite others who are interested in the same focus as you to join. Make your list carefully. This is like inviting people to a very intimate dinner party. You don't want to throw the doors open to just everybody.

Sophia's Wisdom

Belly dancing originally had nothing to do with stripping, seduction, or harems. It was a religious ceremonial dance connected to birthing and was part of the goddess sacred rites. Women danced to encourage the mother and to celebrate the birth. The dance's undulating movements strengthen muscles used in labor and delivery. Its proper name in the Middle East, where it originated, is *Raks Shari,* meaning "the dance of the Orient." Women dance together with their friends, neighbors, aunts, mothers, and cousins to celebrate family occasions. The belly dance is a spiritual connection between mind and body. It brings the dancer a sense of well-being, joy, and freedom. Most important, it's a celebration of the feminine soul and spirit through movement.

Mother Knows Best

"Choose only psychologically stable people." You aren't creating a therapy group, so you don't want to have to be dealing with people's unprocessed emotional "stuff" all the time. This isn't a judgment but common sense. This sage advice comes from *Sacred Circles,* by Robin Deen Carnes and Sally Craig (Harper, 1998).

Take time to really reflect on whom you *want* in the circle. It isn't necessarily appropriate to invite just anybody, and definitely not people you don't want but think you should include. For example, if you have decided that you want to explore the goddess and your best friend finds that idea threatening, maybe you don't need to have her there. This isn't a primarily social group; its intention is to do some deep spiritual work together.

You want people who are doing some other kind of spiritual work, and it doesn't matter if the faith journeys are different. In fact, diversity gives your group depth. We suggest first talking with the different women you are considering inviting and finding out if they are interested in what you are offering. Only then invite them to the membership meeting.

Shaping the Vision

As the core group, you will talk about your vision for the group. In other words, you have already decided on the direction you are going and are asking if there are others who are interested in joining you. Ask each woman to share a bit about herself and also what she would like to have happen in the circle. If the visions don't match, it usually quickly becomes clear. People will have questions that will further sharpen your focus and begin to shape your vision.

The level of commitment to the group is a defining factor. This is a bit like the early stages of dating. You know you are shopping for a deep and lasting relationship. You want to date only people you know have a potential of going there with you, yet you can't get there until you know each other better. If the core group has already made a commitment to doing deep work, then you probably will need to meet together for a couple of years. This probably can't be decided up front with a larger group. We suggest you make a shorter commitment to begin exploration. Those who are ready for deeper work will become apparent as time goes on.

As you begin to design the structure, further sorting out will happen. Practical decisions you will be making include the following:

◆ Where to meet

◆ How long

◆ How often

◆ Topics

◆ Specific form

◆ Style and tone

◆ Leadership rotation

Appendix C, "Resources," offers excellent resources to help you.

Rules Are in Pencil, Not Stone!

The rule-making is a group process. This keeps it from being paternalistic, which means making rules for other people. If you have problems with any of the rules, talk about it. The rules won't be cast in stone; they will only be on a piece of paper. You can even write them in pencil. It might be a good idea to have a copy for each person. Establish a time to review the rules and make the changes you feel will work better.

 **Goddess Guide**

You want your circle to be responsive to the needs of the group and to accomplish what you want it to accomplish. So it is a good idea to have at least a rough idea of what you want to accomplish and establish a regular feedback time when members can talk about how it is working for them. Because everyone is so busy in today's world, you can make this time of reflection and feedback a ritual. This is really one of the ways we can change from the old models and take more personal ownership of our spirituality and spiritual practices.

Things that might help you are …

◆ Have timeframes for sharing and a way of letting people know when they are getting close to the limit. Also decide on the times to begin and end the meeting and respect them.

◆ Learn how to listen without interrupting or commenting.

◆ Agree on a statement of confidentiality.

◆ Don't project your feelings on other members. It is okay to ask someone how she feels, but don't make any assumptions.

◆ Don't "fix" members. Make it a rule from the beginning that if anyone needs anything, even a drink of water, an extra pillow, a pat on the back, or a group hug, she will ask for it.

◆ Respect the inner knowing process. Other than brief readings that can be the source for reflection, avoid bringing books, quotations, and other outside references into the circle.

◆ Empower your leader by allowing her to guide the group through the process, keeping you on track.

And for troubleshooting …

◆ You'll have time when you need to resolve conflict in the group. This is okay! Just find a good process for conflict resolution and work through it. Very good things can happen.

◆ Keep things fair. If one person begins to dominate the meeting with long stories, needs too much attention, or always has a problem, deal with it as a group. It won't go away on its own.

◆ Design a process for someone to leave the group if things can't be resolved—if that is the best resolution.

◆ Avoid telling people what you think or even know is the right answer. This circle is about each one of you learning how to find her own answers.

Here's a partial list of statements that will keep you tuned in and also out of the way while you encourage a person to find her inner knowing:

◆ "You have the answer."

◆ "Stay with it, you'll get it."

◆ "As creative as you are, I know you'll have a really great solution when the time is right."

◆ "Relax—it will surface."

◆ "You know what you need to know when you need to know it."

◆ What would the answer be if you could imagine it?

All of these statements work well any time you are listening to someone express a difficult situation.

The Least You Need to Know

◆ Women find spiritual nourishment in traditional prayer forms, meditation, and also in ancient ways that are "new" to the Western world.

◆ These older forms for prayer and meditation are centered on the physical body as well as the spirit.

◆ The relatively new (1939) Alcoholics Anonymous program has become an important path for many who find recovery from addiction as well as a new revelation of the sacred.

◆ Following ancient patterns and traditions, many women today create circles in which to explore their spirituality.

Chapter 24

Transforming Culture

In This Chapter

- ◆ No barrier is too great for a SISTER
- ◆ Making choices and taking chances
- ◆ Outside the lines and beyond the borders
- ◆ Healing racial wounds with art and ritual

Women's spirituality often is directed toward bettering society and being of service to the world. Since the very earliest days of this country, women have been on the forefront of the major social issues, advocating for justice, instituting social services, and fighting for equality. This tradition continues today. We'll look at three women in present-day society and the programs they represent that show how spirituality is inseparable from life and how women continue to be the guiding force in transforming society.

The Sisters

The SISTER program is a unique and successful alcohol and drug treatment program that is now in its eleventh year of helping African American women get clean and sober. *SISTER* stands for Supported Intensive System of Treatment Empowerment and Recovery. The program began out of the realization that black women faced the same problems that white women faced while battling addiction, yet very few of them were seeking treatment. In 1990 Darlene

Fowler-Stephen, with 21 years of experience in the alcohol and drug unit of Meharry Hospital in Nashville, Tennessee, set out with a team of others to remove the barriers between African American women and recovery. The program creates a strong visibility through their famous bright pink jackets and pink flyers, along with an ongoing outreach directly into the communities, housing projects, jails, and prisons, where women are often trapped in their addictions. The most important ingredient to their success is their heart-felt dedication to their mission.

The Pink Badge of Honor

Fowler-Stephen recounts, "That first trip out into the projects was a little intimidating. We didn't know what to expect. We made our way through drug dealers and teenagers to deliver flyers and talk with the women about addiction." Soon their bright pink satin jackets with the name SISTER proudly displayed on the back became a badge of honor around town and in the projects. On one hot summer day, Fowler-Stephen remembers heading into the housing project without her jacket and being hassled by some young boys who were kicking rocks at her and her companion as they approached. They went back to the car and put the jackets on, and the boys' attitude sharply changed. A voice announced their approach to the others, saying, "Leave them alone! Those are the Sisters—they're here to help!"

 Wise Words _____

"Once a Sister always a Sister! When a woman joins the SISTER program, she is a member for life—regardless of her ability to stay clean and sober. Many have re-lapsed; however, they know they can return without judgment and be met with love and compassion. Some women who are still using refer others to the program, saying, 'I'm not ready yet, but this person needs help. I told her you can help.'"
—From SISTER literature

The bottom line of the SISTER program is, "If you want to get clean and sober, we'll help you no matter what." The program's philosophy is empowerment, and they use every opportunity to encourage, praise, and love women into making a choice for a better life. "It takes a certain type of person to work here," says Dominique, one of the counselors. "Not everyone can do this work. It is very demanding. We stay available to the women at all times." The program takes every woman who wants to come as soon as the space is available. "Some of them arrive in pretty bad shape straight off the street; some have just been beaten by their boyfriend or husband; some are angry and abusive to the staff at first. You have to be able to hang in there with them, and not everyone can do that." Regina, a professional singer and staff member, told about standing at the foot of the bed and literally singing a woman to sleep. "She just wouldn't settle down any other way," said Regina.

The SISTER program's mission statement is …

1. Enabling African American mothers residing in public housing, together with their families, to lead more productive lives by increasing their self-esteem and empowering them to live drug-free.

2. Improving treatment outcomes for the mothers by increasing accessibility of a comprehensive system of treatment services and aftercare programs, including health, mental health, social, educational, and vocational services.

"It Takes a Village …"

"It takes a village to raise a child" is an African proverb. The greatest barriers to women getting into treatment are their children. That's a catch-22. Women won't and can't leave their children because the Department of Children and Human Services will take them, and many women are afraid they won't get them back. They're also afraid they'll lose their jobs, which is often the case, and that they'll get thrown out of their apartment, which is also likely to happen. When a woman is admitted as an inpatient, the SISTER program will find safe places for the children.

"We have surrogate families, aunties, and grandmothers all over town, or we'll pay for childcare," says Fowler-Stephen. If a woman is an outpatient, the SISTER program will often end up taking care of the kids—making the "it takes a village" axiom a reality! Dominique told about how she was waiting to be interviewed for a staff position while three children belonging to a client were climbing all over her. She played with them, not showing any signs of distress. The secretary got up and went into Fowler-Stephen's office and apparently told her "You better hire this one—she can handle the kids!" Dominique got the job!

The SISTER program offers a home environment and a chance to make the choice to trade in misery for a new way of life. Over the years, 850 women have taken that choice. Henny is one of those women, and she is proud of herself today—as is the staff, who sing her praises. Henny is determined to earn a pink jacket! Six weeks of successfully staying clean and sober earns each woman a T-shirt with the SISTER motto, six months deserves a cup, and after one year, she is

> ### Sophia's Wisdom
>
> Over the years, the SISTER program has been featured on NPR and *ABC World News Tonight* and in *The Los Angeles Times*, *Parade Magazine*, and *Family Circle* magazine as well as in local newspapers. The model has been exported to several other towns in Tennessee as well as California, Louisiana, Wisconsin, Florida, Alabama, and Indiana. They also train staff for other programs.

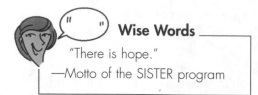

given the highly respected pink jacket bearing the SISTER logo. When the client reaches the three-year mark, she is expected to give something back to the program. Women do that in many ways. Some give their time; others write a song or a poem; and some fix dinner and bring it to the staff and guests.

The spirit of the women who gave up their lunch hour to talk with me was heartwarming. Regina, a long-time counselor, talked about the support she received through hard times—the death of her parents and the recent death of her only child—saying, "Thanks to this program and these women, I can face my life without drugs or alcohol." Frances told how the Sisters are her family: "They're my sisters, I'm a part of their lives, and they are a part of mine." For Brenda, SISTER means that "my boys and I can be together." Narketta says the program "saved my life." Krystal knows "it is way more than a job, it is a ministry." The women all laughed and recounted stories about themselves and each other. I sneaked a sideways glance at Fowler-Stephen, and she was, as I suspected she would be, looking proud of her sisters.

Crossing International Boundaries

I have talked throughout the book about how women's spirituality is focused more on finding common ground than in establishing differences. I thought it would be interesting to see how this works in reality at the institutional level. In looking for a model, I discovered The International Institute of Integral Human Sciences and The College of Human Sciences, a global network of men and women from all over the world who meet and discuss issues relating to human consciousness, healing, education, and ministry.

Crop Circles and Singing Nuns

Looking at the program for the 2001 conference, I saw "An African Evening" with chanting, dancing, and drumming—in full costume!—led by Selby Bheki Gumby, a Zulu priest from South Africa; the Honorable Nokozua Mndende, M.P., also of South Africa; and Chipo Shambare of Zimbabwe and Canada. There were studies on the Kabbalah, a Cosmic Liturgy, "Mystery Schools of Ancient China," the singing nuns, and "Crop Circles: Archetypal Symbols or Code Language and Guiding Images from a Space Science?" There was a class offered called "Staying in Touch with Heaven, a Key Concept in Ancient Judaism, Early Christianity, and other Great World Religions" offered by Fr. John Rossner, O. Tr., Ph.D., D Litt., and another called "Using Intuition and Gifts of the Spirit in Professional Practice and Ministerial Counseling," offered by Marilyn Zwaig Rossner, Ed.D., Ph.D.

I decided to investigate further and discovered that the Drs. Rossner were the founders of the institute and had an interesting story to tell. Here's how they met and the reasons behind the school they founded.

A Vision for Today

Marilyn Zwaig Rossner began having visions as a child and was surprised to find everyone didn't have them. Her grandmother appeared to her regularly and introduced her to an Indian swami who talked to her in Sanskrit, which she mysteriously understood. She now knows it was Swami Sivananda, the great saint of Rishikesh in the Himalayas, who was living in India. In her own words, "I went on to read Sivanandas's works and the story of his life and took part in devotions and yoga classes in the tradition which he had established. I know I made an earthly connection with the Sage of Rishikesh that had already been made in heaven …!"

Rossner describes the events and coincidences that occur throughout life that you know must be "engineered by heaven" or "higher spiritual worlds." She has always felt the presence of unseen hands that have guided her from behind the scenes onto the path that she was meant to follow. At particularly important junctures something coincidental and completely unexpected and spontaneous has happened, leading her on to the next step. She recalls a vision she had at age 14 in which she married a priest. "I didn't know there was such a thing as an Anglican priest. I later met and married my husband of over a quarter of a century, John Rossner, an Anglican priest."

> **Wise Words**
>
> "I have never doubted the existence of God. I was raised in a devout Jewish family and later added Jesus, yoga, and meditation to my spiritual practice, and I find no contradiction to this mix."
>
> —Marilyn Zwaig Rossner

Reconciling Science and Spirituality

Soon after marrying, the Rossners began to explore an emerging field of consciousness and healing, and in 1975 they established The International Institute of Integral Human Sciences. This organization gave birth to an international professional association for people involved in this pursuit called The College of Human Sciences, a global network of pioneering scholars and religious leaders dedicated to developing research and general educational programs for the study of human consciousness and intuition. They created the Spiritual Science Fellowship of Canada, affiliated with the International Council of Community Churches and the World Council of Churches.

> ### Sophia's Wisdom
>
> John Rossner reminds us that throughout history visions, apparitions, prophecies, divination, telepathy, and other psychic phenomena have played a major role in the birth of great religions and civilizations of the world—including Christianity. Today's culture has almost lost contact with its roots in these ancient wisdom sources; however, the world of spiritual insight and modern scientific discoveries have begun to converge. As these two worlds, sometimes seen as conflicting, reconnect, they offer a better understanding of our human religious experience.

The institute offers classes in Personal Spiritual and Psychic Development, East West Spirituality, New Sciences and Healing, and Pastoral Studies in Therapeutic Counseling and Interfaith Ministry. In addition to the course work, the institution sponsors a yearly seminar in which scholars and scientists from all over the world come to lecture and give workshops on a wide variety of subjects relating to spiritualism, shamanism, ministry, the Kabbalah, Christian mysticism, and Tibetan Buddhism—all directed toward the reconciliation of science with spirituality and universal human values.

> ### Sophia's Wisdom
>
> The increasing number of women entering the field of law is resulting in changes in how law is being practiced. It certainly is responsible for the current trend toward mediation as a way of solving many situations that would have previously gone into litigation. E. Finney Clarkson is an attorney mediator who practices "kitchen table law." She finds typical law offices are intimidating for her clients, the majority of whom are women. Sitting around the kitchen table in her office puts everyone at ease. Clarkson sees her job as empowering her clients and helping them realize they have the answers for many of their concerns within themselves. She enjoys helping clients make sense out of their lives. She finds that mediation, especially done around the kitchen table, creates an environment in which relationship can be supported.

Building Bridges

In 1990 Noris Binet, a native of the Dominican Republic, moved to Tennessee and soon after had a vision for a project that could begin the healing process between black and white women in her community. She spearheaded a multilevel project called *Black and White Women Building a Bridge in the Land of the Native American*. It began on the five hundredth anniversary of the European occupation of the Americas. Binet's project unfolded over a four-year period and involved rituals, small group discussions, public forums, and an art show—all focused on issues of race. Binet's qualifications for such a project are unique. She was born and raised in the Dominican Republic and lived for 12 years in Mexico, where she studied with the Huichol Indians. For the past 11 years she has made her home in the United States. Her Caribbean ancestry includes African, Native American, and Caucasian.

Huichol Wisdom

Binet believes women are innate healers and naturally see connections. She had a vision of how women artists could come together and begin to build a bridge between the races to create different experiences of each other and a different way of seeing themselves. She then set out to help design and build that bridge.

Binet brought many years of experience to the project as a sociologist and therapist who had participated in many large celebrations in Mexico, where art, theater, dance, ceremony, and politics all freely mixed on a regular basis. "Every time you look out the window you see the priest, altar boys, men, and women carrying candles and holy pictures processing down the middle of the street. Many are wearing costumes or carrying big masks representing whatever local politics are going on. It's the natural way for Latin people," she said. In addition to her training and experience, Binet brings her particular gifts of creative thinking, tireless energy, and a vision of how even a few can make a big difference.

> **Sophia's Wisdom**
>
> Binet's work has brought her to the realization of the importance of creating environments where women can be truly themselves—places where their visions and identities are acknowledged and validated. When this safe space is created, they naturally explore and learn to embrace who they are, love their bodies, and find their creative and spiritual identities.

Wise Words

"This project explores the multifaceted aspects of bridges. It is not only the physical bridge created by the very existence of the artwork of this group of women, but that this group of women worked together in several workshops, building emotional and spiritual bridges and exploring one of the most important bridges—the one that each individual started to build within herself, with her body, with her inner self, with her creative process and her healing energy."

—Noris Binet, *Women on the Inner Journey* (James C. Winston, 1994)

The model Binet used to create the far-reaching project of social healing is an ancient Huichol Indian ceremonial form. She felt that was particularly significant because the project would begin on the five hundredth anniversary of European occupation of America and because she knew firsthand what a powerful transformational process it offered.

"I had to begin by getting a clear picture of who I was in this project and what my intention was," Binet says. "I saw myself as a bridge. I am not black or white; I am both. I'm also an outsider; I had been codified differently. My culture is more inclusive; everyone is racially mixed. There is a statue outside of the Museum of Modern Art in the Dominican Republic acknowledging the mixing of race. Here in the United States, at least in Nashville in 1990, it wasn't talked about. Yet most blacks have white and Indian blood, and most whites have black and Indian blood. I could look at the women and see how they were alike, rather than different. The issue isn't skin color, it's conditioning—it is how you are taught to see."

Breaking Old Boundaries

"The prejudices I had to deal with were my light skin color, which made the black women uneasy; my 'not white, either,' skin, which made the white women uneasy; and my status as a foreigner from a third-world country. Because of the level of distrust that existed between the two groups of women, I designed this project as a process rather than an event. I knew it would have to be deeper than just a showing of art; we would have to deal with the past. I also knew we should not begin with words, as words would lead to accusations, guilt, and run the risk of further separation. Words express thoughts, and thoughts are always in the past. They are reflections on our experience. If things were going to change, we needed *new experiences* of one another. That would give us something new to reflect on.

 Wise Words

"Perhaps the most essential part of this project is that it is created and developed by common people who believe that something can be done to create change. Using their personal resources, they are taking responsibility for creating a better place to live. It is time for people from small places to be heard. It is not only people in cosmopolitan urban areas who have options to offer."

—Noris Binet, *Women on the Inner Journey*

"The white women were filled with fear, guilt, and denial. The black women were filled with fear, anger, and denial. I also recognized that sheer panic existed just below the surface and the volatility of what we were attempting. I knew we needed to build a common spiritual ground on which healing could happen. We needed an altar, a ceremony, and a new way of being together.

"We began with a series of workshops in which the women could get to know each other. We built our altars, danced, and even created music together. We were breaking through the isolation and individuality of this culture; the women were thirsty for the experience and for the expression of community. We were breaking boundaries—women who had been afraid to touch each other's skin were dancing together. They were looking at each other's faces and seeing into each other's eyes. We were breathing the same air, laughing, and crying together. Soon we had footings for our bridge. By the time the show opened, we could actually stand there together, holding hands, moving together, singing the music we had composed, looking at our art hanging on the walls. Now we had something to celebrate!"

Signs, Symbols, and Synchronicity

Shortly after Binet conceived *Black and White Women*, inside Nashville's Parthenon, a full-scale replica of the ancient Greek temple, the impressive 41'1" statue of Athena Parthenos was unveiled. Artist Alan Le Quire's rendering of the Goddess of Wisdom fills the building, standing over three stories tall. Binet talked about the *synchronistic* meaning of the event for her. "Athena represented a new archetype to the people of Greece. She symbolized a new partnership, birthing a new order of divine and human relationship."

"On the opposite side of synchronicity, the Rodney King riots coincided with the workshop. People were in the streets in 13 cities all across America, and the media was totally focused on it. Suddenly it was clear: We have a racial problem in this country, and we can't hide it. We didn't know what would happen. We even wondered if the Ku Klux Klan might be outside. But we felt that we could make a difference that day, and we did. On a very personal and intimate level and as a society, healing happened. In light of the King riots, I think everyone in the community was pulling for us and praying for us."

Womanspeak

Synchronicity refers to the belief that nothing happens by accident, that there is an intelligence operating in the universe.

Binet feels the project was successful. "We went through a process together, and our lives were changed. We saw how it wasn't always necessary to work on a big scale, that a few coming together could change our perceptions and perhaps provoke a change in the larger culture."

The Least You Need to Know

- Today, as they have always done, women continue to express their spirituality by transforming culture.

- ◆ Successful social programs don't always "follow the rules."
- ◆ People from many different religions and cultures are coming together to study nontraditional subjects and share information about how to build a better world community.
- ◆ There are innovative people with creative approaches to solving societal problems who will help you design your piece of social transformation.

25

Reuniting Body and Soul

In This Chapter

- ◆ Curiosity doesn't always kill the cat
- ◆ Experience remains a good teacher
- ◆ Following the joy
- ◆ Loving the paradox
- ◆ Midwifing the spirit

In this chapter you'll meet three holistic professional educators, trained in both traditional Western medicine and alternative modalities. They approach healing from a spiritual understanding, treating the whole person—body, mind, and spirit. All three women talked about how their intuition guided them toward the people, places, and events that assisted them on their discovery of the healing modalities they would learn and how their personal and professional spirituality developed through the process.

Curiosity Leads Her

Betty Stadler is certified as a family nurse practitioner, healing touch practitioner, healing touch instructor, clinical hypnotherapist, and Reiki master. She is a medical consultant, helping bridge the gap between traditional Western medicine and alternative healing arts. She has had a private practice in mind/body health since 1993 and has been teaching holistic nursing seminars and healing touch since 1991. Stadler sees herself as supporting holistic health as a lifestyle, and her vision is to see conventional health care bridged with complementary-health-care practices to facilitate a philosophy of treating the whole person.

Following the Urge

Regarding her leap from Western medicine to holistic, Stadler believes "It's always a mystery—how we get where we are. I guess the bottom line is that curiosity leads me." Besides her natural curiosity, Stadler credits yoga with facilitating some of the changes in her life. She began practicing yoga at a self-awareness center, which lead to a workshop where she learned intuitive decision-making. Through the process, Stadler found herself making decisions she would probably not have made using a straight-up left-brain logic. From there, her intuition "opened up a whole chain of events," one of which was the study of Reiki, an energetic healing process from Japan.

Wise Words

"Every now and then you should ask yourself why you're doing this work. It helps keep your ego out of the way."

—Betty Stadler's advice to those in the healing professions

From there, "Curiosity led me to the American Holistic Nurses Association, where I found *healing touch*. I felt the urge to investigate, and it turned out to be a major component in my life. I had gone back to graduate school to recapture some of the excitement I had once felt about nursing. As my career developed, I was getting farther away from the people and more involved in administration. I wanted more hands-on nursing. Healing touch brought it to me. I knew almost instantly that I would learn it and teach it!"

Womanspeak

Healing touch is a healing technique that works with the energy field, affecting body, mind, emotions, and spirit. It's philosophy believes all healing is self-healing. The practitioner realigns the energy flow, reactivating the mind/body/spirit connection to eliminate blocks to self-healing. University of Miami's Medical School documented studies showing that the use of hands-on techniques such as healing touch facilitates a person's recovery from surgery and burns. Premature infants have a higher growth rate when healing touch is part of their care. More than 30,000 hospitals in the United States now use such modalities and consider them a legitimate medical technique. In most major cities, it is becoming increasingly more common for teams of medical doctors and nurses to combine allopathic medical skills with hands-on and energy techniques.

Reawakening Spirituality

"I consider healing as a ritual—through my work I have come to a deeper understanding of my religion," Stadler says. Healing touch *reawakened* her earlier sense of spirituality. She was raised Catholic and talks about how religion and spirituality were all wrapped up together in church experiences of her childhood. As meditation became a regular part of her yoga practice, she realized that she had actually learned how to meditate as a child, in time spent silently sitting in church. She talked about the smell of incense, Gregorian chants, ceremonies, and rituals of her childhood—particularly the May crowning. "Girls wore white dresses and carried baskets of rose petals. We had a procession all around the church, singing as we walked. As we passed in front of the statue of Mary, we took hand-fuls of rose petals, kissed them, and dropped them on the floor at her feet." The physical body was very much a part of these rituals—walking, singing, wearing special clothes, carrying rose petals, smelling the incense—"wiring" the brain spiritually and holistically.

Wise Words

"I have recently discovered how great a part food plays in our spiritual development as well as health and well-being. When we eat fresh fruit and vegetables, and eat slowly with intention, our energy field expands, getting much bigger and energized. When we eat denser food, and eat on the run, our energy field compresses. Even during the preparation of fresh food, your energy and the energy of the food begins to interact. It is actually transmitting its life force to you. Food is very spiritual, and preparing food is a spiritual act. I nourish my spirit continually and in many ways: daily meditation, checking with my inner connection with the divine throughout the day, prayer, and nature. One of my favorite ways to feed my spirit is by a walking meditation in the woods. I sleep with my windows open so I can listen to the birds at sunrise."

—Betty Stadler

Stadler went on to say "It is like coming full circle. I draw on those early experiences in the spiritual aspect of my work—I know from *experience* that the body and spirit are one." Stadler considers healing touch and her medical practice as ministry. The course work she teaches incorporates a spiritual history of healing in the Judeo-Christian tradition, grounding it in scripture. For her it was through personal experiences both as the practitioner and as the one who received the work that made the body/mind/spirit connection a physical reality that she experienced, not just a philosophy.

Healing Images

Stadler studied hypnotherapy and found it increased her understanding of how she, as the healer, and the client together enter a state of consciousness in which images come to her that help her know what is going on in her client's inner world. Stadler calls this a spiritual realm in which she experiences the "oneness" in which both she and her client are connected and she is able to receive insight that will assist in their healing.

"There are three things I learned early in my career in healing touch that create the environment in which healing can occur:

- Intention
- Presence
- Acceptance

"Before working with someone, I set my intention, turning the healing process over to God. Presence happens by my staying focused on the client, paying good attention to what I am sensing and feeling. Acceptance is where I as the practitioner completely let go my agenda; that is, I let go of the need for anything to happen and get completely out of the way. Then I can open up to the process. In those moments, something bigger comes through."

The Truth About Aging!

Stadler finds that spirituality differs between individuals, regardless of whether they are men or women. "It comes in many shapes and forms and is often not recognized for what it is. We have so intertwined religion and spirituality that people often don't recognize their own spirituality. I help people find their passion and realize how their passion connects them with the divine. Men are generally farther away from recognizing their spirituality than women because in our current society they are taught to be less connected to their feelings—to "'suck it up,' be strong, and don't show emotions. However, the events following the destruction of the World Trade Center have shown that men are very spiritual. They often express it in action, such as the firemen rushing into the building and the rescue workers who work tirelessly."

Stadler believes that her therapeutic skills get better with age because of developmental shifts that happen as we get older and also because of her own spiritual progress. "At this point in life, I realized it's all spiritual. I've become aware of the interconnectedness of everything and everyone." She talks about finding the intrinsic beauty in even the smallest things throughout each day. "When I was younger, I was busy doing and discovering the world outside myself; now it is about the inner space." It's through this deepening that she is able to provide the freedom for her clients to make the connections for themselves. She smiled a knowing smile and said, "Aging is the opposite of what society tells you it is."

Healing touch is used to assist in the healing of the following:

- Pain control
- Neck and back problems

- Anxiety reduction
- Skin problems
- Wound and fracture healing
- Premenstrual syndrome
- Multiple sclerosis, HIV, or AIDS
- Hypertension and heart and lung disease
- Pre- and post-surgical procedures
- Headaches and migraines
- Autoimmune disorders
- Diabetes
- Cancer
- Grief management
- Arthritis
- Rehabilitation
- Chronic fatigue syndrome
- General well-being
- Disease prevention
- Spiritual enhancement

Ironweed and Other Wild Things

The first time I met Deanna, I found her crouched behind the back porch of her old Victorian farmhouse, planting flowers. She put down her garden tools and asked me if I'd like to see the farm. She disappeared around the corner for a few minutes and reappeared at the wheel of an old 1984 Nissan pickup, which, coughing and gasping, transported us across through fields where ironweed and other wild things towered over our heads. We lurched over hill and dale, finally coming to rest near a beautiful stream. From there we set out on foot, climbing a series of good-size hills, where we checked on the wild ginseng.

On the way back to the house, we crossed a grazing pasture, made our way through a herd of cows, passed two barns, stopped to throw a load of wood into the huge furnace beside the garage, and came through the side door into her kitchen. Without coming up for air, she pulled a couple pieces of salmon and two small steaks out of the refrigerator and began to toss a salad. "How about lunch?" she asked. This was obviously a woman of considerable strength and more than a few facets, I surmised. We ate and retreated to the front porch swing, where we talked for hours, interrupted periodically by a grandchild or two (eight in all) coming through on their way to Grandma's kitchen.

Getting to the Roots

Deanna Naddy holds a Doctor of Science degree in nursing and is the former head of the nursing program at Columbia State Community College in Tennessee. She grew up in Kansas and began her career at the University of Kansas, where she completely accepted the medical model of working with disease. She remembers being horrified to find out her mother was going to a chiropractor. She went on to get her Master's and Doctorate degrees, specializing in mental health. Her career has included working in public health, a medical surgery unit in a small hospital, operating-room nursing, managing a clinic in Jordan for the U.S. Embassy, and 30 years in nursing education.

Naddy credits her transition from allopathic medicine to holistic medicine as following her natural curiosity and the recognition that traditional Western medicine does not get down to the issues that underlie disease. She recalled her mother's trips to the chiropractor and realized that medical doctors could treat back pain only with surgery or drugs; they didn't get to the root causes. She observed her own patterns of stress and how high levels of it often resulted in getting sick. At the same time, people began to come into her life and introduce her to different holistic practices. She was open to explore and receive this new information.

> **Sophia's Wisdom**
>
> In 1995 41 percent of the population of the United States used one or more alternative healing methods to either complement or substitute for traditional medical techniques. It is now estimated that 60 cents of every health-care dollar is spent on alternative therapies.

One of the first people Naddy met was Betty Stadler, a nurse practitioner and healing touch instructor (Stadler's story appears earlier in this chapter). Naddy invited Stadler to teach a class to her nursing faculty (mainly so she could learn this fascinating technique), and she observed the results on the faculty as well as herself. "Despite the fact that many in the class didn't believe in the process, they began to get better anyway—their energy levels rose and they laughed more."

The Joy of Learning

Naddy signed up for subsequent courses in many holistic healing techniques. Her philosophy expanded, particularly regarding the belief that healing begins when people take charge of their health. She was introduced to the important use of herbs and natural products as alternatives to prescription drugs. She began to explore other modalities such as the use of guided imagery, meditation, yoga, tai chi, Reiki, Earth philosophy, and hypnotherapy. The most transformational experience for her came after a class in Bowen Therapy, a gentle hands-on body technique from Australia.

Naddy traveled to Peru and Israel, where she learned to be silent and go inside herself and listen to the voice of creation. "You know, you can be still and learn things," she said to me with amazement in her voice.

Today, she assists people in their healing by listening to their stories and using her extensive background and training to recommend the appropriate therapy. She knows her experience in both the allopathic and holistic worlds gives her expertise and also credibility. Sometimes she uses her own story as a way of connecting with her clients, knowing that her transformation from a straight medical model to holistic healing helps them trust the process.

Naddy believes that spirit is the energetic basis of all life. She nourishes hers in nature and by connecting with God. Rather than an "Aha!" kind of spiritual awakening, she describes hers as a process—a series of smaller steps rather than one big leap. "I know I get guidance; I know I miss some along the way because I don't always listen; but I know it's there when I need it." As to what motivates her to continue to learn and grow, she says simply, "It brings me joy."

Buddhism, Tibetan Medicine, and Nursing Theory

Debra Rose Wilson is a registered nurse, lactation consultant, and candidate for a Master's degree in holistic nursing. Her marriage brought her south from Alberta, Canada, where she was teaching perinatal skills to high-risk street kids and running a breast-feeding clinic. She attends an innovative program at Tennessee State University, one of only a handful of schools across the nation offering advanced degrees in holistic nursing.

Pieces of the Mirror

Wilson's understanding of holism comes from Buddhism and Tibetan medicine as well as the nursing theory of Rosemarie Parse—"The Human Becoming Theory." Wilson identifies holistic nursing as meeting the needs the patient says she or he has in that moment, as perceived by that person. Her experience working with kids on drugs taught her the wisdom of that philosophy. She gives this example: "When talking with a pregnant teenager on the street, regardless of the circumstances—such as homelessness or an active addiction to cocaine, cigarette smoking, or anything else—if she thinks she needs to drink more milk and everything will be okay, that's where you begin. If you try to tell her what you think is the problem, you've lost her. If you go with what she presents as her greatest concern, you've got a way in to the whole person."

Wilson sees spirituality as a developmental process of recognizing her wholeness. "Religion can be one of the ways we develop our spirituality, but there are many ways to do it." She tells the story of God looking in a mirror. "The mirror breaks, scattering pieces of the whole image. If a religion picks up one of the shards and believes it has the whole picture, rather than just a piece, it's problematic."

Debra knows she isn't done learning yet. And when she thinks of graduation, she considers teaching or going on for further study—a Doctorate in philosophy, perhaps. "I like theory because it supports and validates intuitive practice. She loves teaching and watching the lights come on for her students as they experience theory being realized. Her spirituality is about growth—a process she defines as having experiences followed by introspection. Spirituality is about finding wholeness, and that is a process of self-discovery. You must find your truth, stop along the way and sort through your old beliefs, and find out what is true and not true for you.

Out of the Box with Paradox

For Wilson, truth is found in paradox. "The tension between two opposing beliefs can be creative. When you can identify the conflict and sit with it, a solution arises. It is our nature. An example can be seen in her relationship to her grandmother, whom Wilson describes as "a Hungarian healer and extraordinary herbalist. At the same time, she had a mean streak. She sought power from her healing. She could sense vulnerability and go right for it. I could see it even as a child. Do I negate all her abilities because she is mean? Do I pretend she isn't mean so it doesn't conflict with my idea of a healer? Both observations were true. My thinking had to expand and accept the paradox. My grandmother was both those things—a healer and a mean woman!" Wilson believes this is life's essential dilemma and paradox. When we identify the opposing parts in a situation, and hold to them, creative solutions result.

Wilson follows the theory of creative paradox in healing, believing as Buddhist's believe, that disease and other challenges come as both the problem and also the transformer. "When a person can locate the meaning the disease has for them, they can transcend the illness or the challenge they are facing and get on with life. Getting on with life doesn't always mean curing the disease. It can mean changing their relationship to the disease, how they experience it. Disease prevention is an important ingredient in holism, too. Good nutrition and other health practices are part of the process." Her bottom-line philosophy is that the person seeking healing holds the key to their recovery. They know what they need. The job of the practitioner is to pay attention.

Wilson's greatest challenge right now is following the principles of holistic health in her personal life while attending graduate school, working, and keeping up with home life. She describes her relationship with her husband as based on respect and love and as one of the places where she is nourished. She also meditates and finds it a source of renewal.

Integrating Healing Arts

The woman you are about to read about has put a whole new spin on the term "born again"! Sarah Stewart, a health-care provider for more than 30 years, has been a visionary and pioneer using both allopathic and holistic modalities. She draws on her experiences as a nurse, massage therapist, yoga teacher, herbalist, hypnotherapist, mother, and grandmother.

Stewart is a member of the Pre and Peri Natal Association, the American Council of Hypnosis Examiners, the Holistic Nurses Association, and the International Massage Association. Her school, The Institute of Integrated Healing Arts, was founded in 1982. In 1987 it expanded to include instruction on clinical hypnotherapy and yoga. A sister school was opened in the southeast in 1992. Stewart maintains a private practice in Sonoma, California. Here is her remarkable story.

Of the Earth

"I grew up in a small house on the family farm. My grandfather was Cherokee, and my grandmother was pure country. She didn't believe in the God you find at church, but her faith was very strong. She used to say, 'See that rooster over there? God is in that rooster, and he will feed you. We're going to kill that old bird and have it for dinner!' She would grab it by the feet and chop its head off. The feathers would fly, and the rooster would be in the pan before they hit the ground." Stewart talks about life on the farm as holistic in the truest sense of the word. "We plowed the field, planted the seed, harvested the crops, fed the animals, watched the eggs hatch, and saw the horses and cows mating and knew it would result in baby animals in the spring. There wasn't any part of the life cycle we weren't directly involved with—including death."

Sophia's Wisdom

Holistic practices engage a body energy called *chi*, which is the basis of most non-Western medical models. Chi is the living force that runs through the body along meridian lines. If the meridians become blocked (think of kinks in a hose) the energy can't get nourishment to all parts of the body. Systems and organs begin to break down. Massage, hands-on energy work, herbs, acupuncture, acupressure, meditation, or even a walk in the woods can reduce the stress and open the channels again, allowing the life-giving energy to flow. We can pass this healing energy to others (think battery cables and jump-starting a car) and stimulate their innate healing abilities.

"My mother died in childbirth when I was 13 years old, and my brother died with her. She had three other children born healthy and easily at home under the caring supervision of my grandmother—in the same room in which she was born. What went wrong this time? Well, the doctor was going on vacation, and three pregnant women were due at the same time. He put all three in the hospital at once and induced labor. My mother was one of these women. She hemorrhaged to death as a result of being induced and of not being properly attended to during her labor, and my brother strangled with the cord around his neck."

"When she died, her image came to me in a vision. There was peace in her eyes as she looked directly at me and smiled, "Take good care of the kids for me. I have to go now.""

Then she disappeared, and I was left holding my 11-month-old brother and looking at my 11-year-old sister in the corner of the room. A few hours later they came to tell me she had died, but I already knew it. That experience left its imprint on my life in ways that are still being discovered."

"Baby" Consciousness

"I always wanted to be a doctor, but with my mother's death, there would be no chance. I did what many women do: I went to nursing school." In addition to her traditional education as a nurse, Stewart's professional training included many years of practicing yoga. She knows that this spiritual discipline strengthened her and opened up many levels of awareness that she uses in her healing work today. In her 30s she traveled to the Philippines to work with the psychic surgeons she had heard about. Her healing abilities were recognized, and she was allowed to assist them and ultimately to work side-by-side with them. Although she does not use psychic surgery in her practice, she knows the experience opened more levels of healing within her.

Stewart continued to pursue her studies in the blossoming field of holistic health, this time with Dr. David Cheek, a pioneering obstetrician/gynecologist practicing in San Francisco. Dr. Cheek was a friend and associate of Dr. Milton Erickson, who is considered to be the father of hypnosis in Western medicine. Dr. Cheek believed that babies had consciousness in the womb, having both sensory and cognitive awareness. He treated many of his clients with hypnosis to relieve stress during pregnancy and to facilitate pain-free and drug-free deliveries. He encouraged starting the parent-child relationship at the beginning of pregnancy.

Reconception

Building on Dr. Cheek's work, Stewart began to design a process she calls *reconception*, in which she uses regression to take a person back through their experiences of conception, their gestation in the womb, and birth. "The mother's emotional state, her spiritual awareness, as well as her physical health all create the climate in which the baby spends almost the first year of life. Re-birthing is popular, and it's a good way of clearing birth traumas; however, many additional things have already happened to the mother and child at the time of conception and throughout pregnancy that leave lasting imprints on the soulbody."

Womanspeak

Reconception is a process of using regression to take a person back through their experiences of conception, their gestation in the womb, and birth.

"I have worked with pregnant women and their families for many years as a spiritual midwife to the whole family. I prepare them for birthing at home or in the hospital using yoga, breath, hypnosis, massage, and just being there during the pregnancy and delivery. My goal is to help parents and siblings realize that the child within has consciousness. I also emphasize that the family can help this spirit feel loved and wanted. This takes many forms, including stories by the big sister, conversations with the baby, and the traditional preparations of gathering the baby's things. When arrangements are made lovingly with the intention of welcoming the baby, the child is much more likely to be a secure, loving person. This establishes a lifetime pattern that affects every aspect of being a full person, and these positive feelings will be transmitted to everyone he or she meets."

Mother Knows Best

Don't fall into the dualistic either/or trap. Holistic means using both hemispheres of the brain. That means finding the balance between scientific knowledge and intuitive wisdom.

An Integrated Vision

Stewart was on retreat at an ashram in India when a vision of her school came to her, showing her the combination of healing arts that she would offer. She describes it this way, "The body contains our emotional memory. If the memories are good, they contribute to good health. If they are painful, the opposite is true. Combining the hands-on healing of massage with deep relaxation and hypnosis regression along with yoga breathing exercises, emotional trauma from the body can be released." Stewart has worked with hundreds of students, teaching them her integrated approach to healing.

Sophia's Wisdom

Meg, an artist and gardener who recently has begun to develop her healing skills, understands spirituality as how we live. She sees women's spirituality as focused more toward caring, sharing, and nurturing, "perhaps because women have been allowed the opportunity to develop this side of themselves, and maybe because we have a slight inborn advantage." She feels the women's movement betrayed many by undermining women's traditional roles. "All of a sudden feminists were telling us this wasn't okay to be a homemaker. They were insisting that everyone enter the work force. It no longer was about choice." Meg feels that women are starved for spirituality that feeds and comforts the soul. Her spiritual instinct has led her to explore alternative healing. She feeds her spirit in several "hands-on" ways—working in her garden, designing and building sets, baking bread, and cooking.

"Everyone brings individual strengths and offers a little different approach to their healing work. This is important to recognize. The philosophy of Integrated Healing Arts is to use this diversity to create powerful healing modalities that work with the same set of principles yet honor the individual healer. The 'integration' factor of Integrated Healing Arts works at many levels. It integrates right and left hemispheres of the brain by teaching cognitive skills and developing intuitive healing abilities; it integrates new techniques with the body of knowledge each student brings with her; and it integrates past with present, allowing the future to be a transformed one." Stewart reminds her students and clients that "There is no need to carry the pain from the past into the future." The school is licensed and leads to a certification in clinical hypnotherapy, massage therapy, or yoga instruction.

Stewart looks back over her childhood, the loss of her mother, letting go of her dream to go to medical school, and the subsequent events that have taken her all over the world to study with the healers of many different cultures, and she feels a powerful affirmation of being on her true spiritual path. "I am doing the work I feel I was born to do, and I love doing it. I have followed my visions, my intuition, and my inner guidance, and it has served me well. I guess I will continue to follow it."

In Closing

In collecting the material for this book, I realized what a rich spiritual tradition women have to draw on. It was difficult to select who and what stories would be included, and I could have easily filled several books. I hope you use this as a place to begin a deeper and closer look at our collective female history. Check the bibliography in Appendix C, "Resources," for books used throughout that you might enjoy. Appendix C will also tell you how to reach many of the women you read about in this book. As a way of closing, I would like to draw once again on the Lakota prayer honoring all relationships, *Mitakuye Oyasin! All our relations!*

The Least You Need to Know

- Trust your intuition. It will lead you where you need to go.
- Holistic healing often involves both traditional Western medicine and alternative practices.
- The holistic practitioner believes the physical, mental, and emotional aspects of a person are all involved in both disease and healing.
- Holistic practitioners believe the body is self-healing, given support. They work to support this natural ability to heal.
- Spirituality is intrinsic to most holistic healing practices. The practitioner keeps her or his personal beliefs out of the way and allows the client to experience her own connection to spirit.

Women's Spirituality Glossary

'adham A generic Hebrew word for humankind (male and female), meaning "created from the earth."

ambiance The atmosphere or mood of a place.

autonomy Independence; self-government; personal independence; and the capacity to make moral decisions and act on them singularly.

ayurveda A Hindu medical system based on the art of healing and prolonging life.

bards Keepers of the tribal memories. In Ireland, they trained for many years to become great storytellers, poets, and philosophers.

centering prayer A centuries-old form of contemplative prayer in which the practitioner quiets his or her mind, emptying it of all thoughts, to be in silence, allowing God to make any changes God deems necessary.

chakra A Sanskrit word meaning "whirling light." It describes an energy center in the body that generates physical, emotional, and spiritual well-being.

chaos The state of unbounded space and formless matter that is believed to have existed before the creation of the universe. Here it refers to letting go of our structured thoughts so that something new can be created.

chi (*CH'I* or *qi*) The energy or life force of the universe, believed to flow around and through the body and be present in all living things.

collective unconscious   A term used by psychologist Carl Jung to describe the inherited unconscious mind that contains memories, thoughts, and instincts common to all people.

crone   A woman past menopause who is said to have her wisdom. It comes from Rhea Kronia, who was "Mother of Time" in the ancient world, and is associated with Coronis, a carrion crow, because in mythology, crones are often associated with death.

Dianic   From Diana, the Roman version of Artemis, the virgin Goddess of the Moon. Used here to describe a particular branch of modern Wicca that is exclusively female.

divination   The practice of foretelling the future or discovering the unknown through omens, oracles, or supernatural powers of prophecy or prediction; premonition or feeling about something that is going to happen.

dominator   A hierarchical cultural model where one group of people has dominance over another group.

dualism   The philosophical and theological perception that people are inherently dual in nature, that their spiritual and physical nature are separate and opposing forces as in body against soul; the religious doctrine that there are two antagonistic forces—good and evil—that determine the course of events.

duality   The understanding that wholeness has a dual and complementary nature that encompasses seemingly opposites.

druid   A Greek word meaning "oak" and "knowledge" and a title given to learned men and women in the Celtic tradition who were said to possess "oak knowledge" or wisdom. The same word (Druid) describes the religion itself and priests within it.

Druidism   An ancient philosophy that includes both monotheism and polytheism and believes in the sacredness of the earth.

eucharist   A ceremony in many Christian churches during which bread and wine are blessed and consumed to commemorate the last supper of Jesus Christ and his disciples before his death.

ecumenical   The promotion of friendly relations between different religions, or promoting the unity of Christian churches around the world.

Gardnerian   A branch of Wicca that is practiced in mixed groups of men and women, honors both God and Goddess, and follows many of the principles set down by Gerald Gardner.

Hatha   A Sanskrit word combining *Ha*, "sun," and *Tha*, "moon." Describes a type of yoga practice.

hedonism   A philosophical belief that holds pleasure as the highest good.

heresy   An opinion or belief that contradicts established religious teaching, especially one that is officially condemned by a religious authority.

hocus pocus   Irreverent slang from the Latin words of the consecration during Catholic Mass, *Hoc est Enim Meum*, meaning "This is my body."

Holy Spirit   The third "person" in the trinity that is composed of God the Father, Jesus the Son, and the Holy Spirit. The Holy Spirit expresses love and union and is not shown in human form.

hospitality spirituality   Black women's tradition of coming together in their homes as community, sharing food and stories.

idolator   Someone who worships idols or false images of God, a different God from their own.

immanence   God's presence in the creation.

infidel   Someone who has no belief in the religion of the speaker or writer. It is used most often by Christianity or Islam to describe disbelievers.

Inquisition   The relentless process of the Middle Ages in which the church fathers questioned those suspected of heresy or other crimes against church authority. If found guilty, suspects were turned over to the state to be imprisoned, tortured, and put to death.

instinct   Innate intelligence; an impulse that feels natural rather than reasoned; a natural gift or skill.

intuition   Knowing without the use of rational process; sharp insight; immediate knowledge of something.

'ish   The term applied to "man" as the genderless 'adham was separated into two parts of a whole.

'ishshah   The term given to "woman" as genderless 'adham was separated into two parts.

Kabbalah   A spiritual teaching of Judaism; a framework to help in the understanding life and our spiritual journey.

Lilith   In creation stories of some Hebraic traditions, Lilith appears as Adam's first wife. She left him rather than become submissive. Specifically, she refused to lie beneath him in sex. She is a relic of the Sumero-Babylonian Goddess Belit-ili, of Jewish mythology.

Malleus Maleficarum   Literally, *Hammer of the Witches*, the document published by two Dominican priests that became the handbook for the Inquisition in Europe.

matriarchy   A society formed with female values; power is shared between women and men.

matrilineal   A society in which bloodlines are traced through the female and property is inherited through female lineage.

medical intuitive   Someone who can diagnose illness through perceptional insight rather than through the five senses.

Messiah   An anointed king who will lead the Jews back to the land of Israel and establish justice in the world. In Christianity, the belief that Jesus Christ is the Messiah prophesied in the Hebrew scripture.

Mitakuye oyasin   Literally meaning "all my relations," this Lakota prayer acknowledges that all things are in relationship.

moral instinct   The innate ability to discern right from wrong based on physiological information; right action increases the life force.

mystic   A person who belongs to a tradition of prayer and meditation. Mystics are in communication with the sacred presence within them; their writings and teachings are important contributions to religion and spirituality. Mystics traditionally live in monasteries or convents and are found within all religions.

mysticism   A philosophy that is not focused on religious morality, theology, law, or dogma but on the experience of the divine.

Neopagan   A person who reconstructs the religions of the pre-Christian world and follows an ethical and moral system derived from them.

non-Catholic   A term used by Catholics to identify "others." It is no longer considered cool. It is good religious manners to refer to people by their tradition.

old rascal   A patriarch when he is interfering in women's business. You won't find this term in the dictionary; it's pure womanspeak.

omnipresence   The belief that God is present everywhere all at once.

oracle   Somebody or something considered to be a source of knowledge, wisdom, or prophecy; an ancient deity consulted for advice. Such information was received intuitively.

original grace   Not an officially defined religious term; refers here to humans being born naturally graced by their creator, free from sin.

original sin   The Christian belief that humans were created and then "fell" from God's grace by their sin of disobedience.

Pagan   A person who practices a monotheistic or polytheistic religion based on the deities of the pre-Christian world, exclusive of Judaism.

pantheism   The belief that God is present in nature. It is considered heresy in traditional Christianity.

panentheism   The belief that God is present both in creation and in a transcended way, too.

pantheon   All the deities of a particular religion considered collectively.

paradigm   A pattern or model upon which an organization or society is built.

partnership   A nonhierarchical model of society in which people are considered to have equal power. People are considered to be partners with one another, with nature, and with the divine.

patriarchy   A combination of two Latin words, *pater*, meaning "father," and *arches*, meaning "rule." It means rule by father or oldest son or rule by men.

politics   The totality of interrelationships in a particular area of life involving power, authority, or influence and capable of manipulation.

post-Christian   A term used by Mary Daly to describe her theological position as having moved through Christianity to her current position as beyond Christian.

prayer warrior   A member of the church who has an ability to communicate with the ancestors and a particularly well developed prayer life. The ability to communicate is considered a healing gift. The abilities of prayer warriors are recognized by the community and their services are sought after.

racism   The belief that the people of various races have different inherent qualities and that one's own cultural group is superior to another, accompanied by the ability of one group to have power over that group.

reconception   A process of using regression to take a person back through his or her experiences of conception, gestation, and birth.

reformer   A feminist who positions herself within her religious tradition. Reformers firmly recognize that religion needs a transformation, and they believe it can be best accomplished by working from the inside.

runes   Characters from a number of ancient Germanic alphabets usually inscribed on small stones and used like tarot cards to bring insight.

Sanskrit   The old Indo-European language of ancient India.

saved   The Christian belief that salvation happens through the saving power of Jesus Christ, without which, the soul is in danger of eternal loss.

seven generations   The Native American philosophy of making decisions with the understanding that they will impact the world in the future. Morality is determined by how it will effect seven generations of children.

Shekinah   Appears in the Hebrew Bible as the female soul of God. She is part of the teachings of the Kabbalah, the Jewish mystical tradition, in which it is said that she is God's wisdom and creativity and that God is not complete without this female aspect.

soulbody   The unified and nondistinct state of body and soul.

spiritual instinct   The inborn ability to discern thoughts, words, or actions that are positive for us and those that are not based on sensing one's life force.

synchronicity   The belief that nothing happens by accident; there are no coincidences; everything is subject to an intelligence operating in the universe.

thealogy   The study of the divine feminine in the form of the Mother Goddess. It uses cognitive reasoning based on human experiences of the sacred to determine the nature of the sacred.

theology   The study of the divine in male form, usually God. It uses cognitive reasoning, scripture, and tradition to determine the nature of God and what is considered proper relationship and right response.

theory of social equality   The belief that Jesus instituted a reign of social equality reflected in his teaching and in how he organized his ministry with women as central figures. Also the belief that religion and political structures should reflect this model.

transcendence   God's presence in the spirit world above and outside creation.

transformation   A complete change into a more meaningful and helpful interpretation, understanding, or belief.

ultradian   The cycle of right- and left-brain dominance that goes on throughout the day. It corresponds to the dream cycle of sleep.

veda   From the root *Vid*, meaning "to know." Vedas are sacred revelations of the Hindu religion.

virgin   A term used in the classical world to describe the psychological state of autonomy.

Wicca   Stems from the Saxon word *witega*, meaning "a seer or diviner."

witch   A derivation of *wicca*, "sorcerer," and *wiccian*, "to cast a spell." Describes one who engages the practice of Wicca.

womanist   A term created by Alice Walker to describe powerful black women. It is used as a symbol for black women's empowerment.

womanist theology   A body of work written by black women theologians.

yang   Symbolizes the principle of light, heat, action, and masculinity in Chinese philosophy that is understood to be the complement of yin.

Yemaja   One of the African goddesses whose spirit encompasses the enormous creativity of the ocean.

yin   Symbolizes the principle of darkness, negativity, passivity, and femininity in Chinese philosophy that is understood to be the complement of yang.

yoga   A Sanskrit word that describes a physical and philosophical system that includes breathing exercises, postures, and rituals that work to develop awareness of the unity of the practitioner with the supreme being.

Zen or **Zen Buddhism**   A major school of Buddhism originating in twelfth-century China that emphasizes enlightenment through meditation and insight.

Timeline of Women's Spirituality in the United States

1637   Anne Hutchinson is found guilty on charges of heresy in the Massachusetts Bay Colony and banished.

1656   The first Quakers, Ann Austin and Mary Fisher, arrive in America.

1660   Quaker Mary Dyer is the first woman hanged in America on charges of preaching heresy.

1768   The first Methodist church building opens. Barbara Ruckle Heck is credited with being "the Mother of American Methodism."

1787   Sacagawea, Native American guide and interpreter for Lewis and Clark Expedition, is born.

1788   Jemima Wilkinson establishes "Jerusalem," a colony for her society of Universal Friends.

1790   The First Carmel Convent is founded in Maryland under the direction of Mary Xavier (formerly Ann Teresa Matthews).

1812   The Sisters of Loretto, the first American sisterhood, is founded in Kentucky.

1818   Jarena Lee begins preaching for the African Methodist Episcopal.

1819   The Female Hebrew Benevolent Society is founded in Philadelphia, the first of hundreds of women's societies.

1827   Salome Lincoln begins her career as an itinerant minister.

1829   The Oblate Sisters of Providence, established in Baltimore, becomes the first African American sisters in United States.

1832   African American Maria Stewart becomes the first American-born woman to speak in front of a mixed-gender group.

1833   Quaker minister Lucretia Mott leads in founding the Philadelphia Female Anti-Slavery Society.

1836   Mary Lyon receives charter for Mount Holyoke Seminary—the first women's seminary in the United States.

1837   "Pastoral Letter" is issued, berating abolitionists for "agitating."

1838   Quaker Angelina Grimke publishes *Letters on the Equality of the Sexes*, attacking biblical arguments against women.

1843   Former slave Sojourner Truth begins a career as an inspired preacher and itinerant minister.

1845   Transcendentalist Margaret Fuller publishes the classic feminist book, *Woman in the Nineteenth Century.*

1848   The first women's rights convention is held in Seneca Falls, New York, spearheaded by Lucretia Mott and Elizabeth Cady Stanton.

1853   Congregationist Antoinette Blackwell becomes the first women ordained in a nationally recognized Protestant denomination. She resigns one year later due to protests.

1863   Olympia Brown becomes the first woman ordained in the Universalist Church as a pastor. She has a lengthy career.

1895   Elizabeth Cady Stanton publishes *The Women's Bible*, addressing the root causes of centuries of women's oppression.

1904   Mary McLeod Bethune founds a school for African American girls and becomes the first woman to head such an institution.

1912   Henrietta Szold founds Hadassah, promoting Jewish ideals, public health, and nursing education.

1948   The African American Methodist Episcopal Church gives women full ordination.

1951   Paula Ackerman becomes the first woman to perform the functions of a rabbi.

1955   Rosa Parks, American civil rights leader, refuses to give up her bus seat to a white man in Montgomery, Alabama.

1956   The United Methodist Church grants women full ordination rights.

1962   Rachel Carson, marine biologist, publishes *Silent Spring*, heralding the dawn of ecological movement.

1965   The Second Vatican Council of Catholic Church reaffirms that women's domestic role must be preserved in accord with her nature. This translates to no ordination for women.

1974   Sandy Eisenberg Sasso becomes the first female rabbi ordained in the Reconstructionist branch of Judaism. The "Philadelphia 11" (women) are ordained by three retired Episcopal bishops. Their ordination is later declared invalid.

1975   Rosemary Radford Ruether publishes *New Woman/New Earth*, which becomes the anthem of ecofeminism.

1985   Wilma Mankiller becomes the first woman to be named Chief of the Cherokee Nation.

1985   Amy Ellsberg becomes the first woman ordained in the Conservative branch of Judaism.

1988   Reverend Clementine Harris becomes the first female elected Bishop in the Episcopal Church.

1988   Oprah Winfrey makes television history as her company, HARPO Productions, Inc., assumes ownership of *The Oprah Winfrey Show*, making her the first woman in history to own and produce her own talk show.

1992   The Anita Hill/Clarence Thomas hearings shed light on sex discrimination and the fact that men "just don't get it."

2000   Hillary Clinton is elected U.S. Senator from New York, becoming the first First Lady to be elected to the Senate and the first woman to be elected statewide in New York.

Resources

Encyclopedias

Benmowitz, June Melby. *Encyclopedia of American Women and Religion.* Santa Barbara, CA: ABC-CLIO, Inc., 1998.

Beversluis, Joel, ed. *A Sourcebook for Earth's Community of Religion.* Grand Rapids, MI: CoNexus Press; New York: Global Education Associates, 1995.

Cullen-DuPont, Kathryn. *The Encyclopedia of Women's History in America.* New York: DaCapo Press, 1998.

Lyman, Darryl, *Great African-American Women.* New York: Gramercy Books, 1999.

Monaghan, Patricia. *The New Book of Goddesses and Heroines.* St. Paul, MN: Llwellyn Publications, 1997.

Young, Serenity, ed. *An Anthology of Sacred Texts.* New York: Crossroad, 1994.

Goddess

Bolen, Jean Shinoda, M.D. *The Goddesses in Every Woman: A New Psychology of Women.* New York: HarperCollins, 1985.

Chicago, Judy. *The Dinner Party.* New York: Penguin, 1996.

Eisler, Riane. *The Chalice and the Blade.* San Francisco: Harper, 1987.

Gimbutas, Marija. *The Goddesses and Gods of Old Europe Myths and Cult Images*. Berkeley, Los Angeles: University of California Press, 1982.

Monaghan, Patricia. *The Goddess Companion*. St. Paul, MN: Llewellyn Publications, 1999.

———. *O Mother Sun: A New View of the Cosmic Feminine*. Santa Cruz, CA: The Crossing Press, 1994.

———. *The Office Oracle: Wisdom at Work*. St. Paul, MN: Llewellyn, 1999.

———. *Wild Girls: The Path of the Young Goddess*. St. Paul, MN: Llewellyn, 2001.

Sjöö, Monica, and Barbara Mor. *The Great Cosmic Mother: Rediscovering the Religion of the Earth*. San Francisco: Harper & Row, 1987.

Starhawk, Diane Baker, and Anne Hill. *Circle Round: Raising Children in Goddess Traditions*. New York: Bantam Books, 1998.

———. *The Spiral Dance: A Rebirth of the Ancient Religion of the Great Goddess*. San Francisco: Harper & Row, 1979.

Woolger, Jennifer Barker, and Roger J. Woolger. *The Goddess Within: A Guide to the Eternal Myths That Shape Women's Lives*. New York: Fawcett Columbine, 1987.

Native American Spirituality

McGaa, Ed Eagle Man. *Mother Earth Spirituality: Native American Paths to Healing Ourselves and Our World*. New York: HarperCollins, 1990.

Wallis, Michael, and Wilma Pearl. *Mankiller: A Chief and Her People*. New York: St. Martin's Press, 1999.

Ywahoo, Dhyani. *Voices of Our Ancestors: Cherokee Teachings from the Wisdom Fire*. Shambhala Publications, 1987.

Prayer

Cleary, William. *Prayers to She Who Is*. New York: Crossroads, 1995.

Fiand, Barbara, Sisters of Notre Dame de Namur (S.N.D.de N.). *Prayer and the Quest for Healing: Our Personal Transformation and Cosmic Responsibility*. New York: Crossroad Publishing Company, 1999.

Religion

Cole, Susan, Marian Ronan, and Hal Taussig. *Wisdom's Feast: Sophia in Study and Celebration*. Kansas City: Sheed & Ward, 1996.

Heschel, Susannah. *On Being a Jewish Feminist*. (Out of print; available at libraries.)

Labowitz, Rabbi Shoni. *God, Sex, and Women of the Bible: Discovering Our Sensual, Spiritual Selves*. New York: Simon & Schuster, 1998.

O'Gorman, Bob, and Mary Faulkner. *The Complete Idiot's Guide to Understanding Catholicism*. Indianapolis: Alpha Books, 1999.

Women's Spirituality

Binet, Noris. *Women on the Inner Journey: Building a Bridge*. Nashville: James C. Winston, 1994.

Caldecott, Moyra. *Women in Celtic Myth: Tales of Extraordinary Women from the Ancient Celtic Tradition*. Rochester, VT: Destiny Books, 1992.

Cameron, Julia. *The Artist's Way: A Spiritual Path to Higher Creativity*. New York: Putnam, 1992.

Carnes, Robin Deen, and Sally Craig. *Sacred Circles: A Guide to Creating Your Own Women's Spirituality Group*. San Francisco: Harper, 1998.

Crowley, Vivianne. *A Woman's Kabbalah: Kabbalah for the 21st Century*. London: Thorsons, 2000.

Davies, Oliver, and Fiona Bowie. *A Celtic Christian Spirituality: An Anthology of Medieval and Modern Sources*. New York: Continuum, 1995.

Labowitz, Rabbi Shoni. *Miraculous Living: A Guided Journey: Kabbalah Through the Ten Gates of the Tree of Life*. New York: Simon & Schuster, 1998.

McMann, Jean. *Altars and Icons: Sacred Spaces in Everyday Life*. San Francisco: Chronicle Books, 1998.

Pennick, Nigel. *The Sacred World of the Celts: An Illustrated Guide to Celtic Spirituality and Mythology*. Rochester, VT: Inner Traditions International, 1997.

Streep, Peg. *Altars Made Easy: A Complete Guide to Creating Your Own Sacred Space*. San Francisco: Harper, 1997.

Teish, Luisah. *Jambalaya: The Natural Woman's Book of Personal Charms and Practical Rituals*. San Francisco: Harper & Row, 1985.

Tompkins, Peter, and Christopher Bird. *The Secret Life of Plants*. New York: Harper & Row, 1973.

Turner, Kay. *Beautiful Necessity: The Art and Meaning of Women's Altars*. New York: Thames & Hudson, 1999.

Wasserman, James. *Art and Symbols of the Occult: Images of Power and Wisdom*. Rochester, VT: Destiny Books, 1993.

Westfield, N. Lynne. *Dear Sisters: A Womanist Practice of Hospitality*. Cleveland: Pilgrim Press, 2001.

Theology

Christ, Carol P., and Judith Plaskow. *Womanspirit Rising: A Feminist Reader in Religion*. San Francisco: Harper, 1979.

Cone, James H., and Gayraud S. Wilmore. *Black Theology: A Documentary History, Volume Two: 1980–1992*. New York: Orbis, 1993.

Hooks, Bell. *Ain't I a Woman?: Black Women and Feminism*. Cambridge, MA: South End Press, 1982.

Holistic Healing

Achterberg, Jeanne. *Imagery in Healing, Shamanism and Modern Medicine*. Boston: Shambala, 1985.

Achterberg, Jeanne, Barbara Dossey, R.N., M.S., FAAN, and Leslie Kolkmeier, R.N., M.Ed. *Rituals of Healing: Using Imagery for Health and Wellness*. New York: Bantam Books, 1994.

Borysenko, Joan, Ph.D. *A Woman's Book of Life: The Biology, Psychology, and Spirituality of the Feminine Life Cycle*. New York: Putnam, 1998.

Mariechild, Diane. *Mother Wit: A Guide to Healing and Psychic Development*. Santa Cruz: Crossing, 1981.

Myss, Caroline, Ph.D. *Anatomy of the Spirit: The Seven Stages of Power and Healing*. New York: Harmony Books, 1996.

Retreats

Rainbow River Retreats for Artist's and Writers
Star Prairie, WI
Mary Weiland
715-248-3312

Rockhaven Center for Holistic Living
House Springs, MO
www.rockhaven.org

Shekhinah Center's Kathy Norris Breast Cancer Help Program
Knoxville, TN
865-671-2186

A uniquely designed model offering self-discovery and empowerment for women with, and at risk of, breast cancer.

Sisters of Loretto
Nerinx, KY
www.lorettocommunity.org

Seminars, Workshops, and Educational Programs

Donna Fontanarose Raybuck, Ph.D.
The Center for the Sacred Feminine
3400 E. Speedway, #118-130
Tucson, AZ 85716
520-621-5849
rabuckd@netscape.net or drabuck@u.arizona.edu

Women's circles, playshops, and mountain retreats weaving community through music, ritual, and goddess studies.

Combining Forces
Natural Herbal Products, Educational Programs for Adults and Children
Catherine Abby Rich
Larkspur, CA
415-924-5961

Empowerment and Remembering the Earth
Workshops for Wise Women and Crones—also speaking engagements and source materials
Jo Searles, Ph.D., M.W.
State College, PA
Johec75@hotmail.com
814-238-3910

Grace House for AIDS Support
Stories of Grace House by Ronnie Angelus
Minneapolis, MN
www.stjoanofarc.com

Healing Touch and Holistic Nursing Courses in Academic and Community Settings
Betty Stadler
Nashville, TN
615-377-0470

Integrated Healing Arts
Sarah Stewart
Certification in Integrated Massage, Guided Imagery for Healing, Hypnotherapy, Biofeedback, and Yoga
Sonoma, CA
707-291-3499
Nashville, TN
615-383-4449

International Institute of Integral Human Sciences (IIHS)
PO Box 1387, Station H
Montreal, PQ H3G 2N3
Canada
Phone: 514-937-8359
Fax: 514-937-5380

Jill Webb-Hill and Minton Sparks
www.mintonsparks.com
615-665-2127 (to book an appearance with Minton Sparks)

Sparks' *Middlin' Sisters* CD on Dualtone Records is available on Milton Sparks' website, Borders, and Barnes and Noble.

ORIGINS Noris Binet, Ph.D.
PO Box 41761
Nashville, TN 37204
615-297-6654
norisbinet.org

Traveling workshops to the sacred sites of Mexico, Costa Rica, and the four corners of the Southwest United States, and Alaska. Dr. Binet is available for seminars and lectures on creating cultural awareness.

SISTER Program
1005 D. B. Todd Blvd.
Nashville, TN 37208
615-327-6233

Recovery program for African American women and children.

Women's Spirituality
Mary Faulkner
615-383-4449

Workshops, rituals, seminars, and speaking engagements.

Artists

Elizabeth Wise
E.D.M. Wise
PO Box 40878
Nashville, TN 37204
wisespring@aol.com

Sydney Reichman
Franklin, TN
615-799-8094
Friendship Beading Company
Palm Harbor, FL
727-938-4450

Foundations

Photographs of the SISTER Program were taken by Dr. Carlene Hunt, Ed.D., and donated by the HOPE Fund of the Community Foundation. HOPE promotes awareness of the effects of addiction on women and children and sponsors public education through the creation of positive images and messages of women and their children in recovery. It can be reached at 1-888-540-5200 and www.cfmt.org.

Internet Resources

Diana of the Arch of the Moon
Greek Mythology Link Home Page
www.hsa.brown.edu/~maicar/
by Carlos Parada
maicar@swipnet.se

Hosted by HSA Brown University, Providence, Rhode Island

Index

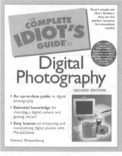